MODERN BUJUTSU AND BUDO

MODERN BUJUTSU & BUDO

THE MARTIAL ARTS AND WAYS OF JAPAN

VOLUME THREE

DONN F. DRAEGER

WEATHERHILL
NEW YORK & TOKYO

TITLE PAGE: Detail of a woodblock print by Kaisai Honen entitled *Chiba Gekken-kai*.

All photographs, except where credit is given, are from the author.

First edition, 1974
First paperback edition, 1996
Second printing, 1996

Published by Weatherhill, Inc.
568 Broadway, Suite 705
New York, New York, 10012

Protected by copyright under terms of the International Copyright Union; all rights reserved. Except for fair use in book reviews, no part of this book may be reproduced for any reason by any means, including any method of photographic reproduction, without permission of the publisher. Printed in the United States of America.

Library of Congress Cataloging-in-Publication Data

Draeger, Donn F.
   Modern bujutsu & budo / Donn F. Draeger
     p.   cm.
   Originally published: 1974 (The martial arts and ways of Japan; v. 3)
   Includes index.
   ISBN 0-8348-0351-8 (soft)
   1. Martial arts—Japan. I. Title II. Series
GV1112.D72 1996
796.8'15—dc20   96-4379
                                                              CIP

Watch out for us!
AKUTAGAWA

CONTENTS

Author's Preface 11

I: THE HISTORICAL BACKGROUND

1. The Emergence of Modern Japan 17
2. The Road to War and the Aftermath 36

II: THE MODERN DISCIPLINES

3. Major Characteristics 55
4. The Modern Bujutsu 65
   Batto-jutsu • Keijo-jutsu • Taiho-jutsu
   Keibo Soho • Tokushu Keibo Soho
   Hojo-jutsu • Toshu Kakuto
5. Kendo 77
6. Judo 112
7. Karate-do 124
8. Aiki-do 137
9. Nippon Shorinji Kempo 163
10. Other Modern Budo 173
    Kyudo • Naginata-do • Juken-do
    Epilogue: The Future of Modern Budo 178
    Glossary-Index 183

MODERN BUJUTSU AND BUDO

AUTHOR'S PREFACE

To investigate Japan's martial culture is to come face to face with a major dimension of that nation's history. To declare that much remains to be said about this dimension, one that is taken for granted by Japanese and Western writers alike, is to state the obvious. Martial activity has made distinct and important impacts on Japanese society, and without seriously examining all aspects of this little-known field of the Japanese ethos, there are a great many historical phenomena in Japan that we cannot fully understand.

In the first two volumes of this series, *Classical Bujutsu* and *Classical Budo,* I made the point that *bujutsu,* or "martial arts," and *budo,* or "martial ways," though related, are distinguishable as separate subjects. Vast differences in the technical characters and purposes of these martial disciplines make this distinction necessary. But if we are to understand the full extent of the development of bujutsu and budo we must also recognize that the *ko budo,* or classical disciplines, have their modern counterparts. The primary purpose of this book is to discuss the general nature and scope of the *shin budo,* or modern cognate disciplines, such as kendo, judo, karate-do, aiki-do, and others less well known.

These modern disciplines are related to the classical martial arts and ways, but there is more to this relationship than can be explained simply by assuming unconscious or conscious imitation alone. Unfortunately, through a lack of true understanding of the Japanese classical disciplines, observers have completely misrepresented the essence and spirit of these disciplines. Their lack of understanding is also evident in their interpretations of the modern disciplines, to such an extent that it has influenced the thinking of those of the present generation who practice these modern disciplines. The latter believe that what they practice is the exact style of technique of the Japanese classical warrior, which has come down to them unchanged and which is entered into in the same spirit as the classical warriors. This is emphatically false. But the belief that it is true has become so solidly entrenched in the minds of modern exponents that it takes considerable wrenching to free them from this fundamental error.

The main aim of this book is to demonstrate that any facet of man's "adaptive dimension," that is, his culture, must obey historical forces. The human experience of the Japanese has been much too rich and diverse to permit any one aspect of culture to stand alone without influencing other parts of that culture. Accordingly, within the realm of the classical martial arts and ways, but not proceeding *pari passu* with them, there has emerged a new stream of endeavor, that of the modern allied disciplines.

Our primary concern is to discover how the modern disciplines evolved, to determine their relationships with the classical bujutsu and budo, and to learn something about their technical and spiritual natures and also the extent to which they are practiced both in Japan and abroad. In this way we are able to learn something about why a modern Japanese society that discarded many of its feudal institutions should have wanted to maintain an interest in feudal martial disciplines, and even create modern ones. We become aware of the connections and interrelationships between the modern disciplines and older traditional cultural institutions, customs, and such beliefs as Shinto and emperor worship; of Buddhism in general, and of Zen in particular; and of the importance of the modern disciplines in the present Japanese educational system.

No less interesting are the political and philosophical ideologies of the exponents of both the classical and the modern disciplines, especially those forms that served the interests of nationalism and ultranationalism during and after the Meiji era (1868–1912); and, with the growth of prewar liberalism, the role of these disciplines in the development of the Japanese militarist state is also of great interest. This latter social phenomenon raises the complex problem of morality in combat; and this in turn raises penetrating questions about *bushido* (the way of the warrior), a long-treasured cultural concept. A comparison of modern Japanese martial records with those of earlier ages leaves us struck by the apparent conflict between theory and practice in the exercise of bushido by the modern Japanese fighting man. Why were the excellent combat ethics of the Meiji fighting man replaced by the brutalities perpetrated by the soldiers of the Showa era (1926–present), as exemplified in the "rape of Nanking" in 1937 and the atrocities committed in Malaya and Singapore in 1942? Is bushido of two types—a classical and a modern form—each with its own standards and values? And if two kinds of bushido do exist, why should the classical variety have been rejected as being too parochial for the Japanese soldier of the Showa era? On the other hand, if bushido is a single code, what factors explain why the fighting man of the Showa era was unable even to approximate the high level of combat morality that was the hallmark of the classical warriors for whom bushido formed the basis of ethical thinking?

Certain psychological factors appear to be peculiar to the Japanese fighting man, and these intrigue us no less. What is it in the character of the Japanese people that allows their fighting men to face death without hesitation? Does what Westerners call "suicidal mania" adequately explain the acts of modern Japanese fighting men in making themselves "human bullets" during the Russo-Japanese War (1904–5), or "human dynamite" in the struggle for Shanghai in 1932, or *kamikaze* fanatics in World War II? Are such sacrificial acts but continuations in spirit of the classical warrior's act of *seppuku* (suicide by disembowelment), or have they another origin? Is the seppuku on November 25, 1970, of Mishima Yukio, who was a dedicated exponent of modern disciplines, a further demonstration of a Japanese friendliness with death that is to be comprehended solely in terms of blind patriotism and loyalty to one's superiors and one's country? These are among the questions to which answers may be suggested by this book.

The modern disciplines form an intrinsic part of present-day Japanese society. The vast majority of Japan's population is engaged in one way or another in these disciplines. Thus the story of the modern disciplines is worthy of our critical attention now, when facts about them are easily obtained. In relating the story of the modern disciplines in this book, however, only a limited selection of material was made. Some readers will cavil at the many omissions, and others will wonder why emphasis has been laid on certain aspects and not on others. In mitigation of these possible criticisms it must be said that this book, like its two companion volumes, is not intended to be a definitive work. Furthermore, the material that was available to me in making this study was almost unlimited, so that some omissions were inevitable. The task has been, rather, one of probing authentic sources and extracting material that I believe best represents and describes the modern disciplines, and obviously many good sources have not been used.

No real understanding of the modern disciplines is possible without viewing them in the context of history. But readers must not expect to find here a chronological exposition. If such an exposition is needed the reader should avail himself of any of the good works on Japanese history to be found in any library. Only such historical facts as set the social scene in which the modern disciplines were originally developed and continue to function will be found in these pages. Moreover, the treatment of the Showa era is less detailed than that of the preceding Meiji and Taisho (1912–26) eras because the Showa era is still in progress and the roles and significance of the modern disciplines at this time are still to be determined.

Two of the many problems faced when gathering material about the classical disciplines do not apply to the modern disciplines. Much of the material about classical disciplines is, by tradition, not available to the public. That for the modern disciplines, however, is relatively free from such restrictions. The modern exponents of the classical systems hide themselves behind a maze of conventions and group traditions, so that there is a tendency to ignore or play down their personal involvement in the activities of the *ryu,* or martial traditions, to which they belong. But in the modern disciplines, where the spirit is more democratic, everything centers on the individual, especially one who is outstanding because of technical skill. This makes it possible for the investigator to obtain directly from those who are most experienced and concerned with the modern disciplines a good cross-section of expert opinions on the nature of these disciplines.

I am deeply indebted to a great number of people for their kind cooperation in helping me prepare this book. Those who were most helpful with its technical content are Professor Watatani Kiyoshi, Professor Otsubo Shigeo, and Professor Watanabe Kenji. I also wish to extend my most grateful thanks to specialists in particular areas of technical expertise, especially to Dr. Sasamori Junzo, Kaminoda Tsunemori, Nakayama Masatoshi, Shiokawa Terunari, Takano Kosei, Kato Masatoshi, Ozawa Takeshi, Yamaguchi Gogen, Oyama Masatatsu, Konishi Yasuhiro, Hayashi Teruo, Yada Hajime, Otsuka Hidenori, Shioda Gozo, Tsuruyama Kenji, Tomiki Kenji, Hisa Tadao, Kuchida Isao, Ueshiba Kishomaru, Sekine Noriko, Shimada Teruko, Sawara Misao, Otake Tadao, Otake Risuke, Kato Hiroshi, and Terauchi Kenzo. I would also like to thank the All-Japan Bayonet Federation, the All-Japan Naginata-do Federation, and the Nippon Shorinji Kempo.

It would not be fair to conclude this preface without expressing my fullest thanks to Dr. John B. Hanson-Lowe, who kindly read the manuscript and made a considerable number of constructive suggestions. I further appreciate the efforts of Kudo Ichiro and Takeda Hideo, whose linguistic skills I depend on, and who have aided in the translations of difficult passages of Japanese documents. Finally, I express my thanks to the photographic processing skills of Kobayashi Ichiro and all the members of his staff, who are responsible for the quality of the photographs used in this book.

Part One
THE HISTORICAL BACKGROUND

CHAPTER ONE

THE EMERGENCE OF MODERN JAPAN

> If a nation in this struggling world should be surrounded by nations of aggressive inclination and should remain inactive, she would certainly be destined to decline and become obscure.
> Yoshida Shoin

THE FOUNDATIONS OF MEIJI JAPAN   The *bakumatsu,* or "end of the *bakufu,*" is the period of the final decay and collapse of the military government, or bakufu, established by Tokugawa Ieyasu in 1603 and maintained until the latter half of the nineteenth century. The bakumatsu was caused by changed domestic and international conditions under which the shogun (originally, "general"; by Tokugawa times, the title of the hereditary military head of state, who paid only the emptiest of lip service to the powerless emperor cloistered in Kyoto) could no longer keep the nation effectively segregated from the outside world. The growing unrest of the first decades of the nineteenth century culminated in the so-called Meiji Restoration, when the hollow structure of the bakufu crumbled and the Meiji emperor assumed titular control of the government in 1868.

All the chief architects of the Restoration proposed to sweep away more than seven hundred years of imperial impotence, during which time Japan had been ruled by a succession of powerful families. These reformers were what Algernon B. Mitford calls "an improvement-seeking class." But among them there quickly arose disparate opinions as to what course of action the new Meiji government should take in effecting the reconstruction of Japan. The progressives saw the need to do away with many feudal institutions, especially those that favored hereditary right over individual merit; in their place they proposed to substitute programs that were more compatible with the ways in which they wished to modernize Japan. Conservative leaders, who had been the chief executioners of the Tokugawa bakufu, having satisfied their hereditary hatred of the

Tokugawa family, aimed at holding important positions in the new government. Many of them wished to reestablish the *ancien régime,* that is, the institutions and spirit of the pre-Tokugawa classical warrior. Thus, as the actual reconstruction of Japan tended to become more and more a progressive movement in which drastic and epochal reforms were brought about, the clash of opinions between progressives and conservatives resulted in a convulsive course of politics that was punctuated by actual combat.

But there were also points of agreement among the Meiji leaders. Their fundamental aim was to win for Japan the respect of Western nations, and thereby to redeem their nation from the gross humiliation that they felt it had suffered through the forcible opening of the country to the West. The fact that according to the resultant treaties foreign laws were to be administered in Japan was a severe blow to Japanese national pride. The Charter Oath, a declaration made in the name of the emperor in 1868, became the platform of the Meiji government. The last of its five articles is significant: "Knowledge shall be sought throughout the world so as to strengthen the foundations of imperial rule." This article was interpreted broadly to mean that, above all, Japan was to be made *fukoku-kyohei,* "a prosperous nation with strong armed forces."

The concept of fukoku-kyohei is an important focal point of the modern Japanese martial tradition. It has a significant bearing on the roles of the classical bujutsu and budo in modern Japanese society, and on the development and uses of the modern disciplines in that society. The authors of fukoku-kyohei made both orthodox and heterodox interpretations of classical philosophy, the individual strands of which must first be grasped if a full understanding of the nature of the modern disciplines is to be achieved.

Three separate streams of thought were united in the minds of Meiji officials and influenced their courses of action. The first of these taught its advocates to inquire, the second to act, and the third the object of the action. All were quiet, narrow streams of academic endeavor at the time that they arose in Tokugawa Japan, and were espoused by visionary thinkers who acted always under official censure, often in exile and sometimes close to death. As the scope of their actions widened, many of these men found themselves victims of the Tokugawa torture chambers, and the blood of some of them flowed vigorously from the sword and spear of Tokugawa "justice." In time the spirits of these men united and caused strife to engulf the entire Japanese nation.

Kogaku, the school of ancient or classical learning, arose at the end of the seventeenth century as a protest against the dogma of Tokugawa academies. Its adherents claimed that the Neo-Confucianism of Chu Hsi (1130–1200), which was the orthodoxy espoused by the bakufu, was not Confucianism at all but a misguided interpretation of Buddhism and Taoism. Therewith the *kogakushi,* the scholars of the school of classical learning, prescribed a "self-awakening," inviting all men to return to the original works of the sage himself, there to find the real meaning of Confucianism. In the original Chinese texts, these scholars declared, would be found not only the evidence for the divine right of the emperor to rule, but the right of his subjects to criticize and restrain the exercise of his power to rule. The scholar Ogyu Sorai (1666–1727), and the *ronin* (masterless samurai) Yamaga Soko (1622–85) were the foremost proponents of the school of classical learning. The former presented utilitarian views in which he defined morality as being determined by social needs, not by natural forces; the latter, for whom "the man of the upper classes grows increasingly stupid," was the prime contributor to shaping the doctrine of bushido. The *han,* or feudal domain, of Choshu in Kyushu was the principle stronghold of this philosophy.

The second stream of thought, also of seventeenth-century origin, was that of *yomeigaku,* the school of intuition or mind; it stemmed from the Chinese Wang Yang-ming (Oyomei) school of Confucianism. Yomeigaku advocates made the definition of knowledge the base of life. For them, to know was to be able to act; as they stated: "Knowledge is the beginning of action, and action is the completion of knowledge." Yomeigaku philosophy was not without higher ideals; knowledge had to be "good knowledge" in the hands of worthy people who would "live the life of a sage" and would "dedicate their whole energies to the service of mankind." The scholar Nakae Toju (1608–48) and the ronin Kumazawa Banzan (1619–91) were the first expounders of yomeigaku in Japan. Nakae maintained that true learning was equated with "control of the mind," a state which "exemplifies illustrious virtue." Kumazawa was painfully aware of the decadent state of the warrior class; he urged a return to a state of readiness for defense of the nation, a concept that was to be implemented by the actions of the "farmer-soldier" rather than by the hereditary type of professional warrior. The domains of Satsuma, Choshu, and Mito became the chief strongholds of this philosophy, which was severely censured by the bakufu.

Another seventeenth-century intellectual product, *kokugaku,* the school of historical or national learning, was the third stream of thought. It called for the recognition of the "true Japanese spirit" and the stripping of alien elements from Japanese culture. A Buddhist monk named Keichu (1640–1701) was the forerunner of kokugaku. The early expounders of this mode of thought include Motoori Norinaga (1730–1801) and Hirata Atsutane (1776–1843). Both these scholars rejected Confucian rationalism and ethics in favor of a more emotional appeal with strong nationalistic overtones. The kokugaku stress on the primacy of loyalty to the throne caused its influence to penetrate all aspects of Japanese culture. It became especially entrenched in the hearts of the *tozama* (outside) daimyo and their warriors.

Following the unification of Japan by Tokugawa Ieyasu (1542–1616) and the establishment of the Tokugawa bakufu, all daimyo and their domains had been divided into two groups: the favored *fudai,* or hereditary vassals, who had been allies of Ieyasu in 1600; and the tozama, those daimyo who had pledged allegiance only after Tokugawa authority was fully established. The tozama domains tended to be farther from the seat of government at Edo, thus more isolated—but by the same token, they maintained a greater degree of autonomy than the territories of the hereditary vassals. There were men from Choshu, from Hizen and Satsuma in Kyushu, and from Tosa in Shikoku (all tozama domains) who, strongly influenced by the kokugaku teachings, were stirred by the social vigor and martial ardor that had characterized the pre-Tokugawa classical warriors.

Numerous pressing problems caused by the social ills of Tokugawa society had to be solved by the leaders of the Meiji government. Amid foreign threats, domestic rebellions, assassinations, the incoming flood of Western technology, complex political and diplomatic negotiations, and economic pressures, they were able, remarkably, to steer a moderate course of action. They faced the problem of creating a workable relationship between nationalism and idealism, and sought to answer the question whether Japan's classical-warrior ethic and institutions fitted the new society. Such sociopolitical puzzles were not likely to be easily, or quietly, solved.

A high degree of outspoken emotionalism permeated almost the entire Meiji era. There were numerous influential men, both within and outside the government, who were proponents of radical activism. As radicals they subscribed to the literal meaning of *sonno-joi*—"revere the emperor and expel the barbarians"—which had originally been fostered by the scholars of the Mito school. In particular, the Meiji leaders were sensitive to the clarion call of Aizawa Seishisai (1827–63), who in his *Shinron* (New Proposals) effectively synthesized Shinto mythology and Confucian ethics of a bushido type. With Aizawa, *sonno* became not only the rallying cry for uniting the nation in support of imperial rule, but also the basis of all morality. In interpreting *joi,* Aizawa's xenophobia caused him to declare: "Smash the barbarians whenever they come in sight." The Mito scholar Fujita Toko (1806–55) qualified this, playing down anti-Western activism by saying: "We must not stain our precious swords with the blood of foreigners." Thus when Mito scholars broke forth with other dramatic slogans, such as *shinju-funi* (Shinto and Confucianism are one), *bumbu-fugi* (literary and martial arts are not incompatible), and *chuko-ippon* (loyalty to sovereign and loyalty to parents are one in essence), the Meiji leaders were able to focus clearly the concepts of *meigi,* or national mission, and *meibun,* or national duty. They produced a synthesis of philosophical thought that became the roots of a nationalistic concept that they referred to as *kokutai,* the "national polity."

The concept of kokutai affirmed that Japanese society had a unique character, evinced as both a political structure and a moral value. This made Japan different from and superior to all other nations. The imperial house was the pivot of national stability, and the incumbent emperor, who was endowed with tremendous divine power and authority, was the living representative of a sacred inheritance from the imperial ancestors. Kokutai thus was moral and just. The emperor was, in fact, the symbolic focus for the best efforts of all citizens. He was the focus of the emotions of the nation. But there was yet another important aspect of the kokutai. Inasmuch as the Japanese people had virtues that people in other lands lacked—loyalty that bound them to the nation and to the emperor, as well as a sense of filial piety that was the foundation of the family unit on which the nation was based—Japanese society was an undivided whole. Japan was therefore destined to be the greatest nation on earth.

Japan's martial strength at the time of the establishment of the Meiji government was particularly incompetent to deal with the international situation. By Western standards the Meiji army and navy were technologically backward. They had inherited the peculiar Tokugawa blend of the principles of feudal militarism and military impotence. Martial deficiencies were many. Yoshi S. Kuno in *Japanese Expansion on the Asiatic Continent,* referring to the quality of the men of the Tokugawa bakufu martial system, observes: "Because of the long-continuing national life of luxury and ease, the military leaders began to neglect and finally to lose their military prowess, thus becoming unfit to command troops. The fighting men, likewise, became unfit to constitute the rank and file of the army. They did not even know how to advance or to retreat in accordance with military regulations, because they had no training. On the whole the officers and fighting men had neither fighting strength nor spirit. These military men attended to the civil affairs of the shogunate government, but as they were military men, and that by inheritance only, they possessed neither ambition nor ability to render meritorious service in civil affairs." The real leadership of the Meiji government came largely from the warrior class of the tozama domains. It was a curious mixture of men. Daimyo were conspicuously absent in roles of leadership. William Elliot Griffis, an eyewitness of the last days of the bakufu, tells us why in his *Mikado's Empire:* "Of all the daimios, there were not ten of any personal importance. They were amiable nobodies, great only in stomach or silk robes. Many were sensualists, drunkards, or titled fools."

THE SAMURAI LEADERS OF MEIJI   Men of samurai origins dominated the major posts in the Meiji government. But their *shibun,* or "samurai status," requires qualification; the meaning of the term "samurai" in this connection should not be misunderstood. In the twelfth century the word "samurai" connoted "service," and did not specifically refer to a fighting man. But by the fourteenth century the term was in common use to describe a kind of *bushi,* or classical warrior, who was both by hereditary privilege and by training a professional fighting man. Samurai at that time, however, were by no means the highest ranking of the bushi, and in the Edo period (1603–1868) there were many different ranks within the samurai class itself.

The image presented by the Edo-period samurai is considerably different from that of the warrior of previous periods. It is that of the docile *hanshi,* or "gentry of the han," the Confucian-educated scholar-officials of the nation. By and large the urban members of this privileged social class were a notoriously effete group of men. It is important to distinguish the urban samurai from those who lived in rural areas. The provincial samurai lived simple and vigorous lives, and because of the rugged environments from which they came, were more hardy than their urban counterparts. But both types were what historian Asakawa Ken'ichi calls "incomplete samurai" because of their lack of martial ardor and technical skills in comparison with the classical warriors of earlier times; the rural hanshi, however, were less "incomplete" than their urban counterparts.

The samurai leaders of Meiji were akin, in terms of temperament and degree of training, to the provincial samurai of the Edo period. However, if only because of their bookish or scholarly tendencies they cannot be equated with the pre-Tokugawa classical warriors; and there are even more cogent reasons why this is true. Samurai at the beginning of the Meiji era were not a class of fighting men prepared through training for instant combat as a necessity in the face of almost constant warfare. They had only the martial legacy of the earlier classical warriors, for the long Tokugawa peace had been a time for taming warriors, reorienting their martial appetites and pointing them toward administrative service and literary achievement. This environment, in which the martial spirit had been devitalized, continued for two and a half centuries, until the bakumatsu. Meiji samurai, therefore, particularly the scholarly ones, were characterized by a relative lack of skill in combat with classical weapons, although easily aroused by matters involving honor or shame.

Despite the general decadence of the Tokugawa regime, however, certain samurai stood head and shoulders above the rest with respect to personal ambitions. These samurai were too much in earnest about solving the challenges of the domestic problems at hand to let the supreme opportunity slip by them, and as the prestige of the bakufu failed, they temporarily united their efforts to bring about a bold *coup d'état* and establish the Meiji government. Kido Koin (1833–77) of Choshu and Okubo Toshimichi (1830–78) and Saigo Takamori (1827–77) of Satsuma formed the original Meiji triumvirate.

Kido, Okubo, and Saigo, together with other provincial samurai, such as Itagaki Taisuke (1837–1919) and Goto Shojiro (1838–97) of Tosa, Yamagata Aritomo (1838–1922) of Choshu, as well as Okuma Shigenobu (1830–1922) of Hizen, though of respectable family origins, were all of lower samurai rank. None of these men was more than a *sotsu*, "trooper," or *heishi*, "man of the militia." Had they lived under the stern martial system of Minamoto Yoritomo, who had established the first bakufu in 1189 at Kamakura, it is doubtful whether any of these men, for lack of the proper hereditary credentials, would have been more than menials to fighting men, or at best foot soldiers, and certainly would not have held high positions of leadership.

Yet it is evident from a close study of the historical records that these leading Meiji samurai were intelligent and forceful men. They had, through great determination, straddled the progressive and conservative elements in their respective han, and at the time of the bakumatsu had emerged as the premier spokesmen of their domains. It cannot be denied that these social engineers of the Meiji Restoration were unusually disciplined men whose lives were shaped to a very considerable degree by their participation in training in classical bujutsu and budo. This training, served by their recollection of the spirit of the classical warrior, gave them a vigor unmatched by other samurai, who no longer trained themselves in martial arts or ways.

The nature and goals of the actions of the "men of Meiji" were determined by their personal ideologies, developed from the three schools of philosophical thought discussed earlier. In the light of what is known of the philosophical ideas of the Meiji samurai, another perspective is provided by the thesis that they were all social iconoclasts. When they rose to power in defiance of the bakufu they were not consciously abandoning any of the traditions of the classical warrior institutions that they may have made their own ideals. They were anti-bakufu because the bakufu represented the Tokugawa family, their hereditary enemy, and because the Tokugawa did not truly represent the classical warrior institutions, which they all to some extent treasured. Further, in appreciation of the fact that samurai like Kido, Okubo, Saigo, Itagaki, Goto, Yamagata, and Okuma had had no experience in combat in the classical tradition, there are fewer grounds for considering their leadership an apostasy against the bakufu. It is best to regard the Meiji samurai as neo-samurai or neo-traditionalists who occupied their positions of leadership within the shadow of the classical warrior traditions. To a man, though, they were *seichushi,* "spirited and loyal samurai," and it is thus worthwhile to sound the depths of their martial interests and to expect that this will give additional clues to the nature of the times in which the modern disciplines were born.

Despite their humble social status and lack of experience in battle with the weapons of the classical warrior, the provincial Meiji samurai were not altogether incompetent martially. This is seen in their readiness to try to solve by combat the problems of state that existed at the time of the bakumatsu. Itagaki, Goto, and Yamagata had had considerable experience in battle during the final struggles of the bakufu. They served with distinction in tactical units that depended on large bodies of commoners bearing firearms to achieve victory in mass engagements. It is not known if any of these men actually participated in single combat, the specialty of the classical warrior. There is only scanty evidence to show that any of these leading Meiji samurai were skilled in the use of classical weapons, such as the *odachi,* or long sword.

When Sir Harry Parkes, the British minister in Japan, was attacked by ronin in 1868, the stocky Goto is reported to have leaped agilely from his horse to decapitate one of the assailants with a single stroke of his sword; which, as George B. Sansom remarks in *The Western World and Japan,* "is not a feat that can be performed without practice." Goto's skill contrasts sharply with that of the Tosa would-be assassins who attempted in 1874 to take the life of Prince Iwakura Tomomi (1825–83). These ronin demonstrated their lack of martial competence, and perhaps, too, the lukewarm quality of their martial ardor, in their failure to carry out their mission because of "the darkness of the night." Yamagata, known as "The Wild One" in his youth, and later as "Pure Madness," a pen name, was an expert in *sojutsu,* the art of the spear, in the style of the Saburi Ryu. It appears, however, that he had no opportunity to demonstrate that skill in actual combat. But in the Yanagawa han in Kyushu, Yamagata defeated all comers, using a wooden *yari* (spear) that had been provided with a *tampo* (padded tip), to demonstrate the efficiency of his technique against swordsmen armed with *bokken* (wooden swords). Sojutsu remained an important interest with Yamagata throughout his life. A man of few words, he believed that the practice of sojutsu was essential for the development of his *seishin,* or spiritual energy. Yamagata is alleged to have practiced daily with a real spear, repeating the fundamental technique of *tsuki,* or thrust, hundreds of times against a large fig tree in his garden; eventually the tree died of his thrusts.

Kido, Okubo, and Okuma participated in martial affairs primarily by directing han policies, supervising such aspects of administration as finance and logistics. Saigo's primary contribution to the overthrow of the bakufu is reflected in the words of the commendation awarded him by the Emperor Meiji for his meritorious services and "skill as a military commissioner in obtaining possession of Edo Castle." And while Kido,

Okubo, and Okuma relinquished all chances to follow the calling of fighting men by becoming absorbed in affairs of state, Saigo's militant spirit afforded him a second chance to display his mettle. Here too, however, in the unsuccessful Satsuma Rebellion against the central government in 1877, which he led, there is little real evidence of Saigo in any role other than that of a tactical leader.

Martial discipline and training in classical bujutsu appear to have played a prominent part in the youth of Kido, Okubo, Saigo, and Yamagata. These martial interests stood them in good stead throughout their lives. In the final analysis, however, the martial disciplines that they undertook served them more as a medium for *seishin tanren,* or "spiritual forging," than as a basis for practical combat skills.

Kido Koin, frail and nervous as a youth, was a filial boy. He was the son of a samurai who apparently lacked all the qualities called for in a man of that social position. As a consequence Kido was adopted into a samurai family of higher rank and enjoined to become a "real samurai." He set out with boyish enthusiasm to master swordsmanship, but at the *dojo* (training hall) of Naito Takaharu, a master teacher of the Hokushin Itto Ryu, his poor physical condition did not enable him to persist in the arduous training required of all members. Nevertheless, Kido maintained a keen interest in *kenjutsu,* the art of using the drawn sword. As a pupil in a school of Yoshida Shoin (1830–59) in 1849, Kido learned about the martial doctrine of Yamaga Soko. After the death of his father, Kido received permission from the Choshu han in 1852 to journey to Edo to study kenjutsu for a three-year period. This proved to be a turning point in his life.

At Saito Yakuro's dojo in Edo, the Rempei-kan, Kido devoted his full energy to mastery of swordsmanship of the Shindo Munen Ryu. In his first year of study he was honored as *jukugashira,* or head student; two years later he achieved the highest award of the ryu, the *menkyo-kaiden,* confirming his expertise in technical skills and his maturity of spirit. After a meeting with Yoshida Shoin in 1853, Kido also enrolled in Egawa Tarozaemon's school of military science, where he displayed a deep interest in Western military technology. Just as Kido's study of kenjutsu tempered his spirit and enabled him to take quick action, the practical teachings of Yamaga Soko, Yoshida Shoin, and Egawa Tarozaemon nurtured his belief that Japan must modernize her military and naval arms along the lines of Western technology.

His yomeigaku- and Zen-educated father inspired Okubo Toshimichi to engage in boyish acts of daring and to shun "cowardice and meanness." Tall and thin, Okubo tended to suffer from ill health as a youth. Nevertheless, like all Satsuma boys, he engaged in martial disciplines in the Jigen Ryu fashion. Okubo took most to the practice of kenjutsu, sojutsu, and jujutsu, but his poor physical condition eventually forced him to give up his training. This early training coupled with his interest in Zen, however, left its impact. Throughout his life he made it a point to live in a frugal, austere manner. His predominantly Chu Hsi Confucian education was augmented by that of the *gochu,* the district youth organization in Satsuma that was designed to make young men into resolute samurai. In the gochu the emphasis was on manliness, self-reliance, and personal honesty. Each pupil wore the *daisho* (combination of long and short sword). Here Okubo acquired his imperturable and self-possessed personality; later, his *igen,* or dignity of demeanor, natural and all-pervading, forced his companions to be overly self-conscious in his presence, and many were those who made hurried efforts to lower their voices and adjust their dress.

Saigo Takamori, together with his close friend Okubo, was a typical Satsuma "warrior boy." Both of these young men were greatly feared by the younger boys of their neighborhood. Formal schooling appears to have been less important in the shaping of Saigo as a man than was the stern discipline of the gochu. At the age of twenty Saigo developed his hatred of the Tokugawa bakufu from the teachings of Fujita Toko at Mito. We know very little of Saigo's participation in classical bujutsu training other than that he did practice the rudiments of Jigen Ryu kenjutsu. As a youth he enjoyed robust health; he grew into a huge and powerful man. Saigo more closely approximates the true image of the pre-Edo classical warrior than any of his contemporaries. Perhaps he believed himself alone to be the true successor of those fearless bushi.

There is copious evidence to show that Saigo was a man of the highest personal integrity. His character formation was completed when he was inspired by his study of yomeigaku philosophy to make bushido the center of his life. This doctrine enabled him to act with frankness, courage, and venom in the matter of Korea's gross insult to the emperor of Japan in 1873. Korea announced that it desired "to cease all relations with a renegade civilization of the Orient." Saigo called for immediate action to punish the insult. He proposed that an official envoy be sent to Korea to protest that unwarranted statement. Saigo reasoned that the Koreans would probably murder the envoy, and thus Japan would be given the chance to declare war on Korea; such an action would, he believed, restore both the martial ardor and the technical skills of the Japanese fighting men, which were at this time at a very low ebb. Saigo offered his services to be that envoy, saying: "If it is a question of dying, that, I assure you, I am prepared to do." Kido gave his strongest support to the daring plan, but Okubo overrode Saigo on the issue and forced the plan to be abandoned.

Saigo, along with other disgruntled samurai, retired from the government in disgust, and from that time onward until his heroic demise in the Satsuma Rebellion, Saigo lived "like a tiger in his cave"; ever planning to take up arms, not against the emperor, whom he dearly loved, but against what he considered to be a "conspiracy against the true interests of the people, an oligarchy which used the imperial name and prestige as a justification of its despotic rule." In Satsuma, Saigo made classical martial disciplines the primary subject in the curriculum of his "private schools," the *shigakko,* where the object of study was to protect the emperor's power from the threats of the Tokyo government. Saigo was not a statesman, nor was he a distinguished strategist. But his charismatic leadership appealed to young men everywhere, and it is perhaps no exaggeration to say that "fifty thousand samurai rallied to his side, waiting on his instructions to lay down their lives at his bidding."

THE MEIJI REFORMS   In their dedicated effort to make Japan a strong and prosperous nation, the Meiji samurai leaders found it necessary to establish a centralized government. This required first the dissolution of the han. Such a proposal was a bold one, and not likely to meet with approval among daimyo and the samurai class in general. Kido made the appeal. He begged the daimyo "respectfully to surrender their han" because the national polity "makes it impossible for a foot of ground to be held for private ends." Kido's argument, supported by liberal financial and titular settlements from the government, induced the daimyo to concede to his wishes, and by 1871 all han were replaced by a prefectural structure that came under the cognizance of the central government.

The disbanding of the han resulted in the dislocation of the many classical martial ryu that were directed by private families who had enjoyed the patronage of the daimyo. Not a few ryu became extinct through lack of purpose and support. Those ryu that did remain active functioned in one of two major ways: (1) in the manner of the Araki Ryu of the Matsudaira family in Echizen (present-day Fukui Prefecture), an undivided unit with a small membership that operated in obscurity, and (2) like the Sekiguchi Ryu, formerly patronized by the branch of the Tokugawa family in Owari (present-day Aichi Prefecture), which split into various units, each gathering substantial numbers of members. There were also classical ryu that had not aligned themselves with any han, such as the Tenshin Shoden Katori Shinto Ryu and the Kashima Shinto Ryu. Alongside the classical ryu, new ryu were developing, none of which could ever hope to match the degree of excellence in combat technique of the older classical traditions; these were the modern cognate ryu.

Approximately two million samurai were affected by the disbanding of the han. Far-reaching financial reforms threatened the loss of the hereditary samurai stipends. And there were other social reforms enacted that made all samurai outside the government join the ranks of the conservatives who longed for a return to the classical-warrior traditions. Class distinctions among nobles, daimyo, samurai, and commoners based on lineage were nominally retained; but class privileges were virtually abolished in 1871. *Kuge* (court nobles) and daimyo became *kizoku*, or peers; samurai of certain ranks became *shizoku*, or gentry; the very lowest-ranked samurai, together with commoners, were reclassified as *heimin*—commoners. Thus a substantial number of the Meiji leaders were on a social par with the commoners.

Resentment among the provincial ex-samurai over the social and financial reforms ran even higher as the Meiji government cautiously recommended that all former samurai relinquish the practice of wearing the daisho, the combination of long and short sword that had been the samurai's distinctive badge and his pride. Few ex-samurai accepted the proposal. In 1873 Shimazu Tadayoshi, the former daimyo of Satsuma, called "the pillar of the nation" by the emperor, was offered a high post in the central government; he was prevailed upon to appear in Tokyo to accept this high honor. Shimazu arrived in the capital accompanied by several hundred samurai, all wearing the old costume of the classical warrior and carrying their two swords. Shimazu in this way registered his protest against the progressive measures being taken by the Meiji government.

It seemed to men like Yamagata Aritomo that the principal need of the nation was military reform. The achievement of the stipulated goal of fukoku-kyohei required substantial armed forces, both for domestic control and for defense against foreign political and economic domination. Yamagata, wounded during the disastrous engagement with Western forces at Shimonoseki during the last years of the Tokugawa bakufu, was convinced that modern firearms would have to replace the antiquated weapons of the classical warriors; furthermore, the archaic system of bujutsu as a primary tactical means of combat had to be discarded. In 1873 Yamagata rose to the post of Minister of the Army in the Ministry of Military Affairs; Saigo was appointed Commander in Chief of the Imperial Land Forces. The Ministry of Military Affairs included a division of ministries between the army and the navy; ex-samurai from the former Choshu han dominated the former ministry, and those from Satsuma the latter.

Yamagata's experience with the *kiheitai*, the "mixed-rifle units" of Choshu, proved to his satisfaction that commoners trained in the use of firearms were superior to the effete samurai of the Tokugawa bakufu; and they were at least the equals of the hardier provincial warriors. Yamagata recalled the emotional teachings of his mentor, Yoshida Shoin, who had declared that the *somo eiyu,* or "grass-roots heroes," were to be the salvation of the nation. Yamagata reasoned: "Feudal conditions spread throughout the country, and there appeared among the people a distinction between the farmer and the soldier [warrior].... Then came the great Restoration of the government [the Meiji Restoration].... On the one hand, warriors who lived without labor for generations have had their stipends reduced and have been stripped of the swords; on the other hand, the four classes of the people are about to receive their right to freedom. This is the way to restore the balance between the high and the low and to grant equal rights to all. It is ... the basis of uniting the farmer and the soldier into one. Thus, the soldier is not the soldier of former days. The people are not the people of former days. They are now equally the people of the empire, and there is no distinction between them in their obligations to the State."

When Okuma strongly supported Yamagata's opinion that all male citizens have a military obligation to the state, saying, "All our sons are soldiers," Yamagata became fully committed to the creation of a universal conscription system. The official notice issued in 1872 with the imperial decree establishing conscription, which largely represents his thinking, sets forth the following justification of universal conscription: "Where there is a state, there is military defense; and if there is military defense there must be military service. It follows, therefore, that the law providing for a militia is the law of nature and not an accidental, man-made law."

In citing indisputable historic facts to buttress his argument for universal conscription, Yamagata reveals the depth of his disgust for the Tokugawa military man: "In the ancient past everyone was a soldier. In an emergency the emperor became the Marshal, mobilizing the able-bodied youth for military service.... When the campaign was over the men returned to their homes and their occupations, whether that of farmer, artisan, or merchant. They differed from the soldiers of a later period who carried two swords and called themselves warriors, living presumptuously without working, and in extreme cases cutting down people in cold blood [*kiri-sute gomen*] while officials turned their faces."

The law of universal conscription called for all men twenty years of age or older, regardless of social background, to undergo three years' active service and then five more years each in a first and a second reserve unit. Officers were to be recruited from the families of former low-ranking samurai. In this way it happened that the peasant masses became the mainstay of a greatly expanded and modernized Japanese armed force.

All the practical measures of reform that were rapidly being enacted by the central government naturally entailed consequences that could not fail to produce suffering and violence. Peasant unrest over matters of social status and taxation grew to substantial proportions. But what worried the Meiji government most was the widespread discontent among the former samurai, who grew openly hostile because of their poor financial condition and their compromised social status. It was this state of affairs that had prompted Saigo Takamori to seek an opportunity to employ the samurai in warfare against Korea. As a recompense for condemning Saigo's proposal, the Meiji government approved a short campaign directed against the Boutan tribesmen on Formosa in 1874, justifying the campaign as a punitive expedition to avenge the slaying of Japanese and Okinawan citizens by these tribesmen. But this token military action did not placate the ex-samurai.

A further bold step taken by the Meiji government was intended to offset potential civil insurrection. An order prohibiting the practice of wearing two swords and limiting the right to bear arms to the members of the regular armed forces was enacted in 1876. This order was prefaced as follows: "Let the effect of this proclamation be well understood. It is not the putting aside of the martial spirit. It is rather the transfer of the sword from the hands of a vast body of men less amenable to discipline to those of a small body much more so." The provincial ex-samurai became greatly angered over the fact that the proclamation, though issued in the name of the emperor, was nevertheless drafted by men in the government who not only were their social inferiors, but men for whom the classical martial tradition had little or no value. Thus, as the highest emblem—the two-sword combination—of the provincial ex-samurai's honor, their very living soul, was taken away from them, the hopes of these men for a government-sponsored restitution of the classical warriors' institutions died. There followed on the order prohibiting the wearing of swords the compulsory cancellation of all hereditary pensions and allowances of the former daimyo and samurai.

These reform measures aroused the ex-samurai to fury. A series of revolts inspired by ex-samurai shattered the government's hopes for civil peace, but all the revolts were quickly crushed by government conscript troops. The bloody fighting culminated in

1877 in the Satsuma Rebellion directed by Saigo Takamori. This was the last time that Japanese fighting men advocating the old order—the classical warrior traditions—showed armed resistance against the government. The victory of the Meiji army over Saigo's conservative diehards proved to the satisfaction of even the most recalcitrant of the provincial ex-samurai that a peasant conscript army, equipped with modern firearms and holding other technological advantages, could impose its will on any group of fighting men armed in the classical-warrior fashion.

THE INTERNAL ORDER   In view of the continued arrogant assumption of cultural superiority by Western nations, the underlying aim of the Meiji government continued to be that of winning the respect of the West. Accordingly, the government directed an intense course of domestic reforms that put increased emphasis on economic strength, national unity, and military power. Ito Hirobumi (1841–1909), a Choshu commoner who had been adopted into a samurai family, was the leading social engineer in the Meiji government. Ito was highly spirited as a boy. He had a massive jaw and unusually big feet, the latter allegedly caused by his practice of going barefoot in order to experience hardship in preparation for his role as a samurai. Yoshida Shoin, one of Ito's teachers, greatly inspired him; the former's execution by the Tokugawa authorities is said to have given Ito his disdain for death. After a brash and unsuccessful attempt to seize the British legation in Edo in 1861, the two-sword-bearing Ito went to England to study; on his return to Japan, he found himself becoming important in the affairs of the Choshu han. He rose to even greater prominence as a commander of a mixed-rifle unit. And in the Meiji era, as prime minister and as president of the Privy Council, he became the personal spokesman for the emperor.

Ito moved to strengthen the government's base of authority—the name of the emperor. To achieve this goal certain efforts had to be made to control and guide popular opinion. Most of the Meiji ex-samurai had had a Confucian (Chu Hsi) education, no matter what philosophy they entertained and were guided by; and their interest in religion was largely a secular one, religion being regarded as a vehicle to serve the nation. Confucianism alone, however, was not well suited to be a guiding philosophy for the state. Shinto, though enjoying a great revival during the first years of Meiji, did not have much to offer the rising generation. Buddhism had been hard hit by the violent reaction against it at the time of the downfall of the Tokugawa bakufu; but that shock had rid it of its lethargy, and though as yet unfit to be named a national religion, Buddhism was beginning to show signs of new vitality. Therefore, Ito reasoned that something new would have to be created, something that appealed to the Japanese mind. It would have to be more in the nature of a state philosophy than a state religion. Ito meant the new product to bring together education, morals, and government.

He began by forcing an important change in Shinto. Ito took away its religious character by abolishing the Daikyo-in, the preaching institute, in 1875. In 1882 Shinto was defined not as a religion in competition with other religions but as something that was more in the nature of an allegiance that took precedence over all religions. In this new role Shinto became the "engine of government." The people were expected to approach Shinto in a patriotic, not a religious, state of mind. In the decentralization of Shinto that followed, the responsibility for the moral instruction of the masses was shifted to the teachers in the educational system.

The Meiji educational system in the mid-eighties changed from its original form as a variety of separate and different programs designed to develop literate citizens for service in all walks of life to a standard national system designed to produce effective workers for the army, navy, factories, and fields. A strong emphasis was placed on moral education. This emphasis was expected to remove the influence of Western culture on Japanese citizens and to replace its undesirable effects with the proper, more desirable Japanese ones. The change culminated in the issuing in 1890 of the Imperial Rescript on Education, which stressed the ideal of social harmony and made a virtue of loyalty to the imperial tradition. Mori Arinori (1847–89), an ex-samurai of Satsuma, became the Minister of Education. He announced: "Japan's schools are for the sake of the nation, not of the pupils." Physical education was an important part of all school curricula. The art of *sumo*, a kind of wrestling, together with modern budo, such as kendo and judo, were taught to all male children; female students participated in *naginata-jutsu*, the art of the halberd, a classical bujutsu.

While stressing the necessity for attaining a high degree of national morality, the Meiji government also clarified its elements. National morality was to be based on ideal values of human conduct. Each citizen was to seek the happiness of the Japanese state, of which he was a part, "happiness" being defined as "perfection." This perfection of the state would be accomplished when every citizen undertook to make wholesome personal conduct his national duty. Bushido was chosen by the Meiji government as a means to instill into the minds of the people the idea of their moral obligation to fulfill their duty to the state. Kido earlier had denied the relevance of bushido to the nation's needs, seeing it as being inherently parochial and inadequate. He had labeled it the remnant of a "fossilized civilization." There was no denying that bushido, the exercise of which was a form of obligation on the part of the classical warrior, was the exclusive patrimony of that privileged social class. But for the leaders of the Meiji, bushido in many ways expressed the national character, and was less the particular province of a given class of people than Kido had asserted.

Bushido, in its elementary form at the time of the Yamato period (c. 400–645)—the oldest truly Japanese society—was an unwritten, tacit code of behavior held in the minds and hearts of men. In the closing years of the Heian period (794–1185) it evolved into an expression of the morality and spirit of the classical warrior, as distinct from a sense of national morality. In the *Kokon Chomonshu* (1254), a treatise concerning the Heian period, are mentioned the so-called "seven cardinal virtues" of the warrior, a very simple kind of moral consciousness developed among those fighting men of ancient times. Briefly stated, the seven virtues urged the warrior to shun violence, to keep his sword sheathed, and to live in peace and amity with his fellow men.

During the time of Minamoto Yoritomo's bakufu at Kamakura (1189–99), the ethic of his bushi evolved further in terms of relationships between inferiors and superiors, and every warrior's personal loyalty to Yoritomo as shogun was the supreme virtue. Thereafter, with the rise of the powerful Hojo family of regents in the thirteenth century until their final defeat by the Ashikaga family in the late fourteenth century, the concept of loyalty was ill-defined. Loyalty entailed a double function: the pro-bakufu warrior owed his loyalty to both the shogun and the bakufu, while the pro-imperial warrior's loyalty was extended only to the emperor. In the misery of the war-ridden days that characterized the Muromachi period (1336–1568) the warrior, whose duty it was to fight, must have felt keenly the uncertainty of life, for such an attitude is clearly reflected in the way in which he regarded the ethics of his privileged class, which were now permeated by a Zen flavor. The obvious conflict between the theory and practice of the warriors' ethic was due to the fact that loyalty rested primarily on one's economic situation, and was observed as long as both sides had common and mutually supporting economic interests. At this time bushido, idyllic and unnamed, was truly a classical warrior's code of ethics, the definition and application of which was fully under the control of classical warriors.

Bushido acquired a complex, highly idealistic form and the major tenets of the code were committed to writing during the Edo period. Yamaga Soko's *Bukyo* (Warrior's Creed) and *Shido* (Warrior's Way) represent the first systematic exposition of the moral aspects of what later came to be known as bushido. In concrete terms Yamaga outlined the social role and worth of the warrior in society. His writings brought a rich content to the social ethics of the warrior class, but he was not alone in shaping the doctrine of loyalty. An eighteenth-century work entitled *Hagakure* (Hidden Behind Leaves) lays down the stern ethical code of the warriors of the Nabeshima family of Hizen (present-day Nagasaki Prefecture). Said to be inspired by the poetic lines of the priest Saigyo (1118–90)—"A mere flower, alive but hidden behind leaves, strikes one as if meeting a soul withdrawn from the world"—the *Hagakure* is the epitome of the canon that once ruled the minds of the Nabeshima fighting men. The spirit of service and loyalty dominates this ethic. Four lines from the work illustrate this:

> We will be second to none in performance of our duty.
> We will make ourselves useful to our superior.
> We will be dutiful to our parents.
> We will attain greatness in charity.

Okuma Shigenobu, a native of Hizen, was obviously aware of the contents of the *Hagakure* when he announced the importance of bushido for the Meiji populace by stating that their ancestors "have attached great importance to bushido, and at the same time hold in the highest respect the spirit of charity and humanity." Ito Hirobumi spoke of "the crust of tradition," in which he singled out bushido as being worthy of application to Meiji society. Bushido, said Ito, "offered us splendid standards of morality, rigorously enforced in the everyday life of the educated classes. The result . . . was an education which aspired to the attainment of stoic heroism, a rustic simplicity and a self-sacrificing spirit unsurpassed in Sparta, and the aesthetic culture and intellectual refinement of Athens. Art, delicacy of sentiment, higher ideals of morality and of philosophy, as well as the highest types of valor and chivalry—all these we have tried to combine in the man as he ought to be."

Thus, whatever their degree of similarity, the one characteristic that definitively separates Tokugawa bushido from that of the Meiji is the latter's emphasis on a primary trait of the pre-Edo classical warrior, self-effacement. Self-effacement was to be cultivated by the people in order to bring themselves into harmony with the prescribed moral standards of the nation. The very fact that the Meiji leaders saw that it was necessary to emphasize the concept of self-effacement reveals something about the personal nature of the average citizen at this time.

Itagaki Taisuke showed a firm grasp of the social situation when he delivered a stinging criticism against the individualists of Meiji society, those who stood aloof from concern for national unity. Itagaki likened them to the socially irresponsible Tokugawa samurai, who were "lacking in a feeling of community." Kido Koin, too, had spoken out boldly about the *gumin*, or "stupid masses," who lacked patriotism and were unenlightened. Mutsu Munemitsu (1844–97), son of a kokugaku-educated samurai of Kii (present-day Wakayama Prefecture) who was in disgrace with the Tokugawa bakufu over financial irregularities, was himself educated in a Confucian manner. Mutsu was contemptuous of cant, preferring instead frank and realistic airing of opinions. His remarkable talents enabled him to emerge in 1883 from five years in prison, where he had been sent for his part in an antigovernment plot inspired by ex-ronin from Tosa, to take up the post of foreign minister, a position in which he served with great distinction during the Sino-Japanese War (1894–95).

Mutsu's acquaintances included Aizawa Seishisai, Kido Koin, Itagaki Taisuke, Goto Shojiro, and Sakamoto Ryoma (1835–67), the last-named a ronin of Tosa. Sakamoto was a great influence in the shaping of Mutsu's thinking. Though Mutsu regarded Sakamoto as "a swashbuckler and unlettered," it was from Sakamoto that Mutsu learned to appreciate the value of persistence in any endeavor. Sakamoto was a menkyo-kaiden swordsman of the Hokushin-Itto Ryu. As a result of his arduous training in swordsmanship he had the ability to concentrate singlemindedly on achieving a given object, even when plans at first miscarried. "Never surrender to failure" and "Make the best of a bad situation," he advised Mutsu.

His prison years had given Mutsu time to reflect on the low state of public respect for Meiji military men. To counterbalance this, Mutsu proposed they be given increases in pay; he made efforts to build up the pride of the individual in being a member of the armed forces, encouraged competitive sports, and made compulsory the study of classical martial arts and ways.

Yamagata Aritomo, new chief of staff of the armed forces, was also acutely aware of the low standard of morality, not only of the general public but also of the members of the army itself. And so the object of universal conscription became, for Yamagata, literally "to transform the commoner into a samurai." This process aimed at making the

Meiji soldier a fully professional fighting man, one who was both morally and technically trained to carry out his responsibility to the nation. Through this training the soldier would be made fit to assume a position of dignity in the nation, and would be deserving of honor because of the great responsibility he assumed in the defense of his nation. There were problems, however, that complicated this transition.

Conscription entailed a mental adjustment by all inductees. Ex-samurai were prone to regard the privilege of bearing arms as a hereditary monopoly, and sharing this honor with the commoners was a blow to their pride. Nor did many of the ex-samurai relish mixing with coarse and ill-bred peasants who had no appreciation of the traditions of the classical warrior. Commoners, moreover, were unversed in the ways of military discipline, and their diverse social backgrounds were not particularly conducive to the creation of the unity of purpose that is of paramount importance in military life. Yamagata sought to blend the ex-samurai and commoners into a harmonious unit. He declared bushido to be the common moral basis of the new army. This being made clear to all inductees, he reasoned, the ex-samurai would take pride in playing a part in the revitalization of the warrior ideals to which they allegedly subscribed; the commoners, too, would realize that by personal participation in the new army their social dignity was being elevated to that of the warriors.

Yamagata, in his promulgation of the Admonition to the Armed Forces in 1878, reiterated those tenets of the Tokugawa brand of bushido that stressed the virtues of loyalty, bravery, and obedience; the virtue of benevolence as interpreted by Kaibara Ekken (1630–1714), a Neo-Confucian samurai of the Kuroda han, was also included. But because he felt the need for a change in emphasis, Yamagata directed the issuing of the Imperial Precepts to Soldiers and Sailors in 1882, the contents of which were made public in order to enhance the prestige of the Imperial Army. This document provided the framework for the moral guidance of soldiers and sailors in the Meiji armed forces. Yamagata regarded the five articles of the Precepts to be "the 'Grand Way' of Heaven." A bare summary of these articles follows:

1. Loyalty is the essential duty.
2. Respect superiors, be considerate of juniors.
3. Valor is to be esteemed.
4. Faithfulness and righteousness must be highly valued.
5. Simplicity in living must prevail.

A Confucian flavor permeates the Precepts, just as it does all the older classical interpretations of bushido. But Yamagata had in fact redefined classical bushido, or had at least modified the order of priority placed on the classical tenets. An outstanding characteristic of Yamagata's brand of bushido is its cautious tone. The emphasis throughout is on prudence, self-control, and a restrained kind of valor rather than on a fatalistic approach to death and the development of a fanatic bravery.

Loyalty, the "essential duty" of the Meiji fighting man, was to be a disciplined devotion that would affect "the nation's destiny for good or evil." When seen in this light,

34 • HISTORICAL BACKGROUND

duty becomes "weightier than a mountain, while death is lighter than a feather." The Precepts are thus in consonance with the *Hagakure's* emphasis on the gravity that is to be placed on dying, but at odds with that type of bushido in that the *Hagakure* explicitly states that duty is to be "held lightly" in order that the warrior may "set his mind at ease." Violence in action, according to the Precepts, is to be shunned because it reflects against the national dignity and makes of its users "wild beasts." In any case, violence is not an indicator of true valor; it must be preceded by "gentleness first," and by qualities that aim "to win the love and esteem of others." Thus the noblest virtue of the classical warrior is eliminated except as it appears vaguely, subsumed under the attribute of valor in the Precepts; as such it is only partially descriptive of what the *Hagakure* terms "a belly full of charity." It is Yamaga Soko's *taigi*, or "Great Righteousness," that is the Precept's ideal of fulfillment of duty, which is characterized by the kind of good faith exemplified by keeping one's word.

The Precepts also urge the Meiji fighting man to consider carefully the consequences of an act *before* acting. On this point, too, the Precepts differ from the teachings of the *Hagakure,* which makes rational calculation an act of cowardice. The importance that Yamagata placed on the need for a fighting man to live a frugal life was brought out in his declaration that national honor is indelibly stained when fighting men grow selfish and sordid through licentious living and thereby sink "to the last degree of baseness," thus gaining "the contempt of the world." No classical interpretation of bushido can take exception to this.

FULFILLMENT OF THE MEIJI DREAM Japan's objective of being fukoku-kyohei in order to redeem its national dignity in the eyes of Western nations was fully realized in the last two decades of the Meiji era. The nation's martial objectives, under Yamagata, continued to be autonomy and security within its own waters; its geographical limits, however, were defined in terms of strategic concepts based on Japan's insular position in relation to continental Asia. Japan's desire to be considered a great power was purely nationalistic in nature. Even when its army and navy won a stunning victory from China in the contest over Korea in the Sino-Japanese War of 1894–95, Japan had not yet moved in the direction of the jingoistic ideals of territorial expansionism.

Twice more, within the short space of a decade following the brief war with China, the Meiji conscripted fighting men fought on foreign soil, in the Boxer Rebellion (1898–1901) and in the Russo-Japanese war (1904–5). Japan's military involvement in the Boxer Rebellion was purely defensive, to protect the lives and properties of Japanese and Western diplomatic agencies from fanatical Chinese who were involved in a dynastic struggle and who had vowed to "sit on the skins of the foreigners" they had killed. The Russo-Japanese War was waged in an effort to offset Russia's territorial expansion into Manchuria. In both of these brief encounters, as well as in the conflict with China that preceded them, the Meiji fighting man gave an admirable account of himself. His displays of bravery and skill in combat won for him and for the Japanese nation the commendation and respect of all Western nations. The Meiji fighting man nobly maintained a remarkably high standard of morality in battle, one that has yet to be matched by any other modern nation. Yamagata's strong hand and influence on the conduct of his nation's fighting men is obvious. Meiji bushido, declared by writers such as Nitobe Inazo (1862–1933) to be "the leaven of the masses," was a synthesis of moral qualities that had been successfully implanted in the fighting men of that era. Theory and practice in Meiji bushido became a harmonious whole. This being so, there were few in Meiji Japan who would declare that the imperial missions of the emperor's army and navy were morally wrong.

The founding in 1895 of the Dai Nippon Butokukai (Great Japan Martial Virtues Association) in Kyoto heralded a significant contribution to the maintenance of the classical martial disciplines. The Butokuden (Martial Virtues Hall), established in 1899 and located adjacent to the Heian Shrine in Kyoto, became the headquarters and central training area of the association. The Butokuden was operated by leading exponents of martial arts and ways. Naito Takaharu, a master swordsman of the Hokushin-Itto Ryu renowned for the high quality of his martial spirit, was chosen to be the head instructor and lecturer of the section devoted to the study of kendo; Isogai Hajime, an outstanding exponent of judo, was named as the head instructor and lecturer of the section devoted to that discipline.

While encouraging the practice of the classical disciplines, the leaders of the Butokukai also stressed the growing importance of kendo and judo in the general education of all citizens. By 1906 they were urging the popularization of these modern disciplines throughout Japan. Famed experts gathered to teach a variety of disciplines at the Butokuden, and periodic meetings of technical commissions convened under its aegis brought about standardization of techniques and methods of training. The establishment of the Dai Nippon Butokukai Bujutsu Semmon Gakko (Great Japan Martial Virtues Association Martial Arts Specialty School) in 1911 gave employment to experts and was a major source of skilled exponents in both classical and modern disciplines. The ever-widening popularity of kendo and judo among the Japanese public was greatly aided by the Ministry of Education directive of 1911 that made kendo and judo compulsory in all middle schools throughout the country; all male students were required to participate in one or the other discipline. This was the first formal governmental acknowledgment of the importance of the modern disciplines in the education of Japanese citizens.

CHAPTER TWO

THE ROAD TO WAR AND THE AFTERMATH

>O, you are busied in the night
>Preparing destinies of rust;
>Iron misused must turn to blight
>And dwindle to a tattered crust.
>   Gordon Bottomley

THE TAISHO ERA   Japan felt herself to be, and indeed was, important. She had been unanimously welcomed into the community of nations and recognized as a member of the Big Five (with Britain, France, Germany, and the United States). Nothing was more natural than for the Japanese people to expect that their nation must continue to be great. But the efforts of the government to modernize Japan further soon revealed staggering problems. Robert J. Kerner has aptly described this time as "an epoch which still casts its ominous shadow over Japan's actions, and, in fact, determines them."

Almost two generations separated the leaders of the Taisho era (1912–26) from the samurai who had engineered the downfall of the Tokugawa bakufu. The decline of the ruling oligarchy of Meiji brought about significant changes in Japan. As assassination, illness, old age, natural death, and retirement into ineffective roles in office took their toll of "the men of Meiji," there emerged a new generation of leaders. But because of lack of unity of purpose, these leaders were unable to cope with the problems of their time. Whereas the problem of the Meiji era had been one of "how," that of the Taisho era was "what for?"

The Taisho ("Great Righteousness") emperor, who succeeded to the throne following Emperor Meiji's death in 1912, was a sickly man, and unable to devote himself to the affairs of state. This situation required changes in the political role of the sovereign. More and more the emperor was isolated from the political scene. And though the leaders of the Taisho government accepted the core concepts of the Meiji *kokutai*, or national polity—loyalty, filial piety, harmony, and moral order—they made subtle changes in the meanings of these concepts. The Taisho legal interpretation of kokutai gradually came under the influence of Minobe Tatsukichi (1873–1948), professor of constitutional law at Tokyo Imperial University. For Minobe the state was a legal person, possessing both sovereignty and authority to rule; the emperor was but the highest organ in the state with executive functions. Minobe's interpretation of kokutai amounted to a reduction of the authority of the emperor, heretofore so sacrosanct as to be unchallengeable. By making the emperor an "organ of state" Minobe intended to weaken autocratic rule and challenge the legitimacy of nonconstitutional bodies. He sought to inhibit those who attempted to use Japan's armed forces autonomously, with the forced sanction of the emperor. In effect, he reduced the Confucian stress on morality and justice. Uesugi Shinkichi, also a professor at Tokyo Imperial University, opposed Minobe's thesis. Uesugi made of the emperor a mystical body, equivalent to a position of absolute authority in a monarchy. Militarists in later decades would use this view of the emperor to justify their extravagant goals.

The Taisho government was composed of separate political elites. The three principal elites were the civil bureaucracy, the armed forces, and the political parties. Divisions within each elite, each hostile to the others, made the Taisho political arena an extremely complex scene, but the political parties finally became the most influential force in government. Grave personal defects of certain party politicians came to be known by the public. Most of these politicians were opportunists, functioning like generals without armies. They had grown influential through their greed for power, attaining positions of advantage from which they forgot their duty to represent the people and which made it easy for them to align themselves with those who were able to further their interests. The general public viewed the politicians as men without principles or morals.

As the goals of the Taisho leaders became ever more diverse, there arose a group of liberal thinkers whose personal ideals and ideologies produced further social and political confusion. On the whole, intellectual activity during the Taisho era was of a high order; its objectives became increasingly more alienated from those of Meiji. The romanticism of Meiji gave way to a kind of realism, then finally to naturalism, because the new generation, having had a less Confucian-oriented education than the preceding one, lacked a strong sense of social responsibility. This trend can easily be seen in Taisho literature. Writers turned away from concern with the emperor, military matters, politics, and economics, and focused instead on the problems of the confused individual in a confused society. Themes of despair, melancholy, and futility dominate the works of writers of the time. The search for identification of the self with nature was a popular theme; nevertheless, in most of these works there is an emphasis on the ethical nature of man.

The problem of self-realization, as portrayed by the Taisho writers, was one not of control but of release of inner forces. Man learns what he is by liberating his natural desires, especially his sexual desires, from the constraints of social mores. Such traditional practices as classical budo, already virtually ignored in the Meiji era, were now regarded as completely anachronistic; the spiritual nature of classical budo ran contrary to the liberal expression of the self. The public preferred instead to engage in less exacting pastimes, such as sports.

The novelist Natsume Soseki (1867–1916) had a great influence on the growing spirit of liberalism in the Taisho era. Soseki's writings ridiculed blind patriotism, holding that individual morality was higher than state morality. Nishida Kitaro (1870–1945), a philosopher dominated by German idealism of the Hegelian type, dabbled in Zen. Upon the failure of "the door to open," however, Nishida turned to the task of providing a philosophical foundation for his countrymen's plight. In his *Nihon Bunka no Mondai* (The Problem of Japanese Culture) Nishida stressed the recognition of a basic Oriental culture, referring to it as "the vision of the shapeless" and "the voice of the voiceless reality." His thinking was characteristically colored by yomeigaku and Zen, especially when he spoke of "active intuition" and "pure experience," seeking to unite these paths of learning in terms of self-identity as well as of the position of Japan in the international community. Nishida's philosophy, like Natsume Soseki's stories, was widely read by the Taisho-era Japanese.

Yamagata Aritomo's authority in government weakened. The powerful position of autonomy that Yamagata had created for the army served those who desired to remove him from politics by giving them the capacity to defy the constitutional government. A demand by the army and navy to obtain larger allocations was rejected by the cabinet. This precipitated the so-called "Taisho Political Crisis of 1912–13," during which the cabinet fell. The political aftermath of "the Crisis" foreshadowed the eventual decline of constitutional power in favor of power by political parties headed by a new generation of high-ranking army and navy officers; these new leaders would prove to be less moderate in their thinking than either the samurai founders of the Meiji government or the transitional leaders of the early Taisho era.

A side reaction to "the Crisis" was the call for more democracy at home. Yoshino Sakuzo (1878–1933), professor of political history and theory at Tokyo Imperial University, endeavored to show that Japan's constitutional monarchy and Western democracy were compatible. His argument rested on his definition of democracy, which included two distinct meanings, *minshu shugi* and *mimpon shugi*. The former meant that "in law the sovereignty of the nation resides in the people," the latter that "in politics the fundamental end of the exercise of the nation's sovereignty should be the people." Democratic trends made their appearance in education. All school texts were revised in 1916–17 to include aspects of Japan's relations with Europe.

World War I was a good war for Japan. As England's ally, Japan committed only a minimal military and naval force but gained tremendous economic advantages in the form of territorial concessions both on the Asian continent and in the Pacific islands. China's neutrality was flouted by Japan, who landed troops on the Shantung Peninsula and put military police in charge of all railway systems there. Okuma Shigenobu, backed by powerful political forces, turned archimperialist, imposing the outrageous terms of the Twenty-one Demands on China in 1915. Control of the Chinese government was virtually in Japanese hands. Yamagata denounced the bullying of China, reasoning that friendship with China and its support for a policy of mutual cooperation in the defense of Asia was a much better alternative. The fact that Yamagata was unable to prevail is further evidence of his lessening power in government and of the fact that cautious nationalistic militarism was being replaced by jingoism.

The Siberian Expedition of 1918–19 was unpopular with the more conservative elements of the government. That campaign had been costly in terms of both lives and expenditure, and had not produced any material gains. Its importance lies in the fact that it was the first outright assumption of authority in matters of foreign policy by the autonomous military clique of the Japanese government. In the final stages of World War I, the Allied forces were anxious to get Russia back into the war against Germany and therefore dispatched troops to Siberia. Japan was requested to participate by sending troops to complement the Allied forces. Yamagata believed that Japan's presence in Manchuria was necessary for the security of China and Japan but was critical of those who desired Japan to expand beyond those territorial limits: "Manchuria is for the Japanese the only region for expansion. . . . Manchuria is Japan's lifeline." He argued: "China might object to the Japanese setting foot in Manchuria, but had it not been for Japan's fighting and repelling Russia from Manchuria, even Peking might not be Chinese territory today." Those of the military clique who favored expansionism urged Yamagata to regard the dispatch of troops to Siberia as a maneuver designed to strengthen Japan's hand in Manchuria, so when Japan responded favorably to the Allied request, Yamagata did not oppose it.

Army Minister Tanaka Giichi (1863–1929), a Choshu general, had other plans, however. He ran roughshod over continental Asians and their national territories as he implemented what he called "a positive foreign policy." Tanaka's highhanded methods alienated China and Western nations alike. At the end of World War I, as the Allied forces withdrew from Siberia, the Japanese troops remained. Only under severe pressure from Western nations did Japan finally consent to withdraw its troops in 1922.

On the domestic scene, while the feeling of national self-confidence gained in the Meiji era had been predominantly nationalistic in nature, in the Taisho era it soon became ultranationalistic. Radicals feared that Japan was becoming too democratic, too Westernized. They made fanatic appeals for the reinstatement of orthodox Japanese institutions and at the same time pressured the government for territorial expansion. For the ultranationalists it was Japan's mission to lead and protect Asia. To carry out their appeals they organized no secret societies but chose to operate openly, believing that publicity would bring them support. The many different groups of ultranationalists operated under a common line of conduct—expediency—shifting their policies as required by the circumstances.

The core of their activities was the Gen'yosha (Black Ocean Society), an organization formed in 1881 by dissident ex-samurai of Fukuoka. Toyama Mitsuru (1855–1944), an influential leader of the Gen'yosha, looked back to the glories of the classical warriors as he imagined them to have been. Toyama was able to attract large numbers of *soshi* (literally, "brave stalwarts"), emotional young activists who thirsted for adventure. They were encouraged to train themselves in classical bujutsu and budo, but many of them preferred modern disciplines, such as kendo and judo. The Kokuryukai (Black Dragon Society), founded in 1901, made *tenno shugi,* the divine rulership of the emperor, its basis for operation, and became the elite group of Japan's ultranationalists. The society was eventually able to exert pressure on the government through its connections with political leaders, business, and the military; financial support was forthcoming from all of these powerful segments of Japanese society. The violent anti-Russian sentiment that permeated the thoughts of the Shina (China) Ronin members of the Black Dragon Society was most useful to the army, which used these men to establish liaison with the Manchurian bandits called *hunhutze* and with White Russians in Siberia, Manchuria, and Korea. From such sources as these the army derived its intelligence and furthered its espionage in Asia in preparation for expansion there.

The defeat of Russia by Japan in 1905 turned the ultranationalists against the important issues of Japanese cooperation in entering into international agreements for naval limitation and a milder policy on the Asian continent. When international trade rights and treaties turned unfavorable to Japan, the ultranationalist radicals became subversive in their own country. The wave of subversive action that swept over Taisho Japan had its roots in the spirit and leadership of the officers of the Kwantung Army, based in Manchuria. Their abortive plot to seize control of Manchuria in 1915–16 had the support of the general staff of Japan's armed forces, and is additional evidence of the rise of aggressive militarism as a feature of Japanese government.

The fanatic Kita Ikki (1884–1937) desired to promote "a revolutionary Asia" and joined the Black Dragon Society to further that aim. In his *Nihon Kaizo Hoan Taiko* (An Outline Plan for the Reorganization of Japan), written in 1919 while he was in Shanghai, Kita stated the measures he believed necessary to make Japan the leader of Asia: (1) the suspension of the constitution, (2) the establishment of martial law, and (3) a *coup d'état.*

Kita's "gospel of the sword" approach appealed to many minds. Asahi Heigo (d. 1921) called for a "Taisho Restoration." He accused Yamagata and other high government officials of corruption. Asahi listed nine points that would bring about the sorely needed civil reforms in "this evil society." He would "bury the traitorous millionaires, . . . bury the high officials and nobility," and "crush the present political parties." As a start toward his ends, he advised his followers: "Do not speak, do not get excited, and do not be conspicuous. You must be quiet and simply stab, stick, cut, and shoot. There is no need to meet or to organize. Just sacrifice your life." Asahi remained true to his principles when, after his brutal slaying of the head of the Yasuda *zaibatsu* (financial clique), he took his own life.

Social and political liberalism effected a sharp shift in Japan's foreign policy. A temporary change from imperialism to internationalism proceeded from the strength of party government in the twenties. This change was also due, no doubt, to the failure of the armed forces to produce material gains, to the growing independence of action of military officers in Asia, and to the galvanization of the Chinese people against the Japanese because of the Japanese army's attempts to dominate them. Yet another contributory factor was the growing hostility of the West, in particular the United States, to Japan's policy of imperialist expansion.

The twenties were characterized by peace, international good will, and energetic democratic action within Japan. A sizable reduction in armament was achieved. At the same time, conservative elements in society who had formed the Kokusuikai (National Purity Society) in 1919 became dedicated to keeping out undesirable foreign ideologies. Their reemphasis on loyalty to the imperial throne and their reaffirmation of the values of bushido, especially the virtues of courage and humanity, inspired a great number of people. The Kokuhonsha (National Foundation Society), founded in 1924, sought to guide the ideology of the people, strengthen the foundation of the nation, and clarify the national polity (kokutai). Both of these societies advocated mass participation in modern martial disciplines, such as kendo and judo.

A stronger civil control over the armed forces in the 1920s had an important effect on the army and navy. The reduction in size of these forces allowed them to modernize with remarkable thoroughness. Those officers who had been relieved of duty because of budgetary cuts found occupation as teachers in middle and high schools, as well as in military camps organized to train young men who did not follow a regular course of academic or vocational training. In the diary of General Ugaki Kazushige, an army minister from Okayama Prefecture who was the first man to break the Choshu monopoly of that position, we find clear evidence of the army's plan for regulating the education of the Japanese citizen: "The right of autonomous command over the emperor's army is, in a time of emergency, not limited to the command of troops, but contains the authority to control the people." Japan's time of emergency was approaching.

THE SHOWA ERA   In the face of the worsening world political and economic situation, Japan ran up the banner of aggressive militarism. This was the calculated and risky policy for survival that ironically involved Showa ("Radiant Peace") era (1926–present) Japan in the greatest buildup of armed forces that she had ever experienced and led her down the destructive path of militarism to national disaster.

By the early thirties there appeared a very distinct cleavage between the ultranationalist ideologists and the ideological conservatives. Youthful, spirited radicals gathered around the former group. The latter, for whom the problems of social change and unrest were to be met by reaffirmation of the traditional institutions of Japan, managed to obtain the backing of respected, established citizens. Shidehara Kijuro (1872–1951), when foreign minister for the second time between 1929 and 1931, took a stand for peaceful cooperation with other countries, and especially for rapprochement with China; he also urged further reductions in the size of Japan's armed forces. His conciliatory attitude and understanding of the necessity for seeking peace earned for his actions the name of "Shidehara diplomacy." Yamamuro Sobun (1880–1950), an important executive of the Mitsubishi zaibatsu, supported Shidehara, saying: "We must absolutely follow a policy of peace."

The ultranationalists, however, continued their activities without moderation. The Black Dragon Society remained steadfast in its belief in "divine rulership" and sought now to heighten the development of "the martial virtue of the Japanese race." In 1930, in a document prepared for its thirtieth anniversary, the society announced: "We shall carry out the spirit of the Imperial Rescript to Soldiers and Sailors and stimulate a martial spirit by working toward the goal of a nation in arms. Thereby we look toward the perfection of a national defense." A considerable proportion of the ultranationalists was especially angered by the fact that the "Shidehara diplomacy" had cost the armed forces a falling off in both size and prestige. The prestige of the army was so low that officers deliberately chose to wear civilian clothing during off-duty hours. It became the pledge of all ultranationalists to restore the army to its former position of greatness.

In general, the high-ranking officers of the armed forces who were the ruling oligarchy under Yamagata had been men of moderate policies. They made Japan's expansionism on the Asian continent a civil matter. The ultranationalists of the Taisho era found Yamagata and his few remaining stalwarts unapproachable and therefore regarded them with great contempt, characterizing them as "military bureaucrats" and "subservient minions of the detestable civil leaders." Yamagata's demise made easier the cooperation already established between ultranationalists both in and out of government. A new generation of officers was now able to dominate the army, and to exercise a heretofore unparalleled independence of action. Their rise to power heralded a shift in balance among the many elite groups and swung control of the government to the leaders of the armed forces, men who always acted under the authority of the emperor, the object of popular respect and adoration.

Among major causes for the assumption of leadership of government by the armed forces was the social tension generated within Japanese society over the rise of militant Chinese nationalism, which now appeared to threaten Japanese interests in Manchuria. Added to the growing social tension was the impression made by undemocratic states that were rising in Europe, many of whose ideologies had found their way to Japan. The political parties were blamed for a depression in the early thirties, which caused ambitious young men to reflect on the merits of Japan's membership in the community of nations as well as on her constitutional form of government.

There were many who urged military expansionism as a sure way of creating an autonomous economic empire that would improve Japan's security by isolating her from the unreliable Western nations. The ultranationalists outside the government were quick to join in the clamor for expansion, and their fervent support greatly influenced the new generation of young officers with regard to implementing radical foreign policy.

As a scramble for empire appeared to the ultranationalists to be the best solution to Japan's social problems, the new generation of officers engineered the Manchurian Incident of 1931, in which the Kwantung Army, stationed in Manchuria, seized Mukden and other points. This eventually forced Manchuria into the status of a military colony of Japan, where the Japanese soldiers' acts of brutality and aggression had disastrous consequences. In the main, the Imperial Army's actions in Manchuria embarrassed the moderate elements of the government, as they felt the eyes of the world were on them, for they revealed the impotence of the government to control the army. The Showa government therefore was forced to give its official sanction to a foreign policy of which it disapproved and provide moral justification for the fighting in Manchuria.

Those who opposed the policies of the army in Manchuria were apt quickly to be made the victims of "patriotic assassinations," the specialty of the ultranationalist radicals in terrorizing their opponents. Minobe's "organ of government" thesis for the role of the emperor was set aside and replaced by Uesugi's "mystical monarch" theory. The intellectual freedom of the Taisho era disappeared, overwhelmed by the repressive acts of the militarists, who achieved complete control over national public opinion. It was an era when the slogan "War is the father of creation and the mother of culture" summarized the attitudes of the militarists, who decided government policy. This era proved to be one in which the moral standards of the Japanese were at their worst, and in its miserable train the Showa soldier through his acts of atrocity left the worst stains on the tablets of Japanese history.

In spite of its high-riding position the army was not a homogeneous unit. Factions formed within it over the fact that Choshu dominance in army leadership had been broken, and thus old clan rivalries came into play as each faction aspired to leadership. Another serious factor in the disharmony among military leaders was the gap that lay between those officers who, after secondary education and special training in military preparatory schools, had gone only to an officer's training school, and those who, after years of field service, had been specially honored in being permitted to attend the Army War College. The latter looked down on the former group of officers because they were from the very lowest families and their military training had been primarily in tactics; this allowed them to take only secondary positions of authority. The officers of the latter group were from families only slightly higher on the social scale, but they had been well educated in such subjects as strategy, science, and ethics, and in addition many of them had traveled abroad to further their careers. Quite naturally they received the best assignments, those of command and staff, and wore special uniforms and insignia to indicate their superior quality. It was the interaction of these two groups of officers that lay at the bottom of moral decay in the army.

The state of moral decay in the Japanese army in the Showa era casts important light on the nature of Japan's martial culture, especially on the modern disciplines. Neither group of the new generation of officers was recruited from the families of ex-samurai, a practice Yamagata had insisted upon. Instead, they came entirely from the peasantry, and literally were Yoshida Shoin's "grass-roots heroes" put in roles of leadership that they had neither the temperament nor the sense of moral obligation to assume. They were men from families that had been completely dissociated from the classical warrior traditions. The result, therefore, could hardly have been different, for these men obviously could have had no real understanding or appreciation of the rigid ethical values of the traditional warrior institutions.

Fiction and drama concerned with the classical warriors' ethos united to produce a general misunderstanding of this feudal segment of society in the mind of the commoner in his new role as a "samurai." He tried to feel noble in his own mind and when faced by his fellow fighting men. The Showa soldier was now a "man of the sword," the very "soul of honor" of his divine country, precisely, he believed, the continuation in spirit and martial prowess of his classical-warrior ancestors. Though he had lived a fully peaceful civil life, which had some negative effects on his fullest development as a fighting man, his education allowed him to master modern military arts and in general to counterfeit a new and exaggerated sense of duty that he believed to be essentially that of the classical warrior. In combat, the Showa soldier acted under the influence of confused ideals that stemmed from a distorted sense of duty forcibly implanted in him; this, combined with culturally determined characteristics dictated by a shame-oriented ethic together with a strong consciousness of social ties and obligations, drove him on with fanatical energy in the hope of attaining future glory and reward. His personal makeup was cloaked with devotion to the sovereign and love of country. This was a combination that enabled him to march to certain death on a word of command, for as Okakura Kakuzo (1862–1913) put it, "love, like death, recognizes no limits."

The activities of the ultranationalist Sakurakai (Cherry Blossom Society) and Ketsumeidan (League of Blood) resulted in a series of assassinations on the domestic scene. Ultranationalist and revolutionary rightist young army officers attempted a *coup d'état* in 1936. They marshaled thousands of troops under a banner that read "Down with the traitors surrounding the throne." Opposition to the coup was substantial, the emperor, the cabinet, and the navy uniting to organize a counteroffensive with a body of troops mustered from outside areas. The defeat of the rebels was followed by the execution of their leaders, including Kita Ikki, who had had a major part in the plot. There followed a series of purges made possible by the reestablishment of strict army control over the public and the increased activity of the military police. General Tojo Hideki (1885–1948) was instrumental in directing these purges. Though the ultranationalists lost influence with the government, they remained hopeful in what were temporarily quiet roles. The army continued in its role of an autonomous elite, its position made even more secure and prestigious by having rid itself of subversive elements within its own structure. The government also moved to clarify the nature of kokutai, the national polity.

This concept underwent changes, significant among which was the attempt to feature Pan-Asianism and the exclusion of the West from continental Asia. The Ministry of Education issued *Kokutai no Hongi* (Fundamentals of Our National Polity) in 1937. This document dealt with the way in which Western influences were to be absorbed without permitting them to destroy Japanese traditional values, and how problems of liberal intellectualism and individualism were to be resolved. Loyalty was redefined: "Loyalty means to reverence the emperor . . . and to follow him implicitly. . . . Offering our lives for the sake of the emperor does not mean so-called self-sacrifice, but the casting aside of our little selves to live under his august grace and the enhancing of the genuine life of the people of a State." As was filial piety: "Filial piety is a way of the highest importance. Filial piety originates with one's family as its basis, and in its larger sense has the nation for its foundation.... The family is the training ground for moral discipline based on natural sympathies."

Then loyalty and filial piety were combined: "Filial piety ... has its true characteristic in its perfect conformity with our national polity by heightening ... the relationship between morality and nature.... Filial piety is a characteristic of Oriental morals; and it is in its convergence with loyalty that we find a characteristic of our national morals."

The document also stressed the quality of *wa*, "harmony," making it a quality of the Japanese spirit and thus a virtue of the state: "Harmony is a product of the great achievements of the founding of the nation.... [It] is a great harmony of individuals who, by giving play to their individual differences, and through difficulties, toil and labor, converge as one." In regard to the martial spirit and bushido, the Ministry of Education had this to say: "Harmony is clearly seen also in our nation's martial spirit. Our nation is one that holds *bushido* in high regard.... But this martial spirit is not [a thing that exists] for the sake of itself but for the sake of peace, and is what may be called a sacred martial spirit. Our martial spirit does not have for its objective the killing of men, but the giving of life to men. This martial spirit is that which tries to give life to all things, and is not that which destroys.... It is a strife which has peace at its basis with a promise to raise and to develop; and it gives life to things through its strife. Here lies the martial spirit of our nation. War, in this sense, is not by any means intended for the destruction, overpowering, or subjugation of others; and it should be a thing for the bringing about of great harmony, that is, peace, doing the work of creation by following the Way [*dō*]."

Maintaining that Yamaga Soko and Yoshida Shoin exemplify the spirit of bushido, the Ministry of Education aimed its ethical canon directly at the Showa fighting man: "The warrior's aim should be, in ordinary times, to foster a spirit of reverence for the deities and his own ancestors in keeping with his family tradition; to train himself to be ready to cope with emergencies at all times; to clothe himself with wisdom, benevolence, and valor; to understand the meaning of mercy; and to strive to be sensitive to the frailty of Nature."

Bushido, seen in this light, has "shed itself of an outdated feudalism" and is "increased in splendor" to become "the Way of loyalty and patriotism" and "the spirit of the imperial forces." The document concludes with this summary of Japan's national mission: "to build up a new Japanese culture by adopting and sublimating Western cultures with our national polity as the basis, and to contribute spontaneously to the advancement of world culture."

The Ministry of Education made no attempt to separate the issues of civil peace and military war. Military reforms were made that found support in, and complemented, the Showa concept of kokutai. The military and naval techniques of Germany, France, and Britain were the patterns for Japan. Two component systems of the classical bujutsu were retained, albeit modified to conform to modern tactics: *bajutsu,* or horsemanship, and *juken-jutsu,* or bayonet art. In the thoroughness of the Showa martial reforms can be seen an unmistakable increase in preparations for war, and one not altogether defensive in nature.

Strategic planning was carried out on the assumption that Russia was the only real enemy in Japan's sphere of interest. It became necessary, therefore, to match Russia's military might. A "Five-Year Plan for the Production of War Materiel" was drafted. Jingoists within the army championed a more aggressive stand against China, urging that the Nanking government of Chiang Kai-shek be crushed before it had time to make an alliance with Russia. The tactical concepts of defense were augmented by strategic concepts of national destiny, moral right, and economic interests.

An unplanned clash between Japanese and Chinese troops near Peking in 1937 spread and developed into general conflict. A Japanese army overran Nanking that same year, determined to deliver a knockout blow to the Chinese. The horrors of the Japanese soldiers' brutalities in Nanking are only too well recalled under the descriptive phrase "the rape of Nanking"; civilian men, women, and children were indiscriminately shot or bayoneted to death. Russia poised its military forces on China's northernmost boundaries and forced Japan to limit tactical deployment of its forces. A puppet government was established in Nanking, and Japan announced the founding of a "New Order in East Asia." This "New Order" was a divided rule. Separate army commands in specific geographical areas, each seeking to dominate the occupation of China, resurrected the old officer rivalries that had riddled the Manchurian front some years earlier. The ultranationalist Japanese, both at home and in China, were spurred on to produce a new wave of terror and espionage.

The limited war in China had an intellectual backing. Okawa Shumei, a civilian conservative, sought to rationalize war by appealing to the citizens' spirit of historical (kokugaku) recall. Okawa reemphasized the thesis that Japan was the leading spokesman for Asia. He likened Japan's military action in China to a holy war, and borrowed an Islamic expression for this purpose: "Heaven lies in the shadow of the sword." In the face of Western criticisms of Japan's expansion in China, Okawa remarked: "The way of Asia and the way of Europe have both been traveled to the end. . . . these two must be united; . . . this unification is being achieved only through war. . . . A struggle between the great powers of the East and the West . . . is . . . absolutely inevitable. . . . It is my belief that Heaven has decided on Japan as its choice for the champion of the East." Hashimoto Kingoro, an army leader of the ultranationalists, called for territorial expansion and challenged the moral myopia of the West in no uncertain terms: "And if it is still protested that our actions in Manchuria were excessively violent, we may wish to ask the white race just which country it was that sent warships and troops to India, South Africa, and Australia and slaughtered innocent natives, bound their hands and feet with iron chains, lashed their backs with iron whips, proclaimed these territories as their own, and still continues to hold them to this very day?"

On the spiritual side, Japan's war potential was mobilized by an undivided national attention to the promotion of martial disciplines, such as classical budo and the modern disciplines. The medium used to develop the frame of mind necessary in time of war was the educational system; kendo and judo became compulsory subjects in the curricula of all schools. Such matters as the standardization of techniques and teaching methods, the qualifications and examinations for instructors, and the issue of teaching ranks and licenses were the province of the Butokukai. By 1941 Japan was sufficiently mobilized to begin an aggressive war.

While Japan kept its eyes on Russia, as far as the Asian continent was concerned, the Imperial Navy looked with alarm at the threatening presence of the United States fleet in the Pacific. Though perhaps the Imperial Army had no fear of risking combat with Russia, the navy was inclined to regard the United States with respect and awe. But in the councils of government the militarists dominated the making of political decisions, and therefore, motivated by their plan for leadership in Asia, drew up operation orders directed against the United States. The militarists rightly felt that the American "Open Door" policy in Asia could not be backed by armed action; the best that the United States could do in retaliation against Japan's opposition to the Open Door would be to invoke economic sanctions.

Japan, a treaty ally of Russia, was put in the embarrassing position of being asked by Germany to attack Russia. After prolonged study of the matter, the general staff decided to wage war against Russia, but when the German attack on the Russian front failed, the general staff switched its strategy and concentrated on Southeast Asia. Japan landed army troops in Indochina in 1941. In retaliation, as military leaders had predicted, the United States and its allies declared a total embargo against Japan. The effect of this embargo on Japan's oil reserves worried the general staff the most. Above the protests of its naval advisers, the general staff drafted a final plan aimed at carrying out "the national destiny of the nation." In essence, the plan outlined how Japan was to secure an area of economic self-sufficiency and defend it. Beyond that major objective lay a vague scheme for the "Greater East Asia Co-Prosperity Sphere," which was intended to harness the resources of Asia into a vast market, integrated and defended by Japan.

The Japanese general staff believed that the risk of war with the Unites States was morally justified, and further, that its plan of operation could not fail; the United States would soon tire of war. China was ineffective, Britain was on the verge of total collapse, Germany appeared to be on the verge of victory, and thus the international situation was such as to leave Japan to face the United States single-handed. The militarists staked their hopes on the fact that Japan's supposed superior spiritual power, its shorter line of supply, and the physical hardiness of its people would offset the admittedly greater industrial advantages of the United States. While the operations entailing the sinking of the United States fleet were being carried out, Japanese diplomats earnestly worked for a diplomatic solution. The decision of the United States in the ensuing negotiations, however, was to brand Japan as an aggressor, and no settlement was reached. The United States' belief that Japan would not attack and the Japanese army's unwillingness to scrap its cherished and "holy" plan were factors that provided Japan with the opportunity to evoke the most fundamental principle of tactical war—suprise—as the general staff ordered the attack on Pearl Harbor in December 1941.

After suffering a crushing defeat at the hands of the Allied Powers in 1945, Japan turned from the smoldering rubble at its feet to the tremendous task of raising itself to the position of a prosperous nation at peace. Its present course continues to be one in which it seeks the respect of the community of nations. Oyama Ikuo (1880–1956), professor of political science at Waseda University, became the "grand old man" in moves for pacificism and socialism but was never directly connected with any specific political stand. In his *Nihon no Shinro* (Japan's New Role), published in 1948, Oyama expressed the postwar sentiments of most Japanese: "As a result of defeat, the wall that secluded the Japanese mind from the outside world broke down.... We also have to realize fully the significance of the declaration renouncing war. This declaration is not a mere accessory, but a guiding principle to regulate our future national life. With this ideal, Japan is going to enter the international stage as an unarmed nation. This is a new role for the Japan that until yesterday was armed from top to toe as one of the imperialistic powers."

Oyama saw a nation without arms as a nation without power, power being defined mainly in terms of military forces and police agencies. He challenged the cynics who might question the ability of a nation without power to be truly a nation by offering a new concept of sovereignty, that expressed in the charter of the United Nations. Such a concept would make of the nation, believed Oyama, "a new Japan." Oyama concluded his aspirations for Japan's future with a penetrating note of concern: "In order for Japan to exist as a nation without arms, everlasting world peace is a necessary premise."

Among the many measures taken by the Allied Powers to eliminate Japan's potential to wage war was a prohibition of all institutions considered to be "the roots of militarism." As a result, the Butokukai and its affiliates were disbanded; the Black Dragon Society was also dissolved. Included in the prohibition were classical bujutsu and budo, as well as the modern disciplines. But the Allied Powers were unable to identify precisely the component systems of the modern disciplines, and one such discipline—karate-do—escaped detection and continued to be openly practiced.

A gradual revival of the practice of all disciplines was begun when in 1947 the Allied Powers authorized the retention of several classical bujutsu and the creation of a new modern discipline, *taiho-jutsu,* as methods of self-defense necessary in the training of Japanese policemen within the greatly decentralized police force. In the following year kendo and judo were also reinstated as desirable training disciplines for the members of the skeleton law-enforcement agency; and, given a sport emphasis, these same modern disciplines were also made available to the general public. The Japanese public's response to sport kendo and judo was, at first, a cautious one, and participation in these disciplines was not widespread. Their popularity grew, however, as men serving with the different branches of the armed forces of the Allied Powers eagerly engaged in kendo, judo, karate-do, and aiki-do; many Japanese experts made their living by teaching these disciplines.

During the late 1940s Japan faced serious domestic problems, among which was the resurgence of ultranationalist ideology. In general, the ultranationalists, through political assassinations and other brutal acts, aimed at disrupting the established pattern of social and political harmony. The Japanese police force, in its greatly decentralized condition, was unable to cope with such outbursts of violence, and as a result the Supreme Commander for the Allied Powers (SCAP) ordered legislative action against all activists. But it remained for the outbreak of the Korean War in 1950 to bring about a marked change in the basic policy of the occupation forces, which until that time had been to demilitarize and democratize Japan.

With the Korean War, the ban on both classical and modern disciplines was officially removed, and the Butokukai was reestablished. SCAP ordered the Japanese government to ensure the maintenance of internal order in the absence of Allied troops, which were needed on the Korean front, and to establish a National Police Reserve. Thus began an unhindered use of classical bujutsu, as well as modern bujutsu created for the purpose of training policemen; and kendo and judo were selected to be the primary means of physical education for all Japanese policemen.

The reactivation of the police force was the prelude to rearmament, which was made necessary by the termination of the Allied occupation of Japan. Though the police force could maintain internal peace and order, it was incapable of defending Japan from external attack. The NPR was therefore expanded in 1952 and called the National Safety Corps, and two years later it was greatly expanded and renamed the Self-Defense Force (SDF), with military, naval, and air arms, but insufficient resources for overseas operations. All military men of the SDF were required to train themselves in juken-jutsu, "bayonet art," a classical bujutsu, and to participate in the practice of *toshu kakuto*, a newly created modern discipline; kendo and judo were used for physical education and given a sport emphasis.

In the 1950s the modern disciplines steadily increased in popularity among the Japanese people. The Butokuden was reopened in 1952, and once again this site served as the focus of activity in the national development of the classical martial arts and ways and their modern counterparts. Generals Curtis B. LeMay and Thomas E. Power of the Strategic Air Command (SAC) of the United States Air Force, both dedicated exponents of judo, were instrumental in accelerating a general revival of modern disciplines in postwar Japan. Under the direction of these two dynamic officers, SAC instituted a combative measures program for its personnel both in Japan and in the United States. Emelio Bruno, America's senior Caucasian judo exponent, was selected to administer the SAC combative measures program. This involved the study and practice of self-defense and survival tactics for airmen, as well as training in self-defense for air police units and a general program of physical education and sport for all SAC personnel. Leading Japanese exponents of the modern disciplines were invited by SAC to teach and demonstrate their skills in the United States. The first such mission was headed by Kotani Sumiyuki of the Kodokan in 1953.

A security treaty signed in 1951 between the United States and Japan, on the same day that a peace treaty was signed, exists to this day. When the peace treaty was implemented early the following year, the Allied occupation of Japan ended and Japan was once again an independent nation. But the security treaty authorized the United States to maintain forces in certain areas of Japanese territory to operate military and naval bases. Considerable opposition to this pact exists in Japan. Those who seek its abrogation frequently incite or resort to violence to such a degree that stern measures must be taken by the Japanese law-enforcement agencies in order to preserve law and order. The fact that ideologies considered undesirable by the Japanese government are involved in such potentially dangerous activities makes it absolutely necessary for the Japanese to maintain sufficient armed forces in support of their law-enforcement agencies to prevent the widescale spread of subversion within Japan.

There are those among the Japanese people who genuinely fear the revival of a military dictatorship. And the subject of Japan's rearmament is a matter of deep concern to other peoples in the world who remember only too well the horrors that accompanied the rapid expansion of Japan's invading armies. On the Japanese political scene the issue of rearmament lies at the base of some of the most heated debates and of civil unrest. Left-wing elements and consitutionalists attack rearmament as a violation of the constitution, while right-wing elements advocate rearmament as a sure means by which to dismiss the need for foreign troops and bases on Japanese soil. The majority of the Japanese people appear truly to cherish the hope that they may contribute, as a nation, to the welfare of mankind in a peaceful world and make true for their country the statement: "The empire, though warlike, stands not for aggression, but for peace."

The effect of such widespread public sentiment has contributed in no small way to the increased desire of the government to reduce the importance of the classical martial arts and ways, and to relegate the classical ryu to positions of obscurity and ineffectiveness. In place of the classical disciplines the government is attempting to foster the growth of modern disciplines under the administration of democratic national federations. Hasegawa Nyozekan (b. 1875), a well-known journalist advocating liberal democratic and social reforms, wrote in 1952 in his *Ushinawareta Nihon* (The Lost Japan): "We must not forget that the Spartan, purposefully militaristic training hampers the development of human knowledge and leads to instinctive, impulsive brute will power. It furnished the impetus for the atrocity cases of Japanese soldiers on enemy soil. True will power of a kind fit for human beings cannot be supplied by such a training." However well-intentioned Hasegawa may be, his criticism of "militaristic training" is not valid. If he means to include both classical bujutsu and budo in his argument, then his position is not secure; it suffers from his lack of understanding of the classical disciplines through having had no direct experience of them. Nevertheless, his observations have influenced a reasonably large segment of the modern Japanese public, for most of whom the classical disciplines are relics of a feudal type of "militaristic training."

Modern disciplines like kendo and judo, which come under the auspices of separate national federations, enjoyed a great deal of popularity in Japan as well as overseas throughout the 1960s because of the strong emphasis that was placed on the application of these disciplines as sport. The establishment of the Nippon Budokan (Japan Martial Ways Hall) in Tokyo in 1964 made this site an important center of activity for the modern disciplines. Adding to the popularity of the modern disciplines is the fact that world championships have been conducted for kendo, and both world and Olympic championships have been conducted for judo. Karate-do, too, has been given a strong sport flavor by the Japanese, and world championships have already been held. In spite of the present tendency to employ some of the modern disciplines as "sport budo," however, there is a growing opposition in Japan to the use of any modern discipline as a sport.

A former vice-minister of industry, Sahashi Shigeru, now retired but influential in government affairs, is an experienced exponent of aiki-do, a modern discipline. Sahashi is a strong opponent of the use of classical and modern disciplines as sport. A distinct yomeigaku flavor informs what he writes in his *Shin no Budo* (The True Budo), published in 1972: "Very few Japanese know what budo really is. Persons of high learning, not those who are directly connected with budo, do most of the writing about it. Theory reigns in most of these writers' minds, but their bodies lack experience, and therefore, there can be no understanding of budo among them. . . . Budo is not a sport. It rests in *bu,* the polished skill needed in martial hand-to-hand techniques, raised to the level of a *dō*, which is a way a man should follow. . . . Budo aims through bu to determine man's final destination in life. Bu, however, is only a first step toward *satori* [enlightenment], the final goal. This satori cannot be revealed by words, but only through actions. . . . It is only the kind of experience noted by Miyamoto Musashi in his *Gorin no Sho* [Book of Five Circles] that is meaningful. This is *tanren,* the secret of successful training, an expression that implies that active training made throughout one's life is the way to mastery of the self [satori]."

Sahashi states that proper training in budo develops the personal quality of *sunao* (literally, "plain and straight"), that is, the ability to accept others for what they say and do. But he emphasizes also the riddance of *kodawari* as a personal attribute gained from practice of classical disciplines; this is the ability to abandon the undesirable mental fixations (kodawari) manifested in prejudice. Sahashi urges young Japanese to train themselves in the true spirit of budo in order to attain genuine peace of mind. Budo performed in classical spirit, if not in classical style, is believed by Sahashi to be the ideal training for all citizens, as the mind will be made first "to open," then "to be aimed," and finally "to be brought under control." He further suggests that much of what passes for Japanese budo today is not really budo at all. True budo, says Sahashi, "is to place oneself between life and death and to train the mind. Judo and kendo [as practiced today] are not true budo. They [the exponents of modern kendo and judo] should adopt the spirit of classical disciplines, and not that of pure sport. The technical aspect must not override the spiritual side of budo. To train properly is to establish *hontai* [literally, "main body"], which is morality. To establish morality is to increase a man's ethical conduct and benefit mankind. . . . If the body and mind are made secure [at peace], morality flows from man just as naturally as flowers open from the bud."

Part Two
THE MODERN DISCIPLINES

CHAPTER THREE

MAJOR CHARACTERISTICS

O imitators, you slavish herd.
Horace

The modern cognate disciplines can be described in various ways. To the traditionalists and to those who regard classical bujutsu from the viewpoint of actual combat, the modern disciplines are nothing but an ass in a tiger's skin. An adherent of the spiritually oriented classical budo may view the modern disciplines as a brash and colossal sham, a mere empty shell. Conversely, the adept at modern disciplines is prone to regard the classical bujutsu as crude and anachronistic methods of bloodletting, and the classical budo as methods of seeking oblivion in the idealization of folly. He offers, as a more worthwhile goal for man's endeavors, the modern disciplines, which to him are the beacons of material progress illuminating the realization of useful and wholesome social aims.

The history of the modern disciplines begins after the overthrow of the Tokugawa bakufu in 1868. At that time, as we have seen, Japan was plunged into a period of modernization. The nation suddenly became aware of its crumbling defenses against the outside world, of its disrupted economy, and of the confusion in its social and political systems. Traditional institutions were being challenged, and the leaders of the Meiji government acted with revolutionary vigor to restore national and cultural unity. In the conflict that arose between the conservatives and the progressives, the course of leadership swung in favor of the latter, who maintained that almost all classical bujutsu were nothing but archaic technologies incapable of sustaining national defense. Bujutsu was quickly replaced as the national form of training for members of the armed forces by superior Western military and naval methods and technology. These gave to Japan a combat capacity better suited to its foreign policy of imperialistic expansion.

Though the condemnation of the classical bujutsu as fighting arts by the government was a matter of official national policy, these disciplines did not simply decay. It was primarily their romantic element, coloring the opinions of a minority of conservatives who envisioned the retention of classical warrior virtues as admirable personal values in modern society, that kept the classical bujutsu from disappearing completely. Classical budo, being spiritual disciplines divorced from all considerations of actual combat, and standing against the rising tide of personal liberation in the Meiji and Taisho eras, also did not enjoy a wide following. These disciplines primarily, and oddly enough, served the interests not only of a nonradical group of conservatives but also of radical activists and progressives; in the latter two cases classical budo was not so suprasocial as to be indifferent to politics.

Ultranationalists and militarists, both in and out of government, distorted the intrinsic purpose of classical bujutsu and budo, thus proving the truism that new uses can be found for any product of man's ingenuity; indeed, a hammer can be used to paint a house if it satisfies the expectations of whoever uses it in this absurd fashion. The forced change in the primary purpose of the classical disciplines entailed discarding certain of the integral elements of their respective compositions and a subtle shift in emphasis on the priorities of the remaining elements.

The intrinsic nature of classical bujutsu is manifested by the threefold relationship: (1) combat, (2) discipline, (3) morals. The forced change modified this relationship to the following: (1) discipline, (2) morals. Similarly, the intrinsic nature of classical budo comprises (1) morals, (2) discipline, (3) aesthetic form. This was changed to (1) discipline, (2) morals. It will readily be seen by these changes, made approximately a century ago, that the people advocating them made no distinction between bujutsu and budo; in their eyes, the two were equated. This is the overriding reason for the general misunderstanding of classical disciplines that prevails today, which helps explain why the majority of modern Japanese are unable to distinguish between these two very different kinds of classical disciplines, and furthermore, why they are unable to make any distinction at all between classical and modern disciplines.

But there is more behind the effect of these gross changes than is apparent at first glance. These changes were made to accommodate a new role for such ryu of classical martial arts and ways as could be adapted to the needs of the government. This new role was their use as a means of discipline for citizens. They created a new mentality and spirit in those who were forced by the educational system to participate in such activities, which they would not have done of their own volition; for as surely as the degree of brightness is not the only difference between a kerosene lamp and an electric light, the minds of the people using such disciplines will also differ. Because an external mode of life dictated what the inner life was to be, the activist disciplines altered the internal lives of the Japanese people. The Japanese government fully expected that this change in its citizens' mental outlook would take place.

A basic element of the inner self of any human being, called "spirit," is that inner being which controls the external self; no life is independent of spirit. The Japanese government sought to develop and control the spirit of its citizens by ordering them to participate in bujutsu or budo. *Seishin,* or "spiritual energy," which is generated through training in classical disciplines, was expected to heighten such attributes as courage and patriotic spirit, especially in the case of the soldier or sailor. In reality, the emphasis on enforced discipline tended to exaggerate the importance of spirit in physical endeavor. Every fighting man came to believe that seishin would enable him to perform on the battlefield with a mind that would make possible unfaltering and unerring decisions in any emergency. This concept of seishin helped to fabricate the myth that the Japanese fighting man was invincible in battle.

Along with the change in the primary purpose of the classical disciplines, the personal sentiments and morals of the modern Japanese citizen also differed from those of the classical warrior. "Change" means the creation of a new mode of life, as well as of new ideals in life and new morals for life. But it is also true that both the mode of life in the days of the classical warriors, and the attitudes of mind and spirit fostered by those times, did in some way affect the creation of a new Japanese mind and spirit. All changes are influenced by a spirit of reminiscence, and thus, so pervasive was the influence of classical martial culture on the Japanese people that it enabled them to attempt to preserve the stoic values of the warrior virtues in an entirely new form that was much more acceptable to their modern generation. And so appeared the first of what are today called the *shin budo,* or "new budo." "Shin budo" is a generic expression that encompasses the modern cognate disciplines, that is, those disciplines created after the collapse of the Japanese feudal system in 1868. Both bujutsu and budo forms are included in shin budo and must be differentiated.

For reasons already discussed, the modern disciplines are linked more in technique than in spirit to the classical martial arts and ways. This is partly because the modern disciplines center on the individual's rather than the group's concern for self-protection, and are also focused on the individual's desire to improve his physical and mental health. The developers of the modern disciplines were spurred in the task of creating new bujutsu and budo forms by the fact that many of the classical ryu were closed to them; the classical budo ryu, however, were less restrictive in membership than the bujutsu ryu. Classical ryu appeared to many people in Meiji Japan to be filled with unscientific attitudes and practices. Many of the ryu lacked realism. They functioned in a sphere of activities that were concerned with particularly narrow and vague values in which training was conducted in such a manner as to enable trainees to imagine that they had conquered figments of the mind that there was no question of actually surmounting.

The founders of the modern disciplines borrowed liberally from both the theory and the practice of such classical disciplines as they had studied or practiced. In order to enhance their own personal prestige and that of their new creations, many of these founders made exaggerated claims regarding connections with classical disciplines, cleverly choosing ryu genealogies that could not be proved to be false. But the great expenditure of thought and energy involved in synthesizing different elements of the classical disciplines into new forms also gave rise to numerous innovations that brought to many of the modern disciplines a substantial degree of originality. On the whole, the first modern disciplines founded exhibit a freedom of individual expression and a virility unknown in the classical disciplines.

CATEGORIES AND CHARACTERISTICS   The modern disciplines are usually characterized as methods of self-defense, or as tactics for sparring and grappling with an opponent. In the strictest sense none of the modern disciplines is a true martial art; it is even debatable whether these systems are genuine martial ways. Because of the wide range of their stated purposes and their emphasis on self-defense, there is really very little martial—warlike or combative—quality in these disciplines.

There are two major types of modern disciplines: bujutsu and budo. Both types are alive and vigorous in modern Japanese society, though their purposes are different. Budo forms enjoy a greater popularity because they serve a wider range of purposes, which are determined simply by personal interests and tastes. In order that something of the general nature of the component systems of the two major categories may be understood, it is useful to examine each category in terms of purpose, spirit, and technique.

BUJUTSU

PURPOSE   The major purpose of many modern bujutsu is to provide officially approved methods of hand-to-hand combat for people authorized by the government to deal with offenders against the social order; all study and application of such modern bujutsu is thus confined to the members of law-enforcement agencies and the armed forces of Japan. Other modern bujutsu are purely for use by average citizens as methods of self-defense and spiritual training.

SPIRIT   A spirit of combat morality, which is defensive in nature and which is intrinsic to the classical bujutsu, applies to their modern counterparts. A substantial number of systems of modern bujutsu are made even more highly moral, because of the need for humane application in civil life, by changing the ethical concept of the classical bujutsu of sanction for killing an enemy to the concept of endeavoring to restrain an assailant. Violence is to be met and controlled by restraining those responsible for it, not by taking their lives.

The classical emphasis on *seishi o choetsu,* or transcending thoughts about life and death, is carried over into modern bujutsu, though its significance there is somewhat less meaningful. This is because classical bujutsu are intended to be applied as principal systems of combat on the battlefield, where they operate on the basis of *buai shinken shobu,* or combat to the death between professionally trained and highly skilled equals. The modern bujutsu, however, not only are secondary methods of combat that are mainly (but not exclusively) intended for use in civil life rather than on the battlefield, but always pit a highly trained professional technician against an almost always less-trained assailant. Thus, combat for the exponents of modern bujutsu becomes *shobu,* a matter of winning or losing in a serious hand-to-hand encounter. For these reasons the modern bujutsu are only quasi-martial arts.

TECHNIQUES   The care taken over the selection of techniques that brought the modern bujutsu into existence and that allows them to approximate their classical ancestors in spirit also allows the modern forms to be practical means of hand-to-hand combat for civil applications. Training, therefore, depends entirely on the use of *kaho,* or the method of practice that relies on the use of *kata,* prearranged form. So effective are the techniques of modern bujutsu that it is impossible to practice them in any form of free exercise; consequently, they are not sports.

The teaching of modern bujutsu is conducted by skilled licensed professional instructors. The method used by these instructors is a mixture of intuitive (*kan*) or psychological and rational or logical learning practices, the latter no doubt stemming from the influence of Western methodology. But by and large a yomeigaku flavor permeates all teaching and learning.

Modern bujutsu deal with all aspects of unarmed and armed combat: armed defender against armed attacker, armed defender against unarmed aggressor, unarmed defender against unarmed attacker, and unarmed defender against armed assailant; defense against multiple assailants is also considered. All techniques are uncomplicated, and all are direct responses to attacks. The club and stick are the most prized weapons used in the execution of techniques because these instruments permit a wider range of controlled punishment of the assailant than do bladed weapons or firearms.

BUDO

PURPOSE   Modern budo consists of various systems used as spiritual training and religious cultism, forms of physical exercise or education, methods of self-defense for individuals in daily life, athletic and recreational activity, and sport. All of these systems purport to improve and integrate man's mental and physical energies in such a way as to bring him into harmony with the mores of a peace-seeking international society.

SPIRIT   The high degree of social tolerance that characterizes modern budo forms is an outstanding feature of these disciplines. They are open to all people, regardless of occupation or social station. In furtherance of their varied purposes, modern budo ignore the essence of the classical "sport of death" and substitute for it the "sport of life." The universalistic interpretation that is placed on *senjo,* or the place of battlefield combat, by the classical disciplines becomes for modern budo a kind of arena, the *embujo* for exhibitions and athletic performances or the *shiaijo* for sport contests. In the latter arena the idea of shinken shobu or shobu is replaced by that of *shiai,* a trial between two people in which an opponent replaces the enemy. The uncompromisingly severe martial spirit of the classical disciplines is alien to the modern budo systems. Moreover, the execution of modern budo techniques is never more than an approximation of real hand-to-hand combat, because the taking of life is only symbolic and the action is more in the spirit of a game or sport competition. Exponents of modern budo are required to adhere to highly restrictive rules that limit not only the techniques that may be used but also the precise manner in which they may be executed. Seishi o choetsu is thus at best only symbolically present, and in some modern budo this spirit is completely disregarded.

Dō, or *michi,* which in the classical martial arts and ways is a "way" to be followed or that should be followed, is given a different emphasis in modern budo. Dō becomes the way that *must* be followed by all exponents, a compulsion that gives to modern budo the nature of a forced activity.

TECHNIQUES Kaho, the reliance upon the use of prearranged forms in training, is depreciated in all but a few modern budo in favor of a controlled kind of free exercise. Group instruction, led by *sensei* (instructors) of all levels of competence (and incompetence) replaces the classical method of a direct and highly personal relationship between *shihan* (master teacher) and *monjin* (disciple). Intuitive learning (kan) is less important than is a rational approach to training. The trainee is made to participate in "lessons" taken over a prescribed period of time. These lessons are neatly scheduled as "package courses" of instruction and are expected to be the means through which the trainee eventually will become expert.

The majority of modern budo systems are applied as unarmed methods of grappling or sparring. The grappling systems are the descendants of the polytypic series of tactics that had its beginnings in the martially ineffective styles of classical jujutsu of the late Edo period; the sparring systems developed under the influence of Okinawan peasant arts of hand-to-hand combat. In the emphasis given to unarmed combat, modern budo exhibits a shallow eclecticism, and this is especially true of the newest forms. The founders of these new systems demonstrate that they have substantially forgotten, or perhaps have never understood, the fire in which the techniques of the classical systems were forged. Their lack of familiarity with weapons and with the exigencies of actual hand-to-hand armed combat has resulted, when combat becomes the prime purpose of study or application, in the creation of impractical exercises.

MODERN DISCIPLINES AND CLASSICAL CONCEPTS It is useful to discuss further the connections between the classical and modern disciplines. When the nature of these connections is known, it is possible to understand that much of what passes for original thinking in the design of modern disciplines is, in reality, merely the repetition or amplification of ideas that have served the spirit and function of the classical disciplines for centuries.

Various institutions, customs, and beliefs of traditional Japanese culture—including both those that are indigenous to Japan and those borrowed from alien sources—are to be found in the modern disciplines. Shinto, Taoist, Confucian, and Buddhist concepts that are acceptable to the modern Japanese are revealed when the elements of modern disciplines are critically examined.

Those modern disciplines in which the sword is used as the principal weapon are regarded as the highest forms. It is highly unlikely that this preference will ever be destroyed. This is because the sword continues to be the premier weapon of Japan. But few modern swordsmen are consciously aware, as they wield their blades, of the fact that the precedence of the sword stems from ancient Shinto beliefs. Shinto's highest deity, Amaterasu Omikami (literally, "Heaven Shining Great August Deity"), the ancestral deity of the imperial family, considered the sword as enabling its possessor to "distinguish right from wrong, for the sword stands for justice, and helps the weak against the strong for humanity's sake." Thus, the sword is a divine object of worship, not merely an instrument for killing. For the early Japanese people, the sword always had the qualities of being "firm, sharp, and quickly decisive, wherein lies the true origin of all wisdom," in the words of the *Jinno Shotoki* ("The Records of the Legitimate Succession of the Divine Sovereigns," by Kitabatake Chikafusa; 1293–1354).

Taoist and Confucian concepts combine to form a complex philosophical amalgam that is not intended to be divided. In this view, the cultivation of the self through rigid disciplines is equated to "illustrious virtue," and it is considered axiomatic that one cannot perfect one's self without perfecting the selves of others. Furthermore, aside from the very obvious integration of Taoist and Confucian concepts in the overall doctrine of dō, "cultivation of self" and "illustrious virtue" have yet another significance for exponents of modern budo.

The *Great Learning* (the *Ta Hsueh,* a chapter of the Confucian classic the *Book of Rites* and later designated one of the Four Books of Chu Hsi) makes reference to the "eight minor wires," that is, the eight steps to be taken in spiritual cultivation of the self. The second of these "minor wires," or "the investigation of things," can be interpreted in several different ways, but the result always involves a multiple, not a single, aspect of personal endeavor. The very fact that most modern exponents miss the significance of this multiplicity of endeavor in relation to their study and training in modern disciplines is reason enough why the matter should be explained here.

An exponent who proposes to strive for self-perfection through the medium of a single-system type of discipline fails to abide by the aspect of plurality in "the investigation of things." The criticism of T. S. Eliot comes to mind: "People are always ready to consider themselves people of culture on the strength of one proficiency." And it is patent that the dō cannot be grasped by a single corner, let alone be achieved in this fashion. To attempt to do so is to alter the classical concept of the dō. Thus the tendency of modern systems to develop as all-and-only specialties, that is, only an empty-hand or only a one-weapon system, is rejected by traditionalists as not being characteristic of true budo forms. The traditionalists offer, as proof of their case, the fact that all genuine masters (*meijin*) of classical disciplines, without exception, studied a wide range of different disciplines, never specializing in one alone, at least not before having achieved meijin status. As further evidence, the traditionalists point to the modern scene, where the absolute lack of true masters of the modern dō forms among pure specialists, no matter what their technical perfection, corroborates this thesis.

Many of the dualisms of Chu Hsi Confucianism are found in the modern disciplines, where they have been transferred from the classical disciplines. The modern kendoist who crosses his training weapon with that of his opponent regards that act as *yuken* (in kendo terminology, "shinai contacting shinai"); when these same two training weapons are held apart, this action is termed *muken* (in kendo terminology, "no contact between shinai"). All kendo techniques operate from one or the other of these two aspects of Confucian thought. Yet it is doubtful whether the average modern kendoist realizes that the former condition stems from the Chu Hsi concept of *yukei*, or "having form," and the latter from its complement, *mukei*, or "having no form."

In fact, the ranking system used in many modern disciplines to popularize their teachings, the so-called *dan-kyu* system, is itself based on this very Chu Hsi dualism: exponents having *dan* (graded rank) are designated *yu-dansha* (those having graded rank), while those having no dan are termed *mu-dansha* (those having no graded rank). In the execution of kata, or prearranged form, the judoist or the adept of karate-do who exhibits the right proportions of stillness and movement utilizes the Chu Hsi concepts of *sei*, or passivity, and *do*, or activity, in his mental and physical attitude. The modern bowman, as he performs the necessary operations for shooting a single arrow in *kyudo* style, may scarcely be aware that he has performed yet another act of Chu Hsi dualism; that of *tai*, or essence, and *yo*, or function. Nor does the exponent of some styles of aiki-do generally realize that in spite of the great emphasis placed on *ki* (vital force), the Confucian reverse, *ri*, or reason, must be equally operative if harmony of spirit and action is to prevail.

Whether they are stated or unstated, believed or disbelieved, known or unknown, the dualisms of Chu Hsi can be identified as being operative in all types of modern disciplines, just as they are in the classical forms. Only through the operation of these polarities can the exponent demonstrate a quality of performance that gives a typically Japanese character to the physical action and the necessary emotional mood to accompany its presentation. A performance shorn of any aspect of the many Chu Hsi polarities is a "dead" performance, the result being evident in a lack of "body feeling" on the part of one or all performers. This defect indicates the lack of an "inner life" in those who are exhibiting their skill, the "inner life" that is an essential quality of the true expert, the meijin.

All modern disciplines, as well as the classical martial arts and ways, are activistic in nature. They appeal to the essentially nonreligious nature of the Japanese people but are not without distinct concepts of morality and religious feeling. The modern budo, in particular, seek a metaphysical foundation for their concept of morality. The ethical stimulus that modern budo aims to give its exponents proceeds naturally from Taoist and Confucian concepts more than from Zen precepts, which many modern exponents believe to be the essential source of their ethics; the classical concepts of bushido are only remotely reproduced in modern budo teachings. The Confucian way elevates the mind to a state in which the individual becomes one with the universe, in contrast to the Taoist way, whose basic concept is a negation of the self; this self-abnegation must be made through an identification with nature, which in turn produces an elevation of the mind above mundane distinctions like "this" and "other." Both the Confucian and the Taoist concepts find support in modern budo. At the same time, the modern budo forms follow the theme of social expediency postulated by Ogyu Sorai, which tends to weaken the relevance of many of the highly stringent ethical concepts of Confucianism.

So far as modern exponents are concerned, the natural dispositions of modern man including those in which his inclinations may produce immoral conduct, which were well understood by Motoori Norinaga and Ogyu Sorai, take precedence over abstract, idealistic moral patterns of behavior. For example, the ethical teachings of Confucianism and Taoism that underlay much of the ascetic conduct of the classical warriors have become, in modern budo, little more than romantic ideals. The naturalism of Hirata Atsutane, with its appeal to the Japanese spirit, is a good summary of the goals of Japanese exponents of modern budo today: "To comply with those natural dispositions is called the Way. . . . Since the True Way is as facile a matter as this, one should indeed stop acting like a sage and completely abandon the so-called mind, or the way of enlightenment, and all that is affected and Buddhaish. Let us, instead, not distort or forget this *Yamato-gokoro* [spirit of Japan], but train and regulate it so that we may polish it up into a straight, just, pure, and good spirit of Japan."

A similar naturalistic tendency, which conditions the acceptance of Confucian ethics in modern disciplines, also plays a strong role in the way in which modern exponents accept the influence of Buddhism. At the time that the first modern disciplines were being founded, all sects of Buddhism broke away from strict observance of rigid discipline; and the lessening of the old spirit of austere discipline, together with the growth of liberalism, had an effect on the nature of the modern disciplines. Then too, Buddhism has always had much more significance as the "business of state" in Japan than it has had as a religion for individual Japanese. Therefore, Buddhism influences modern budo only insofar as it is useful for the realization of absolute truth within secular life. The recognition given by modern exponents to the sacredness of physical effort is a dominant feature in any sense of religion they may possess. Thus, if an exponent puts his whole heart and soul into his training, he is practicing "good Buddhism" in the sense that the Zen priest Takuan (1573–1646) meant when he said: "The law of the Buddha, well observed, is identical with the law of mundane existence. . . . The Way [Dō] is practical only."

In the remaining chapters of this book, representative modern disciplines are discussed. While it is important not to lose sight of the connections between the modern and the classical disciplines, it is more important to recognize that, by and large, in the exercise of the modern disciplines in this age of scientific rationalism little attention is paid to the cryptic and intuitive world of the classical martial arts and ways.

Though the earliest of the modern disciplines can be evaluated with some degree of reliability as to their essence and their roles in and effects on society, nevertheless it should be borne in mind that these disciplines are constantly undergoing change. In addition, new modern disciplines are emerging. We hear of systems called *taido* and *aikiken-do,* and still other disciplines. At the time of writing these are too young yet for any hard and fast conclusions to be drawn about their intrinsic nature, and their roles in society have yet to be determined. Therefore the remaining chapters of this book will deal in detail only with well-established modern disciplines, which are not necessarily the oldest of the modern disciplines.

Rather than repeat much of what has already appeared in reliable books on the history and development of the modern disciplines, and on the explanation of their techniques, each of the modern disciplines selected for discussion here will be treated along a new line. Emphasis is placed on the intrinsic nature of these disciplines as stated by their founders and by some of their most qualified and respected exponents. This presentation has a twofold purpose: first, the practicing exponent of modern disciplines will be furnished with a basis for comparing the original form with what is being practiced on the modern scene. In many cases a glaring difference between essence and modern interpretation will be revealed. The recognition of this difference may then be used by serious and dedicated exponents to help rectify the malpractices observed on the modern scene.

Secondly, for the uninitiated, for whom the modern disciplines are perhaps no more than an object of curiosity or simply an academic issue, this presentation will give a true picture of what the disciplines really stand for, an understanding that might not be achieved if one had to rely on chance observation of the perverted practices that riddle the modern scene and are made to pass for the genuine article.

CHAPTER FOUR

THE MODERN BUJUTSU

> Though our sandals be changed,
> our journey continues.
> Okakura Kakuzo

Batto-jutsu

Many classical ryu feature *iai-jutsu*, the art of drawing a sword from its scabbard; but they prefer to call this art *batto-jutsu*. The expression "batto-jutsu" is equivalent in meaning to iai-jutsu, but the former more clearly states the harsh act of "striking instantly with the sword" in dealing with an enemy. When combined with the practice of *tameshi-giri*, the art of testing the cutting ability of a sword and the skill of its user, batto-jutsu implies actual combat.

The establishment in 1873 of the Toyama Gakko, a special school for training army personnel, led to the founding of the Toyama Ryu in 1925. Contained in the martial curriculum of this ryu is *gunto soho,* or the method of using the army sword. Gunto soho, or Toyama Ryu *iai,* as it is more popularly called, stems from the experiences of many *kenshi* (expert swordsmen), notably those skilled in the techniques of the Omori Ryu *tachi-iai,* or drawing (and using) the sword from a standing posture. Seven techniques comprise the Toyama Ryu iai. All are practical methods to be used to kill a foe instantly.

Nakamura Taisaburo (b. 1911) is a master technician of Toyama Ryu martial studies; he is skilled in gunto soho, juken-jutsu, and *tanken-jutsu* (short-sword art). He is also a master teacher of classical iai-jutsu and such modern disciplines as kendo and iai-do; in addition, he is highly skilled in kyudo and judo. Nakamura has brought a total of thirty years' experience to fruition in the founding of his Nakamura Ryu, and makes batto-jutsu its central subject.

THEORY AND TECHNIQUES Nakamura purposely chooses to classify his system of sword-drawing techniques as a *jutsu* form in order to preserve the dignity and martial character inherent in that system. A sense of the practical thus dominates all of his teachings, and no special attempt is made to embellish techniques with a network of fanciful philosophical concepts. Nevertheless, a positive spiritual essence lies at the base of all training in the Nakamura Ryu.

Nakamura Ryu batto-jutsu draws its spiritual essence from what is suggested by the expression *eiji happo,* which is, literally translated, "the ideogram 'eternal,' eight laws," a fundamental concept of *shodo* (the way of calligraphy). But it is the deeper, Buddhist figurative meaning for "eight," that is, "myriad," that is intended here; thus the expression "eiji happo" means "the myriad eternal ideograms." This special meaning implies the infinite variety of patterns possible for the calligrapher's brush as it is used to write various ideograms, and applied to Nakamura's batto-jutsu this becomes *happo-giri no tosen,* or "the myriad patterns (sword trajectories) for cutting."

The very practical elements of Toyama Ryu iai have inspired Nakamura to include them in his brand of swordsmanship. As in the Toyama Ryu techniques of iai, *seiza* (the formal Japanese sitting-kneeling posture) has been entirely eliminated from Nakamura's batto-jutsu; all techniques are executed in a standing posture. Nakamura has extended the scope of the five standard *kamae* (combative engagement postures) of modern kendo (*chudan no kamae, gedan no kamae, jodan no kamae, hasso no kamae,* and *waki no kamae*) to eight by making left and right variants for the kendo standards of jodan, hasso (happo), and waki no kamae. Eight cutting techniques, known as happo-giri, make up the entire repertoire of the Nakamura Ryu batto-jutsu, and therewith literally fulfill the designated requirement of eight actions indicated by that expression; but these are fundamental patterns, and the expert is free to improvise within the latitude afforded him by the Buddhist interpretation of eight as myriad.

Batto-jutsu, as taught by Nakamura, is not specifically intended to be an art of killing; but on the other hand, it is not intended that the exponent of batto-jutsu be killed should he be forced to face an enemy in combat. Nakamura's batto-jutsu abides by the classical concept of *bu,* which is always a defensive interpretation of combat. The purpose of Nakamura's system is to provide a means for the *seishin tanren,* or "spiritual forging," of the individual. Through dedication to training, the exponent of Nakamura Ryu batto-jutsu improves himself mentally as well as physically and thereby elevates his character. *Kokoro* (mind, spirit, mentality) must be brought into all training efforts. As a spiritual aspect of the self, kokoro enables the exponent to prepare for the arduous discipline of training. Kokoro frees his mind from distracting thoughts and enables him to concentrate his energy on what he is doing as he trains. *Seigan no kamae,* a combative engagement posture that resembles the chudan no kamae of kendo but differs from the latter in that it specifically threatens the foe's eyes, according to Nakamura "is a projection of the exponent's kokoro"; it readily reveals to an expert like Nakamura the user's state of mind and his degree of skill with the sword.

No matter what level of spiritual perfection may be derived from the practice of

Nakamura Ryu batto-jutsu, and regardless of how high a degree of skill in the pure form of the happo-giri may be attained, Nakamura believes that without some way of testing practical effect, the art becomes a meaningless exercise in form. He suggests, therefore, frequent use of tameshi-giri (test cutting) as a necessary adjunct to batto-jutsu training. Through sufficient experience with cutting against targets made of bamboo and rice-straw, the exponent of batto-jutsu can evaluate his physical technique in terms of effect; this serves to indicate his mastery of indispensable fundamentals, such as proper use of kamae and *ma-ai* (combative engagement distance), and his skill in focusing the cutting power of the sword through hand actions.

IAI-DO TODAY   Nakamura is as traditional in his thinking as he is practical. He does not consider any modern budo to be a martial art. Referring to systems of iai-do in particular, Nakamura views them as nothing but disciplines for mind and body, many exponents of which use their individual skill to bolster their egos and to impress viewers. According to Nakamura, modern iai-do technique has purposely been made both artificial and pointless from the point of view of combat; iai-do is beautiful according to the concept of *tadashii katachi,* or "correct form," which is exercised in accordance with the *seitei-gata,* or standard form of sword-drawing techniques, created by the Zen Nihon Kendo Remmei (All-Japan Kendo Federation) and the Zen Nihon Iai-do Remmei (All-Japan Iai-do Federation). Nakamura views the seitei-gata as concessions made to the demands of today's public.

The practical, combative aspect of sword drawing, which is the essence of jutsu forms, is lost when such techniques are adapted to the requirements of iai-do. Beginning a sword-drawing technique from seiza, for example, "was not the manner in which the classical warrior employed his sword," notes Nakamura, "for it is not a practical posture when one is armed with the daisho [long and short sword combination]." Neither is Nakamura content with the form of execution of the four technical characteristics of sword drawing when made in iai-do fashion. *Nukitsuke* (drawing the sword from its scabbard) is generally done far too slowly, and in a manner that withdraws as much as eighty percent of the blade from the scabbard before any appreciable speed of action occurs. "This is not *nuki*," the instantaneous action of the blade, says Nakamura. The slow draw further exposes *suki* (weaknesses in defense) in the swordsman's technique. *Kiritsuke* (cutting action), as made by the majority of modern swordsmen, is also "ineffective," says Nakamura, "because they lack experience with tameshi-giri." *Chiburi,* or manipulating the blade in such a way as to "shake off blood" that supposedly has accumulated there from the immediately previous cutting action, is also inefficiently done. "No warrior ever did chiburi as it is performed by the iai-do exponent of today." The only real cleaning action after striking a human target "is to wipe the blade with a piece of cloth or paper, an action never omitted by the warrior before returning a blade to its scabbard." The final act of *noto,* or returning the blade to its scabbard, does not escape Nakamura's critical attention either, for not only does it follow on the inefficient action of the chiburi, but it is made quickly for no other purpose than a demonstration of skill. In reality, "the return of the blade to the scabbard, as it was done by the warrior, was a rather slow, careful action made as *zanshin* ("alertness remaining-form"; continued domination over the opponent characterized by complete, continuous concentration and evinced through both mental attitude and physical posture) prevailed.

Modern exponents engaged in iai-do also have little understanding of the manners and customs of the classical warrior. They appear to Nakamura a careless lot. "I have carefully examined many hundreds of swords belonging to modern swordsmen, and scarcely have I found one of which the *koiguchi* [the open end of the scabbard] was unscarred." The classical warrior evaluated his skill, and that of others, by the condition of the koiguchi. The koiguchi was not to be scarred by cutting it, which occurs when the action of drawing the sword or the return of the blade to the scabbard is improperly done. Inasmuch as the koiguchi is an integral part of the sword, virtually a part of the warrior's "living soul," to scratch or cut it is tantamount to scarring one's own soul.

Nakamura offers sound constructive advice that would evoke a greater sense of discipline from exponents of modern iai-do and bring them to maintain traditional, practical values in the use of the sword. "There should be established a balance of the old and new in all training," says Nakamura, "but the tendency for showmanship must be removed, sport or competitive aspects eliminated, and the relationship between kendo and iai-do recognized." Many modern kendoists know nothing of true swordsmanship simply because "the *shinai* [bamboo practice sword] is not a sword." Only the live blade can instruct in kendo, the "way of the sword," believes Nakamura.

Keijo-jutsu

At the time of its establishment in 1874, the modern Japanese police force assumed responsibility for the maintenance of civil law and social order throughout Japan. The problem of modernizing police methods of hand-to-hand combat has been a continuing concern of police officials since the late Meiji era. The sword served as a standard item of the policeman's equipment until the end of World War II, augmented by the revolver or pistol. But in spite of the effectiveness of blade and firearms, these weapons are obviously inappropriate in many common situations.

A seven-man technical commission was appointed for the purpose of creating a more suitable method of armed hand-to-hand combat. Shimizu Takaji and Takayama Ken'ichi, two expert technicians of classical bujutsu, gave a demonstration of *jojutsu* (fighting-stick art) before the technical commission in 1927. Their demonstration was so impressive that police officials decided to adopt several techniques of jojutsu and to incorporate them in the special training programs of Japanese policemen. The training of patrolmen in jojutsu requires expert supervision, and in 1931 Shimizu was called to Tokyo to be the resident police jojutsu instructor. Under his technical guidance the *tokubetsu keibitai,* or special police unit, was created; policemen of this unit were specially trained in the use of the *jo,* a medium-length hardwood stick.

Jojutsu, as adapted for modern police purposes, is officially referred to as *keijo-jutsu*, or police-stick art. As taught by Shimizu, this is a system used to restrain unruly groups or to quell riots. The ban imposed on martial arts and ways by SCAP in 1945 exempted keijo-jutsu because it was a necessary subject of training for Japanese policemen. But the general stability of the domestic scene gave few opportunities for the application of keijo-jutsu, and thus its role in police work was less essential than had been anticipated.

THEORY AND TECHNIQUES   Keijo-jutsu is based on the classical martial art of jojutsu, specifically teachings that stem from the seventeenth-century Shindo Muso Ryu. The defensive rationale of classical jojutsu applies equally well to keijo-jutsu.

When used in a systematic fashion, the stick is the ideal weapon with which to restrain an aggressor. It offers a wider range of application than any other weapon. In civil law-enforcement work the use of firearms or bladed weapons is restricted to a very narrow range of application. The user must either dole out drastic punishment with his chosen weapon or return it to its carry position, thus making the weapon useless. There is no guarantee when using firearms or bladed weapons that serious injury will be avoided; and if too little use is made of these weapons, there is no guarantee that an aggressor can be subdued. The great difficulty in knowing how to use either firearms or a bladed weapon for restraining an aggressor reduces the effectiveness of these weapons. The stick, however, can be used against an assailant to inflict whatever degree of punishment is necessary to produce submission.

Techniques of keijo-jutsu can be applied with the intention either of causing enough pain in an aggressor to discourage him from further action, or of using sufficient force to break bones and contuse tissues and then to incapacitate him; when the techniques are directed against anatomical weaknesses, called *kyusho*, they result in stunning or knocking out the aggressor. In the hands of an expert, the stick (jo) is used to strike, thrust, sweep, block, parry, or cover the aggressor's attack and neutralize it; both unarmed and armed assailants are readily subdued. The rapid manipulation of the jo produces a bewildering series of actions that are most difficult to defend oneself against, and in trying to do so the aggressor must expose some vital weakness that can be exploited by the person using the jo.

KEIJO-JUTSU TODAY   In modern Japanese society, police units rely upon keijo-jutsu as the primary means of coping with certain difficult situations. During times of social unrest, when rioters threaten the security of average citizens, keijo-jutsu is the ideal defense. The mass demonstrations that characterized Japanese urban life in the mid-to-late 1960s and in the first years of the 1970s offered excellent opportunities for refinements in the use of keijo-jutsu. A constant study of keijo-jutsu techniques and tactics is carried out by Shimizu; he is ably assisted by Japan's leading police experts, Kuroda Ichitaro, Yoneno Kotero, Hiroi Tsuneji, and Kaminoda Tsunemori. In ordinary times, however, the jo is a symbol of police authority and justice. Police guards on duty in all Japanese cities carry the jo for this purpose.

Taiho-jutsu

Many urgent problems had to be solved before the modern Japanese police force could carry out its important mission. Neither the severe martial techniques of classical bujutsu nor the spiritually oriented ones of classical budo proved to be entirely useful in their pure forms when applied to civil problems. From the time of the late Meiji era, the modern disciplines of kendo and judo have been useful to the Japanese police primarily as systems of physical education. It remained essential that the police design their own formal systems of hand-to-hand combat that would be more appropriate methods of self-defense.

A technical study committee was convened by the Tokyo police bureau in 1924. The committee members consisted of high-ranked swordsmen who were exponents of kenjutsu, kendo, and iai-do, and specialists in *goshin-jutsu* (self-defense methods of jujutsu and judo). Members of the former groups were Nakayama Hyakudo, Hiyama Yoshihitsu, Saimura Goro, and Hotta Shitejiro; Nagaoka Shuichi, Mifune Kyuzo, Nakano Seizo, Sato Kinosuke, and Kawakami Tadashi represented the latter group. This committee devised a series of self-defense techniques based on unarmed defense and recommended that these techniques be taught to all policemen. The police board approved the techniques and incorporated them into police training procedures with the proviso that the techniques be given extensive study and testing.

The prohibition of martial arts and ways and modern disciplines by SCAP forced the Japanese government to request SCAP to allow the police force at least to develop and use a system of self-defense. Upon receiving approval of this request, the Tokyo police bureau convened a new technical committee headed by kendoist Saimura Goro; judoist Nagaoka Shuichi; Shimizu Takaji, the twenty-fifth headmaster of the Shindo Muso Ryu; Otsuka Hidenori, founder of the Wado Ryu; and Horiguchi Tsuneo, a pistol expert. This committee reviewed the techniques of classical kenjutsu, jujutsu, and jojutsu, and adapted several techniques from each of these disciplines for police use; the committee also selected techniques from modern disciplines, such as jujutsu, karate-jutsu, kendo, and judo, for incorporation into the proposed system of self-defense; and further ideas were gained from a study of Western boxing. A system comprising these elements and called *taiho-jutsu* was created in 1947, and *Taiho-jutsu Kihon Kozo* (Fundamentals of Taiho-jutsu) was published as an official manual for policemen. Taiho-jutsu was revised in 1949, 1951, 1955, 1962, and 1968.

THEORY AND TECHNIQUES   The techniques designed by the first police technical study committee were largely based on classical disciplines as modified by modern judo *kihon*, or fundamentals, such as posture, gripping, and body movement. Ten techniques of *nage*, or throwing, were the basis of the taiho-jutsu system. Eight techniques dealt with *idori*, or situations involving sitting postures; and six *hiki-tate* tactics, or those which bring an unwilling assailant to his feet so that he can be led away, were also devised. Little concern for the victim was shown in the execution of these techniques, which remained in use until after the end of World War II.

Whenever taiho-jutsu is used in modern Japanese society it is applied so as to cause minimum damage to the assailant. An aggressor is to be confronted, controlled, and subdued with safety for both the arresting officer and the prisoner; killing or maiming are measures to be avoided except in the most extreme emergencies. To accomplish this delicate task certain acts in hand-to-hand combat are fundamental.

The concept of *kobo-itchi*, in which the priority of offensive or defensive action depends on the appropriateness of either to the situation, is fully recognized in taiho-jutsu, where it is manifested as *sen*, or initiative in combat. Sen is of three degrees. The first of these, and the most desirable level, is *sen-sen no saki*, or the ability of the arresting officer to act to control his assailant before the latter can launch an attack. *Saki*, the second level of sen, enables the arresting officer to join in an assailant's attack, already started, and then gain advantage over and control the assailant. *Ato no saki*, the third level of sen, is the ability of the arresting officer to receive a surprise attack and to counter it.

Patrolmen study taiho-jutsu in two ways: in *toshu*, or unarmed fashion, and also while armed with the *keibo*, a short wooden club. Considerable study is made of postures, especially those of *kamae*, that is, the postures adopted when an arresting officer prepares for confrontation with an assailant. Fourteen *kihon-waza*, or fundamental techniques, of defense are augmented by sixteen *oyo-waza*, or advanced techniques; mastery of all techniques enables the policeman to deal effectively with all normal hand-to-hand encounters. In addition, the patrolman learns six techniques dealing with *seijo*, or handcuffing; *soken*, or searching methods; and *hiki-tate oyobi*, the restraining methods that bring an unwilling assailant to his feet and enable him to be led away, all the while under control. Throughout the application of all techniques the patrolman must make good use of ma-ai, or appropriate combative engagement distance; he learns to position himself so that he is close enough to his assailant to control him effectively but too far away to be effectively attacked.

But techniques of taiho-jutsu alone are not enough. Every Japanese policeman is expected to develop *heijo-shin*, the normal and tranquil state of mind that is manifested in relaxed posture, normal breathing rhythm, and confidence in what is being done. Through training in taiho-jutsu the patrolman overcomes fear of an assailant. Judgment of the situation and the ability to make the proper use of techniques is the product of experience in depth in training exercises. Among the many aspects of judging a hand-to-hand situation are: (1) the attitude of the assailant (offensive or defensive), (2) the number of assailants, (3) the use of weapons, and (4) the capabilities of the assailant or assailants. Practical situations involving armed and unarmed combat are part of taiho-jutsu training. Trainees wearing protective armor are allowed to wage combat against each other, and the result of each encounter is entered into a record for future evaluation.

TAIHO-JUTSU TODAY Taiho-jutsu is under constant study for further possible revision.

Great changes in social environment in Japan have made it necessary for the police to modify and so improve the system of taiho-jutsu. Though the emphasis on the simple restraint of assailants and other social offenders has not been removed, severe measures have had to be incorporated into the system so that the police can cope with the excessively violent tactics of some radical activists. Taiho-jutsu has also been modified to permit the use of its techniques when the user is garbed in heavy protective equipment (helmet, bulletproof vest, gloves, and shin guards).

Keibo Soho

Keibo soho is the police method of using the keibo, the patrolman's short wooden club, in hand-to-hand combat. The systematic use of the keibo is an essential subject of study in the training of all Japanese policemen.

The keibo became a standard part of the Japanese patrolman's equipment in 1946, during the Allied occupation of Japan. Formalized techniques for the use of the keibo appeared in connection with the creation of taiho-jutsu the following year. The first keibo used by the Japanese was a length of hardwood approximately a foot and a half long; it was necked at one end to distinguish the handle from the body. This design proved unsatisfactory. As a weapon it was too short, broke easily at the neck, and could not easily be reversed by a hand-sliding action. A keibo with a uniform diameter, and approximately two feet in length, was adopted in 1949, but this weapon proved to be too heavy. The short stick of the United States Navy Shore Patrol was finally adapted and standardized as the Japanese keibo in 1956. Shimizu Takaji, the highest authority on stick and club techniques in Japan, headed a technical commission for the study of keibo tactics and recommended the formalization of effective methods. This commission made a constant study of techniques and tactics during the 1960s.

THEORY AND TECHNIQUES   The concept of defense that is essential in law-enforcement work is basic in keibo soho. Shimizu has incorporated many of the defensive aspects of the jojutsu of the Shindo Muso Ryu, of which he is the current headmaster, in keibo soho; patrolmen are taught to use the keibo to respond to an unprovoked attack made by an aggressor, and to subdue the aggressor by knowledge of the kyusho (anatomical weaknesses). The actual techniques of keibo soho, however, are more closely allied to the *jutte-jutsu* (the art of using the single-tined iron truncheon) of the Ikaku Ryu, a seventeenth-century martial-arts tradition; Shimizu is also headmaster of this ryu. These techniques include striking, thrusting, parrying, blocking, and covering actions. All keibo techniques must be used in connection with fundamental methods of body management taught in taiho-jutsu; posture, evasive turning actions, and proper use of ma-ai are important.

KEIBO SOHO TODAY   Because every patrolman carries the keibo as a standard item of equipment, Shimizu conducts a continuing study of its use. The keibo is the single most useful tool of the Japanese policeman to effect the submission of an assailant. But the tendency of radical activists to employ violent tactics that involve the use of various weapons of considerable length makes it necessary to improvise new keibo techniques for use by patrolmen who are responsible for controlling such difficult situations.

Tokushu Keibo Soho

The most recent development in police combat arts involves the use of a weapon called the *tokushu keibo,* or special police club. This is a collapsible tubular truncheon made of metal alloy; because of the rapid manner in which this truncheon can be extended from its fully telescoped position it is also referred to as *tobi-dashi jutte,* or "jump-out truncheon." The tokushu keibo appeared in 1961, at which time it underwent a five-year period of study by various police technical commissions. Essential in its development were the police combat instructors Shimizu Takaji, Kuroda Ichitaro, and Kaminoda Tsunemori.

In 1966 a series of standard techniques for the tokushu keibo was announced, and the system of using this special weapon was called *tokushu keibo soho.* The tokushu keibo was given to police officers who were assigned to special missions. A revision of techniques was carried out the following year, and these revised techniques are currently undergoing extensive testing.

THEORY AND TECHNIQUES The basic techniques of tokushu keibo soho stem from the teachings of the Ikaku Ryu. The single-tined iron truncheon called the *jutte* is the special weapon of the Ikaku Ryu. The jutte is to be used defensively, in response to an unprovoked attack, and it is this same defensive attitude that applies to the use of the tokushu keibo in modern police work.

All ways of using the tokushu keibo require that the operator be fully trained in the fundamentals of body control, such as posture and stance, as well as turning movements. Through *kihon renshu,* practice of fundamentals, the operator improves his reactions in executing prescribed tactics for avoiding an aggressor's attack and in making an effective counterattack with the collapsible truncheon. The *kote-uchi,* or blow to the aggressor's weapon-bearing or attacking arm, must be perfected. Other methods of striking, thrusting, blocking, parrying, and covering the assailant's attack to neutralize it make up the basic methods of using the tokushu keibo. Five techniques are designated as standard, though a considerable number of variations are also practiced. So that these techniques may have a full element of surprise when used, they are divulged only to policemen designated to use them.

TOKUSHU KEIBO SOHO TODAY Essentially, the tokushu keibo can be used in the same manner as the normal wooden keibo, but the durable construction of the collapsible truncheon gives the latter a wider range of application. Except for its relatively high production cost, its advantages over the wooden keibo are many. Its smaller size, when fully collapsed, makes it easy to carry and less susceptible to being seized by an aggressor in a scuffle; it is also easily concealed.

The bodily harm caused by a blow from the tokushu keibo appears to be less than that from the wooden keibo, perhaps due to the metal club's tubular construction, but at the same time its effect exceeds that of the wooden weapon.

Hojo-jutsu

In connection with the work of a police technical commission in 1927, Shimizu Takaji included in his demonstrations made before that body the classical bujutsu called *hojo-jutsu*. Shimizu, assisted by Takayama Ken'ichi, showed the art of restraining and immobilizing an aggressor through the use of a tying-cord. The great interest of the police officials in this little-known art led Shimizu to recommend the adoption of several techniques by the police for use in controlling prisoners.

The adoption of hojo-jutsu for police training methods remained under formal study until 1931, when Shimizu became jojutsu instructor to the Tokyo police. Shimizu then organized formal instruction in hojo-jutsu for all patrolmen. His basic teachings remained in use until after Japan's defeat in World War II. The subsequent ban on classical martial arts and ways did not include hojo-jutsu, as this art was considered an essential part of the training of Japanese policemen. Special studies made in 1949, 1951, 1955, 1962, and 1968 by Shimizu produced some modifications in his original methods of hojo-jutsu and made them more suitable for use in situations likely to arise today.

THEORY AND TECHNIQUES   A seventeenth-century classical bujutsu, hojo-jutsu of the Itatsu Ryu, forms the basis of modern police hojo-jutsu. Though the classical art is distinguishable as a separate formal system of combat, it is in reality only the final stage of action in the classical martial art of *torite*, the art of seizing and restraining an aggressor; the aggressor must first be brought under control before he can be rendered helpless with the tying-cord. In modern police work one can accomplish with taiho-jutsu what the Edo-period policeman did with torite; the application of keijo-jutsu, keibo soho, or tokushu keibo soho techniques may also precede the use of hojo-jutsu.

Modern hojo-jutsu, as used by the Japanese police, consists of five *kihon*, or fundamentals, of handling the tying-cord; three techniques of *tote-nawa (hoshu-nawa)*, or frontal tying; and four techniques of *inchi-nawa (goso-nawa)*, or rear tying. The operator using hojo-jutsu must be capable of keeping his victim under control while tying him. Tying a victim must also be accomplished quickly, and a great deal of training is required to develop the necessary manual dexterity. The various methods of tying make possible different degrees of control. For instance, there are methods that restrict the use of the arms without immobilizing the hands, needed for eating and the like. Some methods permit the prisoner to use his legs for limited walking, but he is unable to run;

still other methods completely immobilize the victim. Certain patterns of tying are used to produce pain in the victim if he struggles to escape, while still other patterns cause loss of consciousness if he tries to escape. A trained policeman is also able to subdue and tie a number of people by himself.

HOJO-JUTSU TODAY   It may appear strange to some that so primitive a method as tying a prisoner with a simple cord should still be used in police work. But in this day of mass arrests during violent demonstrations, the simple tying-cord is not only more economical than metal handcuffs and other restraining devices but also, when hundreds of prisoners are to be immobilized, more readily available. Shimizu and his assistant Kaminoda Tsunemori are carrying out constant study of the use of hojo-jutsu in modern police work.

Toshu Kakuto

Japan's defeat in World War II brought about the complete abolition of its armed forces, and therewith Japan's capacity to wage war. In the years that followed on the Allied occupation of Japan, it was evident that no nation could continue to enjoy a position of prestige in the community of nations unless it maintained some form of national defense. The Self-Defense Force was established in 1954, and continues today as the core of the Japanese armed services.

Every military agency requires an efficient method of instruction for hand-to-hand combat. The fact that this is the so-called nuclear age does not in any way rule out the possibility that a soldier may be required to fight an enemy hand-to-hand; it is his duty to do so with confidence and efficiency. The Japanese tactical method of fighting for use by individual soldiers is called *toshu kakuto*.

The system of toshu kakuto was founded in 1952 under the technical direction of Major Chiba Sanshu (then a captain). Chiba is an expert in various arts of hand-to-hand combat, especially classical jujutsu; he is also skilled in modern disciplines, such as Japanese *kempo* (fist way), judo, karate-jutsu, and *aiki-jujutsu,* and is trained in Western boxing and wrestling. Chiba combined tactics from these various systems to develop his synthesis of toshu kakuto.

THEORY AND TECHNIQUES   Toshu kakuto, a thoroughly military art geared for use in self-defense, is not without elements of offense in accordance with the concept of kobo-itchi, whereby the appropriateness of offensive or defensive action in a given situation determines which of these aspects receives priority.

Certain modifications made in classical and modern disciplines make toshu kakuto practical when used on the modern battlefield. The present-day soldier can expect to fight while wearing considerable clothing and possibly laden with equipment. All movement, therefore, must be simple and direct if it is to be effective; a high degree of agility may be impossible because of the burden of clothing and equipment. All techniques must be valid under conditions in which the terrain may cause its own hazards. There must also be included in toshu kakuto techniques that can be used to dispatch a foe quietly but effectively, for this may be required when dealing with enemy sentries.

Because the striking and kicking methods of toshu kakuto are to be used against an enemy who may also be heavily clad, they must produce the highest possible shock effect if they are transmitted into vital areas. Thrust-punching actions are made with the fist held vertically, not with the screwed-in action that is common to many karate-like systems. The former method of punching not only guarantees a stronger impact on the target but is less liable to damage the wrist. Kicks are delivered with the heel in a thrusting manner. This method of kicking produces the greatest amount of shock-impact and protects the foot from injury; karate-like use of the toes or instep may injure the foot even when boots are worn.

CHAPTER FIVE

KENDO

*Keep up your bright swords,
for the dew will rust them.*
Shakespeare

Kendo is the senior, most respected and popular of the modern budo disciplines. Unlike many other modern disciplines, kendo owes its present standardized form not to the endeavors of a single person but to the collective experiences and skills of many; both classical warriors and common citizens have influenced the creation of modern kendo.

Neither classical kendo, as it was first designed and taught by the founder of the Abe Ryu in the seventeenth century, nor kendo as it is practiced today is either a fighting art or a pure sport. The most experienced devotees of modern kendo consider it to be primarily a system of spiritual discipline; but certain of kendo's inherent characteristics allow its use in physical education, sport contests, or athletic training, or as a recreational activity. But there is in kendo's fascinating technique a spiritual essence whose depth and complexity make it possible for the average modern-day Japanese, who are insufficiently familiar with kendo, completely to misunderstand its intrinsic nature.

Modern kendo is based on a legacy of classical Japanese swordsmanship that is at least as old as the history of the Japanese nation; traditional accounts place the beginnings of Japanese swordsmanship in the mythological age of the deities. Without a doubt the deities, the men, their weapons, and the formal systems of swordsmanship that are subsumed under this legacy all, in one way or another, have inspired the creation of modern kendo. Though the precise national form called Nippon Kendo was developed after the close of World War II, centuries before that time the essential spirit, the prototypes of the equipment used, the theory, and the mechanics of kendo techniques were already being created.

The bushi, or classical warriors, used their swords in *kenjutsu* (aggressive sword art) fashion to establish and maintain social order in Japan from the ninth to the middle of the seventeenth century. Thereafter, the role of the classical warriors as a ruling group became largely a symbolic one. It was but a façade for authority being wielded by a confusing assortment of *buke* (martial families) who acted through the samurai, who were only nominally warriors. Throughout it all, however, the samurai and his sword was viewed by the commoners with an awe generated by a respect born of fear.

One key to understanding why the sword was and even now is regarded by the Japanese as the premier weapon of their land, and also why kendo stands at the head of the hierarchy of activistic disciplines, lies in recognizing a special trait of the Japanese people. The Japanese possess a distinct fondness for sword-fighting at close quarters. Combat in the earliest eras of the classical warriors was generally fought under conditions in which great distances separated the contending forces. The primary tactic was shooting volleys of arrows directed at the enemy by bowmen deployed behind covered positions. Experience, however, proved that this method of combat was indecisive. The classical warrior thus modified his tactics. He began fighting at close range, both in *kiba-sen* (mounted combat) and *toho-sen* (combat on foot), when he was able to attain a decisive result. Thus the *zan-totsu*, or "close and strike," tactics that characterize the methods of the classical warriors became the standard manner of fighting. This style necessitated the use of weapons that were held in the hand and used to pierce and strike. The *odachi*, or long sword, proved to be the best weapon for zan-totsu tactics; and kenjutsu was its most efficient vehicle.

Kengo, or strong and skillful swordsmen, made *kengi*, or sword technique, famed and feared throughout the land. These swordsmen, however, were not without spiritual feelings. In the arduous process of gaining their formidable skills with a variety of weapons, many swordsmen began to reflect on metaphysical questions. The most famous of these swordsmen sought to perpetuate both their physical skills and their philosophical outlooks through the creation of formalized systems of techniques, which they embodied in ryu, or martial traditions. By the time of the establishment of the Tokugawa bakufu in 1603 there were thousands of ryu. Each had its own special philosophical doctrine that centered on swordsmanship in terms of its spiritual essence, theory of techniques, and views on morality in combat, that is, the aims and ethical practices of fighting men. The teachings of the classical ryu greatly influenced the thoughts and actions of the leaders of the Tokugawa bakufu, as well as those of men opposed to the rule of Japan by the Tokugawa family.

Each *ryu-gi*, or style of a ryu, in the pre-Tokugawa systems of classical kenjutsu is designed for waging hand-to-hand combat in defense of a specific local group. In this kind of kenjutsu, self-protection is important only to the extent that the solidarity of the group is concerned. The strategic concerns of attack and defense are subsumed in the doctrine of kobo-itchi, that is, that offense and defense are one and the same thing.

Kenjutsu is used to force victory over an enemy through the use of relentlessly aggressive tactics that cause the enemy to create suki, or weaknesses in his defense, by his reflex actions. Because the pre-Tokugawa leaders of government gave moral sanction to the right of swordsmen to kill, fighting men were guaranteed every opportunity to develop what they regarded as the "positive style" of swordsmanship; kaho, or the use of prearranged formal exercises, was the central training method for this kind of swordsmanship, and shinken shobu (combat to the death) the only possible test of a swordsman's skill.

One of the best examples of the positive style of kenjutsu, as it influenced the political and social history of Meiji Japan, is that of the Jigen Ryu. The Jigen Ryu was founded by Togo Bizen no Kami (1563–1643), and became the foremost martial tradition for the classical warriors of Satsuma. The Jigen Ryu style of kenjutsu features the use of provokingly aggressive tactics in which the swordsman is ready at any instant to strike down his enemy.

During the relatively peaceful centuries of Tokugawa rule, however, battlefield combat was virtually impossible, and civil brawling with the live blade was illegal without specific bakufu sanction. Thus, in this relatively tame social environment, the positive style of kenjutsu quickly became anachronistic. In its place the so-called "vacant style" of swordsmanship was created. This is characterized by a dominantly "wait and see" attitude, the tactic of *suki o mitsukeru,* observing and taking advantage of a weakness in defense (suki) of the enemy created through an error in judgment. Kaho is also the central training method in the vacant style of kenjutsu; but far less dynamic exercises than those of the positive style make up its repertoire.

The social strictures of the peaceful Edo period irritated numerous martial-minded swordsmen. A classical example is that of Yagyu Jubei (c. 1607–50), the one-eyed son of the originator of the Edo Yagyu line of the Shinkage Ryu, Yagyu Munenori (1571–1646). Jubei was a highly spirited warrior and a staunch supporter of the positive style of combat. In his great remorse over the fact that the vacant style of swordsmanship was growing in popularity, Jubei sought and obtained shogunal permission to test his skill against swordsmen trained in the vacant style. The combat was to be made with live blades. Jubei arbitrarily selected seven swordsmen standing in a group and provoked them to attack him by deliberately insulting them and other crudities, which included spitting upon them. In the clash that followed, Jubei severed the arms of two, who ran away, blood gushing from their wounds, then killed another outright, while the remaining four ran for their lives. Jubei's display of skill called attention to the superiority of the positive style over the vacant style, and incidently increased his personal fame as a swordsman; young men inspired by the deed eagerly sought Jubei's teachings.

During the remaining years of the Edo period, however, the popularity of the vacant style of kenjutsu grew enormously. This indicates the degree to which the combative ardor and skill of swordsmen at that time had been suppressed by the bakufu's deliberate policy of reducing and reorienting the warriors' martial appetites toward literary achievements. Successors to classical ryu that once featured the positive style of kenjutsu therefore were inclined to develop the vacant style. A display of skill made with grace and dignity became the criterion of good swordsmanship. The majority of ryu founded after the mid-seventeenth century proceeded on this basis.

By the mid-eighteenth century there were three methods of sword training generally available to those aspiring to develop or maintain skill in kenjutsu. These methods made use of (1) the live blade in *katana* or *tachi* form, (2) the *bokken,* or wooden sword, and (3) the *shinai,* a lightweight mock sword. Actual combat (shinken shobu) or trial engagements (*shiai*) were conducted between combatants who were identically armed with one of the three instruments. But combat with the live blade required shogunal permission and so could not be carried out as a standard practice. Combat with the bokken was originally approved by the bakufu. *Taryu-jiai,* or trials between swordsmen of different ryu, were avidly sought by many ryu. But when it became obvious that these engagements almost always resulted in serious and crippling injuries to the participants, and sometimes in needless deaths, the bakufu banned the taryu-jiai.

The shinai method of testing skill, called *shinai-shiai,* though not matching the precise but severe results resulting from the use of either the live blade or the bokken, nevertheless protected the combatants from serious injuries and death. Use of the shinai became popular, and the method of training in swordsmanship with this mock weapon was called *shinai-geiko.* Kaho, as a training method, was reduced in importance because of the priority given to free exercise in which opponents attacked each other vigorously, but always observing certain rules to ensure safety. Shinai-geiko is the direct forerunner of modern kendo.

The earliest use of the shinai is traditionally credited to Hikida Bungoro (c. 1537–c. 1606), founder of the Hikida Ryu (also called the Hikida-kage Ryu). Hikida studied the Shinkage Ryu, and is immortalized as one of the *shi tenno,* or "four kings," of the sword; the others are Yagyu Tajima no Kami of the Shinkage Ryu, Kurando Marume of the Taisha Ryu, and Shingo Izu no Kami of the Hikida Ryu. But Hikida's shinai was a crude instrument. Its hardness and weight made it almost as dangerous as the bokken. Kamiizumi Ise no Kami (1508–78), the founder of the Shinkage Ryu, and Yamada Heizaemon (d. 1578), the founder of the Jikishin-kage Ryu, also used the shinai in their training methods. But these great swordsmen used the shinai to analyze the techniques of combat; they did not consider it an instrument for regular training conducted entirely in shinai-geiko fashion.

The earliest uses of shinai-geiko as a regular method of training for swordsmen were crude attempts to eliminate injuries among participants. To make training safer, protective equipment had to be developed. The Jikishin-kage Ryu is the first known ryu in which this was carried out, around 1711. Yamada lamented the general lack of martial ardor in swordsmen engaged in the vacant style of kenjutsu practice. He was uncertain whether kaho training alone, without at least an occasional real combat, would maintain the fighting efficiency of a swordsman. In his own training, Yamada made kaho the first step in learning swordsmanship, but he longed for decisive results in combat that unfortunately, he believed, could not result from the use of kaho. This led him

1. The Butokuden, Kyoto.

2. The Budokan, Tokyo.

3 (above). Shimizu Takaji, Japan's highest authority in police combat training. He has been decorated by the emperor for his distinguished service to classical and modern martial arts and ways.

4, 5. Nakamura Taisaburo, master swordsman of Toyama Ryu batto-jutsu and founder of the Nakamura Ryu, demonstrates tameshi-giri (test cutting) with a sword against a bamboo pole.

83

84

6, 7, 8. *A young exponent of* iai-do *demonstrates* chiburi *(the gesture of shaking blood off the sword) followed by* noto *(returning the sword to its scabbard) after delivering a sword cut.*

9, 10. Left: Police combat instructor Kaminoda Tsunemori (left) demonstrates the use of the keijo *(medium-length police stick) against an assailant armed with an iron pipe. Right: Kaminoda (right) applies a wrist lock in* taiho-jutsu *fashion.*

13, 14. Kaminoda uses a tying-cord in modern hojo-jutsu *fashion to restrain an aggressor. The entire tying process whose first and last steps are shown here takes about ten seconds.*

11, 12. Left: Kaminoda (left) uses the keibo *(wooden police truncheon) to block an attack to the head by an assailant wielding an iron pipe with the* tokushu keibo *(collapsible metal police truncheon). The* tokushu keibo *is approximately six inches long when closed and about eighteen inches long when extended.*

15, 16. Major Chiba Sanshu, founder of the toshu kakuto *system of unarmed combat used by the Japanese Self-Defense Force, demonstrates a kicking technique (above) and a punching technique (below).*

17. Yamaoka Tesshu, founder of the Itto Shoden Muto Ryu of kendo.

18. Yamada Jirokichi, fifteenth headmaster of the Jikishin-kage Ryu. (Photo courtesy of Kato Masatoshi)

19. A British competitor (right) at the First World Kendo Championship, held in 1971 at the Budokan, Tokyo, uses the uncommon combination of long and short shinai.

20. Both competitors in this National Police Kendo Championship at the Budokan, Tokyo, are attempting men, a strike to the top of the forehead.

21. *The competitor on the right is attempting a* men, *while his adversary prepares to block it. This photo was taken during a National Police Kendo Championship at the Budokan, Tokyo.*

22. *Kano Jigoro, founder of Kodokan Judo, as a youth (c. 1877) in his pre-jujutsu days. (Photo courtesy of Otaki Tadao)*

23. *Kano Jigoro in 1915, as president of the Kodokan. (Photo courtesy of Otaki Tadao)*

24. Kano Jigoro (dark clothing) and Yamashita Yoshiaki demonstrate koshiki no kata (ancient forms) in this rare 1930 photograph.

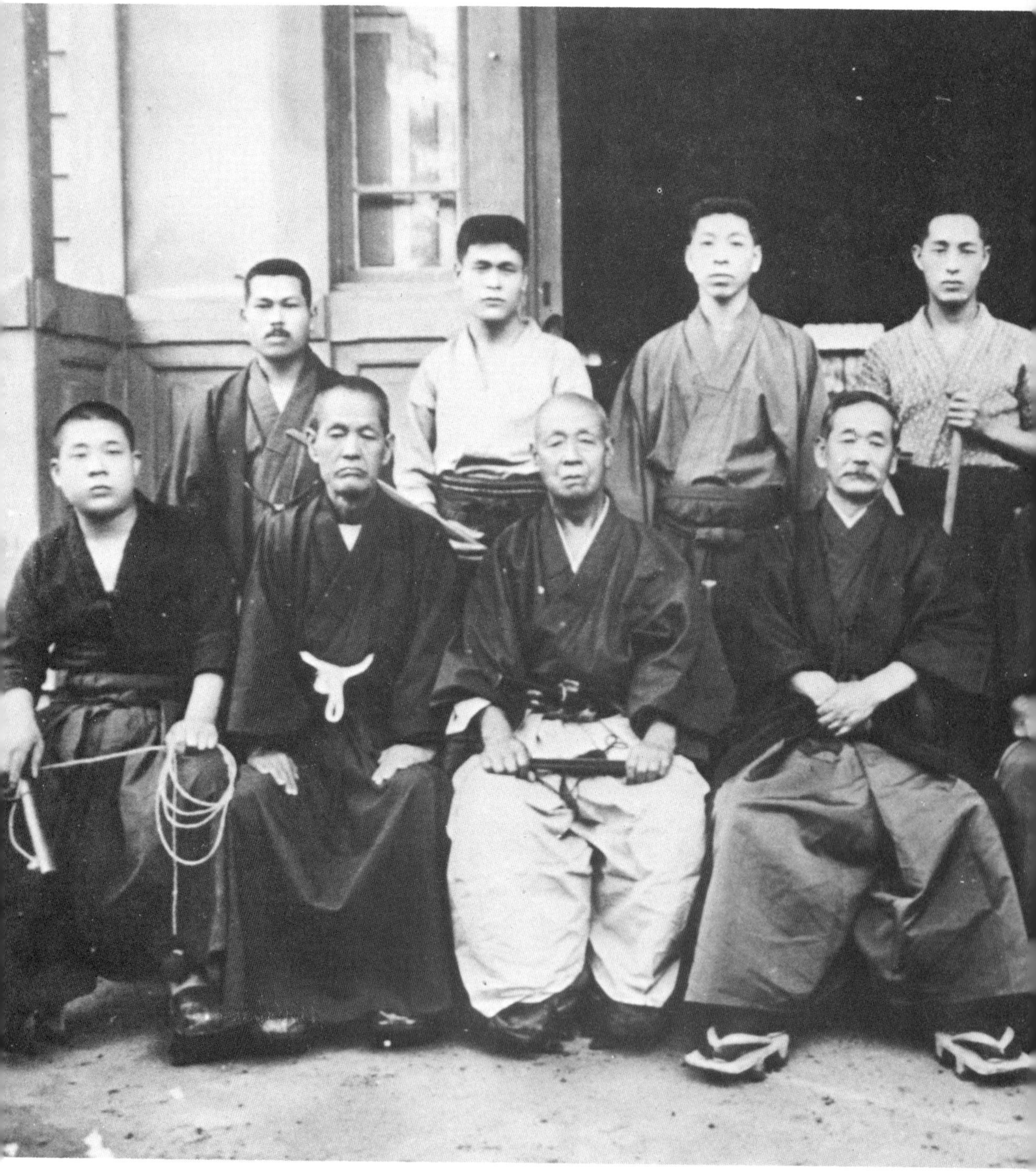

25. *Kano Jigoro (seated, fourth from left) in 1921 with classical* bujutsu *exponents. Seated at far left is the young Shimizu Takaji, who had just been appointed the Kodokan* jojutsu *instructor.*

26. *Anton Geesink of the Netherlands (left) in action at the first Olympic judo championship, held in 1964 at the Tokyo Olympic Games. His opponent here is Japan champion Kaminaga Akio (fifth dan). Geesink was the Olympic gold medalist.*

to experiment with pieces of protective equipment that covered the head and lower arms. Trainees wearing this kind of simple armor could engage in spirited exercise without fear of injury. Yamada's successors made the wearing of protective equipment in connection with shinai-geiko a standard practice for members of the Jikishin-kage Ryu. Many young men of samurai families were attracted to the Jikishin-kage Ryu, where they could wage mock combat and romantically imagine that they were participating in the fighting art of their classical ancestors.

Nakanishi Chuta (fl. 1751), formerly a member of the Ono-ha Itto Ryu, established his own style of swordsmanship under the banner of his Nakanishi-ha Itto Ryu. In order to attract more disciples, Chuta followed the example of the Jikishin-kage Ryu. He first improved the *mune-ate* (today called the *do*), the torso protector; he also modified the *kote,* or protective gloves, of the Ono-ha Itto Ryu. His redesigning of the shinai made that instrument lighter and stronger.

In the nineteenth century shinai-geiko, conducted with the participants wearing protective gear, quickly became a very popular practice. The appeal of its dynamic action was much greater than that of the relatively static kaho of either classical kenjutsu or kendo, especially that of the vacant style, and so thousands of young men thronged to the dojo. Rigorous training in shinai-geiko style also afforded a healthful means of exercise, a factor which attracted older people. With the increase in its popularity, by the mid-nineteenth century a substantial number of commoners was engaged in the practice of shinai-geiko. Over five hundred ryu specializing in shinai-geiko were created and operated by commoners, who regarded shinai-geiko as their opportunity to share in a glorious tradition heretofore the monopoly of the classical warriors. But there were also more mundane reasons for the plethora of ryu. Dojo vied with dojo for members, for if he had numerous trainees the head of a dojo gained not only social prestige but also financial solvency. There was thus the unavoidable tendency of many dojo to cater to the wishes and whims of the trainees, forsaking the rigid disciplinary values of the older classical ryu that were focused on cultivation of the spirit. Most trainees toward the end of the Edo period preferred to train solely for the purpose of winning matches in sport fashion, and thus the emphasis on contests (shiai) dominated in most dojo.

The bakufu recognized shinai-geiko as a spiritual discipline, certainly not as a fighting art, and therefore encouraged its development. Shinai-geiko was useful in dissipating the energies of people who might otherwise put such energy to uses not in the best interests of the Tokugawa regime. Bakufu logic in this matter, however, seems to have been unsound, for despite the bakufu's vast network of spies, who kept surveillance over the activities of its citizens, there were dojo that became hotbeds of anti-bakufu sentiment. Being a skilled swordsman at the end of the Edo period quite often entailed complicated political issues. We cannot go into this complex matter here, but a discussion of a few general relationships that are relevant to the development of the modern disciplines, swordsmanship in particular, will be both useful and interesting. In the free mingling of men who held different political opinions that affected the course of the Japanese government we see the significant fact that these men were bound together by a spiritual outlook instilled in them through a common interest in swordsmanship.

One of the greatest swordsmen in the period just prior to the bakumatsu, the decline and fall of the Tokugawa bakufu, was Otani Shimosa no Kami Seiichiro (1789–1844). Otani was a menkyo-kaiden-ranked technician whose great skill earned him the undisputed honor of being called *cho-ichi-ryu,* or a superswordsman. He became the thirteenth headmaster of the Jikishin-kage Ryu and was head of the Kobusho, a government training school. Otani's personal integrity was as great as his skill with the blade, a fact that is witness to the depth of spiritual cultivation made possible by sufficient training in the positive style of classical kenjutsu. It was Otani who introduced Chiba Shusaku (1794–1855), founder of the Hokushin Itto Ryu, to the Mito han officials, who then made the *kumi-tachi* (kenjutsu) of that ryu their official style of swordsmanship. Chiba operated the Gembukan dojo in Edo and boasted of a membership of five thousand trainees.

One of Chiba's disciples was Sakamoto Ryoma, a ronin from Tosa. Saito Yakuro (1799–1872) was a skillful swordsman trained in the Shindo Munen Ryu style. He operated the Rempeikan dojo in Edo. Here the anti-bakufu teachings of Mito scholars like Fujita Toko, Aizawa Seishisai, and gunnery expert Egawa Tarozaemon influenced his many disciples. Prominent among Saito's disciples were Kido Koin and Takasugi Shusaku of Choshu. Momono-i Shunzo (1826–86) was of the Kyoshin Meichi Ryu, and skilled in the use of a great variety of weapons. He attended the bakufu Kobusho. Later, Momono-i established the Shigakukan dojo in Edo, where Takeichi Hampeita, an anti-bakufu swordsman from Tosa, trained. Takeda Sokaku, destined to become important in the development of modern disciplines, was a promising young swordsman training in the style of the Ono-ha Itto Ryu. In 1874, at the age of sixteen, he appeared at the Shigakukan and defeated Momono-i in two out of three matches using a shinai in shinai-shiai style.

Adverse reaction to the popularity of shinai-geiko was concurrent with its development. Expert swordsmen were unanimous in their opinion that an overemphasis on training for gaining match points in shiai destroyed the intrinsic purpose and aims of classical kenjutsu and kendo; furthermore, to win matches was not the same as winning a real combat. These opinions, however, because they were held only by the foremost swordsmen, advocates of the positive style, were in the minority. The average swordsman was content with his practice of shinai-geiko because he had no direct experience of positive-style classical substitutes.

Oishi Susumu (1798–1865) was the strongest master of shinai-shiai in Kyushu. Originally trained in the Shinkage Ryu, Oishi had devised his own style and founded the Oishi Shinkage Ryu. He was a tall, powerfully built man. His special technique with the shinai was *kata-zuki,* a one-handed thrusting action powerful enough to stun its victim. Oishi was primarily concerned with gaining the match point, and is the best example of how an overemphasis on shiai training can lead to the loss of spiritual values. Oishi's fame in shiai spread rapidly across Kyushu, and the fact that he used a shinai of extreme length in his bouts became legend; his shinai ranged from four to over six feet in length. This gave him a very decided advantage in making his thrust against an opponent. But the unusually long shinai was not the only aspect of Oishi's perversion of kendo values. He also constructed his *men*, or protective mask, with a pronounced peaked grillwork so as to deflect any blows or thrusts made at his head; the *men-tare*, the mask flaps for protecting shoulders and throat, were very narrow and numerous, a feature that interfered with any attempt of an opponent to strike or thrust at Oishi's head.

Oishi used his great skill to make money. He freely toured Kyushu in *dojo arashi* (literally, "dojo storming") style, a combination of challenge and blackmail. Heads of dojo that Oishi visited, and who accepted his challenge to shiai, would be soundly and publicly beaten with resultant personal humiliation and loss of professional prestige; few disciples were willing to remain with an instructor who was ineffective in shiai. Those dojo instructors who wished to avoid the embarrassment of defeat at the hands of the boisterous Oishi would make handsome payments to him in the hope that he would leave and never return.

Otani, in support of his opinion that the positive style of swordsmanship was superior to shinai-geiko training and to show his great contempt for Oishi, engaged the latter in a match. Using a shinai so as not to injure Oishi, Otani inflicted a quick and exceedingly humiliating defeat on Oishi, needing only one stroke made in the positive style of the Jikishin-kage Ryu to do so.

Chiba Shusaku, like both Momono-i and Saito, was far below the level of skill possessed by either Otani or Oishi. But Chiba was a good technician, and supported training for matches. He made shinai-shiai a sport, on occasion pitting men and women armed with wooden naginata against swordsmen armed with the shinai. The general public greatly enjoyed these matches and would pay an admission fee to see their favorites in action. Chiba's son, Eijiro (1832–62), was famous for using a one-handed swing of the shinai made from a position high above his head. Upon spotting an opening (suki) in his opponent's defense, Eijiro would strike furiously with a whiplike action of his shinai to score the match point. Antics such as these became popular with audiences, who came to contests primarily to be entertained.

Another stalwart of the Jikishin-kage Ryu, and its fourteenth headmaster, was Sakakibara Kenkichi (1829–94), a disciple of Otani. Sakakibara, while disapproving of some of the technical aspects of shinai-geiko, was himself an advocate of the use of the shinai in training. But he despised the use of "small" quick techniques that were indicative of a cautious vacant style of swordsmanship. While training with those who were capable of using such techniques to "tap" or "touch" his body, Sakakibara ignored these tactics and sought to deliver *ippatsu*, "at one stroke," a devastating conclusion in the form of a strike made in the manner of cutting with a real sword, not simply touching the opponent's body with his shinai. The quality of Sakakibara's cutting action was well known and respected after his appearance with Momono-i before Emperor Meiji in 1886, when he successfully cut halfway through a helmet that was considered to be indestructible; Momono-i had failed in his attempt to do likewise. One of Sakakibara's best disciples was Takeda Sokaku, who had joined the Jikishin-kage Ryu to polish his skill with the sword.

A lack of agreement among Edo-period swordsmen on standards for techniques, training methods, training garb and equipment, and the conduct of matches prevented an early development of a truly national standard of kendo. But there were signs that there was recognition of the need for acceptable standards. The Kobusho set the length of the shinai at three *shaku* eight *sun* (approximately three feet eight inches) in 1856, but the problem of length continued for some time thereafter to be a vexing one. There were swordsmen who insisted that if a modern form of swordsmanship like kendo, "the way of the sword," was to develop on a national basis, then the principal instrument used in its practice, the shinai, must at least be the length of a normal sword (approximately three feet three inches), even if not having its shape and weight. The Ono-ha Itto Ryu confirmed these opinions, and the shinai was limited to a length of approximately three feet three inches and was not to exceed three pounds in weight; the cylindrical shape of the shinai, however, could not be changed without jeopardizing the margin of safety that it provided.

In the Meiji era, social conditions were such that Japanese citizens favored Western culture over their own. Classical martial arts and ways, and even shinai-geiko, fell into disfavor with the general public. The objections of the Japanese police force were one of the major reasons that swordsmanship did not disappear entirely from the scene. Founded in 1874, the police force was charged with the responsibility for maintaining law and order at a time when civil disturbances were many. The name of the Batto-tai, or Sword Unit, of the police became famous during the Satsuma Rebellion of 1877. Police swordsmen held the Satsuma warriors of the Jigen Ryu in check, a feat that led to the official acceptance of swordsmanship by the police in 1879; iai-jutsu was also made an official study. Master swordsmen who were hired by the police as instructors included Matsuzaki Namishiro of the Shinkage Ryu; Ueda Umanosuke of the Kyoshin Meichi Ryu; Shibae Umpachiro, Watanabe Noboru, and Neigishi Shingoro of the Shindo Munen Ryu; Takao Tesso of the Tetchu Ryu; Mitsuhashi Kan'ichiro of the Togun Ryu; Tokino Seikishiro and Okumura Sakonda of the Jikishin-kage Ryu; and Shingai Tadatsu of the Tamiya Ryu.

Sakakibara, too, made great efforts to renew the popularity of swordsmanship. Backed by notable swordsmen of his day, Sakakibara planned a tour of Japan for experts who were to demonstrate swordsmanship to the general public. This plan was not without a professional motive, for many instructors had fallen into financial difficulties because of the social conditions. The Meiji government approved Sakakibara's plan in 1873, and the tour proved to be popular with the public. But the decline of interest in swordsmanship continued.

The founding of the Dai Nippon Butokukai in 1895 and the establishment of the Butokuden in 1899 made possible significant contributions to the classical martial arts and ways, as well as to the development of shinai-geiko under a harsh style known as *gekken,* "severe sword." Higher institutions of learning preferred to develop what they called kendo; in 1909 a university kendo federation was formed. This caused the government to accept kendo as a subject of physical education in all middle schools in 1911.

Many modern kendo authorities regard the Meiji era as the time when the intrinsic values of classical swordsmanship were discarded. The spiritual essence of classical swordsmanship was perverted in order to allow swordsmanship to survive in public use. Kendo, as gekken, was used by the militarists to bolster a sense of nationalism among the people in preparation for war. This special use of kendo had far-reaching effects on the growth of its popularity and the nature of its techniques. The founding of the Zen Nippon Kendo Remmei (All-Japan Kendo Federation) in 1928 made possible the standardization of kendo on a national basis. This organization provided technical guidance on the quality of instructors by conducting periodic examinations for the right to hold ranks and teaching licenses, and set standards for techniques and training methods.

With Japan's growing commitment to nationalism and imperialistic expansion, kendo became increasingly important, not as a fighting art but as a spiritual discipline and a form of physical education that was aimed at binding together the Japanese people in a common sense of national responsibility. Kendo became a compulsory subject in all primary schools in 1941. But upon Japan's defeat in World War II, and with the occupation of Japan by the Allied Powers, kendo was banned. Its revival in 1948 led to broader aims and less harsh techniques, which have since been avidly accepted by the international community as the basis of a desirable and wholesome sport for all people.

ESSENCE AND AIMS   The essence of kendo is spiritual. Kendo, "the way of the sword," has at its base the will to triumph over adversity in life, but lying far deeper than this aim is its primary concern for improving one's individual character and living a virtuous life.

It is most difficult for the average modern person to understand that the main purpose of kendo is not the acquisition of technique. The sword is no more than a measure with which to improve one's spirit, to nourish one's moral nature, to deepen one's personality, and to stabilize one's moral sense. In the teachings of the Itto Ryu *heiho* (swordsmanship) as Ito Ittosai (1560–1653), the founder, prescribed them, it is stated that he who is without a wholesome moral character cannot achieve great heights in swordsmanship. All training must be directed toward the improvement of spirit rather than toward the acquisition of technique; and in that training, sincerity is absolutely essential to success. The swordsman without right conduct will only succeed in destroying himself.

Ken no shinzui, or the real aim of kendo, is to learn to settle the problems of life without drawing the sword. This line of thought stems from pre-Tokugawa concepts, such as the *mutekatsu* (no-hands victory) principle of Tsukahara Bokuden (1490–1571) and the *muto* (no-sword) doctrine of Yagyu Tajima no Kami (1527–1606). Standing in even closer chronological relationship to the philosophical essence of modern kendo are the teachings of Yamaoka Tesshu (1837–88), founder of the Itto Shoden Muto Ryu. Yamaoka lived at a time when the social turmoil that accompanied the fall of the Tokugawa bakufu and the rise of the Meiji government easily provoked swordsmen of lesser spiritual maturity than he to settle issues with the blade. Yamaoka had many chances to fight when his great skill certainly would have prevailed; but because he believed in the classical concept of bushido he never drew his blade in actual combat.

Yamaoka, originally trained in the Jikishin-kage Ryu positive style of kenjutsu, was the most skillful swordsman of the so-called *san-shu*, the three statesmen whose names used the common ideogram *shu*: Yamaoka Tesshu, Katsu Kaishu, and Takahashi Deishu. All three men were firm supporters of the bakufu, but Yamaoka held the most objective perspective on the political issues that necessitated its abolition. In spite of his great loyalty to the Tokugawa family, Yamaoka held that his greatest loyalty was to the Japanese nation as a whole. His influence on bakufu leaders was phenomenal. Keiki, the last Tokugawa shogun, is frequently accused of weakness of character in succumbing to the demands of Saigo Takamori, Okubo Toshimichi, and Iwakura Tomomi, that is, in surrendering the power of the Tokugawa family to rule. Actually, Keiki was the savior of the nation, whose decision to surrender was conditioned by Yamaoka's teachings of Muto Ryu heiho. And when Yamaoka had been made secretary to Emperor Meiji on Saigo's recommendation, Yamaoka's teachings greatly influenced that sovereign. The emperor was a robust man, proud of his physical strength. On a playful boast he engaged Yamaoka in grappling, only to be rudely thrown down "in a twinkling of a star." His defeat by a man of apparently lesser physical strength so impressed the emperor that he was forever convinced that the use of sheer power is not the best way to resolve problems. After this event kendo in general, and Yamaoka in particular, stood in great favor with the emperor.

Yamaoka believed that the bearer of the sword must conform to the spirit in which it was traditionally forged. Swordsmiths like those who made swords in the tradition of the famous Masamune family of swordsmiths (c. 1250–c. 1600) did so in the spirit of *nukazu ni sumu*, which means settling issues "without drawing the sword." A sword is to be borne for the purpose of maintaining peace and saving life, not for making war and taking lives. Yamaoka always abided by this spirit. As applied to kendo, Yamaoka realized that this spirit is most difficult to master, for it must begin, paradoxically enough, with learning how to draw and use the sword. Cultivation of this spirit is based on the yomeigaku concept of the individual's engagement in activistic discipline. In kendo, the development of the individual's spiritual maturity, his "inside skills," depends on his having sufficient training with the drawn weapon in the execution of "outside skills." The effort to be made in training toward achieving the goal of self-perfection (*satori*) is "catalyzed" by *shugyo*, or austere training, in the process of seishin tanren, or spiritual forging. Spiritual maturity can be recognized in swordsmen who have achieved that state by their proclivity for reflective thought and introspection.

Kendo also draws its essence from doctrines established by famous bladesmen who came under the influence of the Zen priest Takuan or of his teachings, among which is that of *fudoshin*, the "immovable mind." Miyamoto Musashi (1584?–1645), the founder of the Emmei Ryu, expressed that concept as *iwao no mi*, the "rock body";

Kamiizumi Ise no Kami, the founder of the Shinkage Ryu, came out with a plethora of similar concepts; and Ito Ittosai, the founder of the Itto Ryu, declared *isshin itto,* or "one mind, one sword" to be the culmination of spiritual maturity. Yamaoka referred to this same essence as *shingi ittai,* that is, "mind and technique are one," implying that the perfection of technical skill and the development of the spiritual man are inseparable. Yamaoka was, of course, under the influence of the Jikishin-kage Ryu doctrines. A short look at Meiji and post-Meiji Jikishin-kage Ryu teachings will further explain the essence of modern kendo.

Yamada Jirokichi (1863–1931) is a splendid example of the unity of technical skill and spiritual perfection in a swordsman. As a boy Jirokichi was sickly. Inspired by the physical strength of his younger brother, who could easily lift and press overhead a straw bag filled with rice, Jirokichi began the study of gekken, or "severe sword," as kendo was commonly called in the Meiji era. Jirokichi was a filial boy, under the influence of a kogaku-educated family. He grew into manhood with a sense of humility that was genuine. "I think I'm worthless," he would often remark to friends, but among those who knew him well there is no question of his merit as a great swordsman and teacher of kendo.

Jirokichi became the fifteenth headmaster of the Jikishin-kage Ryu. He demanded that the strictest attention be paid to fundamentals and made all trainees in his dojo undergo rigorous exercise. "Practice hard," he advised swordsmen, "so as not to shame your ancestors." Kendo training for Jirokichi was simply a matter of "killing the self [ego] in order to succeed." He took issue with the trend of Meiji-era kendo to cater to sport or entertainment and amusement. For Jirokichi, earning money through public displays of kendo was particularly reprehensible. All his efforts for kendo were directed toward maintaining its intrinsic spiritual essence.

Jirokichi devoted his life to seeking self-perfection through training in kendo. In that process he influenced many people who were also instrumental in developing kendo. It was Jirokichi's nature to be sensitive to the qualities of a man's character. He never turned a man of bad reputation away from his dojo, but would rather attempt to give him subtle clues on how to improve his life. Jirokichi reasoned that the teachings of a virtuous man can bring others less ethical in conduct to change their ways. His personal dealings with people were based on his honest and calm approach to every situation, even in the face of agitation and violence, an ability he developed from his training in swordsmanship.

The moral essence of kendo, as summarized by Jirokichi, appears in some of the precepts listed in his *Kendo Ron* (Treatise on Kendo) and in the injunctions that comprise his *Shuyo Shosei Ron* (Treatise on Mental Training and Life). In the *Kendo Ron* are the following maxims:

1. The mind must be an unclouded mirror! Do nothing not [socially] good; keep quiet [suppress ardor], but be active at all times.
2. Make shugyo an aspect of your daily life [outside as well as in the dojo].

12. *Ken no michi* [kendo] is Zen. *Ken Zen ichi mi* [sword and Zen have the same goal], that of killing the ego.
13. He who practices [kendo] is apt to be rude or bold in manner, and if skilled may wish to demonstrate his skill. Always remember these points:
    (a) avoid rude behavior;
    (b) honor *ri* [human relations] by being polite and not forgetting *gi* [moral obligation];
    (c) don't seek popularity or power;
    (d) be prudent, not flippant;
    (e) refrain from using violence.

From the *Shuyo Shosei Ron* come the following precepts:

1. Dō is facilitated [mastered] by giving regard to the exponents of past ages, not to those of the present day.
2. One's real merit is determined after death.
4. Have pride in yourself, but base pride on [balance of] *bun* [academic learning] and *bu* [martial learning], not on riches and prestige.
5. Be careful in manner and words.
6. Be gentle, with a sense of dignity.
9. Don't think only of your own convenience [don't be selfish].
11. Human relations [the interdependence of men] must be recognized.
24. Devote your life to spreading good. Don't judge others, for one day you will make a mistake and wish to avoid being judged.
26. Be satisfied with your development only at death.

It is most difficult for the average person to understand that kendo should not be considered a sport, especially today in view of the increasing popularity of national and international kendo championships, of which Japan is a staunch supporter. To practice kendo purely as a sport is to pervert its essential purpose. Kendo is not a sport because, instructs the *Kendo Ron,* "sport is not life itself." Whereas sport occupies only a portion of one's life, kendo monopolizes life. Sport is conducted for the purposes of improving health and physical fitness, for financial gain or increasing personal prestige, and not the least important reason is that sport is intended to bring enjoyment and amusement to both participants and spectators alike. Yamaoka despised the tendency in Meiji Japan to make kendo a sport. Jirokichi, too, spoke of the fact that when one begins "to enjoy kendo, then the element of shugyo must of necessity be missing," and one's practice degenerates into sport or simple amusement. However spirited one's participation in sport may be, it cannot reach the required level of dedicated intensity and austerity inherent in the spiritual essence of dō.

Takano Kosei, the current headmaster of the Nakanishi-ha Itto Ryu, criticizes the attitude of "sword play" that is so prevalent among modern kendo exponents. Takano sees the attitude of "play" as detrimental to the real spirit of kendo. "Kendo may be practiced, or one trains himself through kendo," says Takano, "but one must never just 'play' kendo."

Takano regards the Meiji era as the beginning of the "dark ages" for kendo. It is from that time onward that the essential spirit and purposes of classical tradition become clouded over by superficial values. And with the growth of militarism, the militarists recognized kendo as being useful in promoting a distinctive strong nationalistic Japanese spirit among all citizens. Consequently, the characteristics of kendo in the Taisho era show a clear emphasis on *shin-shin shugyo,* or "mind-and-body training," for the development of a unified national sense of spiritual ardor and morality. This modern emphasis differs from the classical interpretation of dō in that it was less concerned with the individual's self-perfection as an individual than with the fact that individual citizens must be spiritually bound together to perfect the country. Kendo thus became a social cohesive force to harness spiritual energy for the purpose of buttressing nationalism. This use of kendo continued unabated as Japan faced grave national emergencies that culminated in World War II.

The stress on kendo for bolstering national physical and spiritual fitness to increase the sense of nationalism among the Japanese people may be seen in Taisho-era publications, such as *Kendo Shugyo no Shiori* (Kendo Training) by Makino Toru, a swordsman of the Hokushin Itto Ryu. Makino wrote: "Many styles of kendo [kenjutsu] were born in the age of warriors in order to instruct them how to regulate their conduct and lead virtuous lives. But at the same time the prejudiced idea arose that swordsmanship was only for warriors. Even now it is still prevalent even though the universal conscription system has been formulated. This prejudiced view stems from the idea of class distinctions in the Edo period. Kendo [today] is indispensable for the enlightenment of the people and for the protection of the national structure. Therefore every Japanese should study kendo for the glory of the nation." Makino also wrote that improvement of skill is only a means, not the aim of kendo training, a declaration that dispels the erroneous idea that kendo is a fighting art: "I don't say the improvement of technique is of little importance. What I mean is that the prime object of kendo exists in the clarification of the true relations of sovereign and subjects, cultivation of loyalty and patriotism, and reformation of one's character so that it attains a state of perfection."

On self-sacrifice, and particularly the Zen concept of learning to transcend thoughts of life and death (seishi o choetsu), Makino wrote: "One who sets one's heart on studying kendo must not forget the great duty of loyalty and filial piety. In case of emergency, he must lay down his life for his mother country. In addition to that, he must fully understand the Imperial Rescript on Education as being his standard of conduct. This instructs him to be a loyal Japanese subject by polishing his personality, and to serve the sovereign. He must also read the imperial instructions given to warriors [Imperial Precepts to Soldiers and Sailors] both night and day, and must endeavor to be a warrior in a real sense, using their standards of conduct as his."

Makino's words suggest that the spirit of self-sacrifice is to be applied to the practice of kendo, but also that it is to be drawn and fostered from sources external to the teachings of kendo. This opinion agrees with that of most modern masters of kendo, who feel that the shinai, though a symbol of the essence of the sword, cannot really prepare the way for the development of seishi o choetsu. This *utsukushii tamashii,* or "beautiful spirit," can be developed only through extended experience in disciplines made with the live blade. Kendo therefore aims at developing the person as a "perfect personality, as a member of society and his nation, through the assistance of the sacred living sword."

TECHNIQUES AND TRAINING METHODS   Kendo technique follows the doctrine of *ju-go awase,* or combining "softness" with "hardness" in all aspects of its scope. Through ju-go awase, kendo becomes a highly efficient system for the integration of human energy. Kendo thus becomes an extension of the technical theory of swordsmanship as it appears in the classical styles of kenjutsu and kendo. Since these older sources of swordsmanship have greatly influenced modern kendo techniques there must of course be certain important considerations that underlie that influence; numerous modifications in classical technique were necessary to create the modern kendo techniques. These modifications are indicative of the change from swordsmanship as used in combat to its use on the level of spiritual discipline and that of sport.

Modern kendo is a dojo budo, that is, it is intended that kendo be performed under the ideal conditions obtaining in the training hall, or dojo. Here the smooth, level floor on which trainees practice makes it possible for them to move with a degree of speed and assurance not guaranteed when swordsmanship is performed under natural conditions out-of-doors. Thus one of the first modifications made in classical techniques involves the swordsman's posture.

The typical modern kendo posture is an extremely erect one. It requires that the exponent stand with his feet quite close together, not widely spaced, and with his toes pointing directly forward; additionally, the rear heel is raised from the floor, a stance that is traditionally attributed to the secret teachings of Ito Ittosai. None of these requirements is honored in classical kenjutsu, where they would lead to precarious balance and the inability to reinforce efficient cutting actions that depend on a sinking action of the waist. The full frontal posture generally assumed by the modern kendoist also stands at odds with the *han-mi,* or half-frontal position, of classical kenjutsu, which is preferred on initial engagement with the enemy because it protects the vulnerable region of the heart. But the upright posture observed in modern kendo permits the kendoist to make ideal quick starts and changes of direction on the level surface of the dojo floor. Movement from orthodox kendo posture is usually made with a sliding-step kind of displacement, in which the rear foot, heel raised, offers a good purchase against the floor from which to launch the body forward into the attack. The slide-step type of movement is rarely possible on natural terrain.

Closely connected with the swordsman's posture and movement is the matter of the protective equipment he wears. In actual combat the classical warrior often wore *katchu,* a lightweight but durable, flexible armor; the techniques and tactics of classical kenjutsu reflect this use of armor. Modern kendo armor is only a very rough approximation to that used on the battlefield in terms of weight and durability, and consequently the posture and movements of the modern kendoist are less restricted; accordingly, the form and execution of his techniques differ from those of the classical swordsman.

It is important also to realize the consequences imposed by use of the shinai. The shinai is responsible for much of what characterizes modern kendo technique, making it essentially different from that of classical kenjutsu. The shinai is a mock sword, though whether it is even a reasonable substitute for a training sword is a debatable point. It is, in reality, little more than a lightweight tubular stick. Its lack of weight and *sori* (curvature), together with the extreme length of its *tsuka* (hilt), permit it to be used differently from a real sword. All these factors affect the speed with which the shinai is used, and consequently, the very technique of kendo. The almost cylindrical shape of the shinai makes it aerodynamically superior to the real sword; and the length of the tsuka results in the shinai being used as a *teko,* that is, operated on the lever and fulcrum principle, a fact that accelerates the tip of the shinai so that it reaches fantastic speeds not possible with a real sword. But the shinai is ideal for the purpose of modern kendo, which is not that of actual combat, and must be constructed as it is to be safe.

There are very obvious differences between the cutting action made with a real sword and the striking action of the shinai in modern kendo. The relatively straight-arm action used for striking with the shinai against a chosen target stems from Itto Ryu teachings. It is never seen in classical kenjutsu technique of the positive style, for arms held in that locked-out position when a genuine cutting impact is made not only lack the force necessary to effect penetration but can injure the swordsman's elbows; this is especially true when the sword strikes forcibly against armor. The touch-stroke of kendo makes possible a rapid attack that can be sustained with the lightweight shinai to a degree impossible with the sword used in kenjutsu fashion. Thus the touch-stroke of kendo is ideal for the noncombative purpose of kendo because there is no concern about either penetration on impact or self-injury.

Only eight areas of the body may be struck by the shinai in kendo training; seven kinds of blows and one thrust are permitted. In classical kenjutsu any part of the enemy was a potential target, and the weak points in battlefield armor influenced the choice of these targets. Each classical ryu has its specialty in tactics for exploiting these weaknesses. Kenshi of the Tenshin Shoden Katori Shinto Ryu slashed the enemy's wrists from underneath, penetrated his groin and thighs, as well as cut deeply into his insteps, in the execution of their techniques. Kenshi of the Shinkage Ryu often chose to sever a single thumb, a simple act that made it impossible for the victim to grasp or hold a weapon; or they would cut both hamstrings at the backs of the enemy's thighs in order to disable him. These are but a few of the considerations that make the shinken shobu in classical kenjutsu style a lethal matter, one that is entered into only after great preparation and always without any concern for limiting rules. But the arbitrary limits placed on which parts of the body may be used as targets in kendo technique are said to be due to the desire to provide a margin of safety for the participants and to improve the accuracy of specific and fundamental attacks. The choice of these limited targets is, therefore, a logical one compatible with the intrinsic purpose of kendo.

Kendo techniques are based on the mastery of mechanically performed fundamentals, among which footwork is important. This footwork makes an erect posture possible and is conducive to making the body and shinai move in unison, which enables the kendoist to attack with speed, accuracy, and vigor. In learning kendo, emphasis is traditionally placed on the tactics of attack, but without the proper spirit to sustain those mechanical aspects, techniques quickly degenerate into meaningless form. *Ki*, or "material force," as presented in the doctrine of Chu Hsi, lies at the base of this spirit. This is the ki mentioned by Tsukahara Bokuden in his discussion of *fudo no seishin*, or the spirit of the "immovable mind," and later stressed as an important element of life by the Neo-Confucian Kaibara Ekken, who defined it as "life force." This ki is the same as that mentioned in the teachings of the Itto Ryu's *shin-ki-ryoku* doctrine; here ki is the "inner power" by which one carries out what he judges to be good or right.

The harmonizing of one's ki with that of the opponent, that is, *ki-ai*, characterizes good kendo. Ki-ai is manifested in the spontaneous "full spirit" of the swordsman. It is a condition of, and essential to, proper training. Ki-ai consists of inseparable and mutually assisting mental and physical elements that act to combine and bind the energies of the exponent into a course of live action, even when the exponent is standing motionless. Ki-ai in kendo must not be thought of as being simply the high-pitched, shrieking sound that is emitted by exponents as they train. The use of audible ki-ai is essential for learning the proper execution of techniques, for only then can the trainee "fill" himself with enough concentration to enable him to trigger the release of his total spirit and therewith "propel" his physical technique. But ki-ai made ventrally, not just vocally, can shatter the composure of all but the most highly developed swordsmen.

Asari Matashichiro, of the Nakanishi-ha Itto Ryu, used ki-ai effectively in connection with the delivery of his *tokui waza*, or favorite technique, the *tsuki* (thrust). It is said that Asari's ki-ai knocked his opponent off balance even before the impact of the thrust. The acme of ki-ai, however, is reached not in noise but only when, notes the *Sun-tzu* (*Sonshi* in Japanese; the ancient Chinese classic *Art of War*, by Sun Tzu), "at last practice is silent." The most skillful kendoists are able to execute their techniques effectively and exhibit the very highest quality of ki-ai, if they choose to do so, without resorting to continuously making noise.

Yomeigaku and Zen concepts involving intuitive learning underlie most modern kendo teaching methods in Japan. This pattern of self-activity promotes a natural kind of learning, one that brings a depth of knowledge to the exponent that is not possible through a purely rational approach to study. But kendo training methods are based on two main streams of thought in which priority is given to the study of either theory or technique. Sasamori Junzo, the current headmaster of the Ono-ha Itto Ryu, relies on technique first in his approach to teaching. Takano Kosei of the Nakanishi-ha Itto Ryu favors what he calls the method of *ri-gi ittai*, or the idea that theory and technique are one. The kendoist training under Takano's guidance begins with physical action.

"If theory came first," notes Takano, "there would be gaps in the kendoist's mind, and this would be detrimental to his progress." Kendo theory is not particularly useful to the novice; it is only "body action," says Takano, "that can teach the trainee how to move his body properly."

Kakari-geiko, or "attack training," is the basic training method for kendo. In this method the junior trains with a senior who serves as a target for the former's blows. The junior executes his techniques without fear of reprisal, but all his actions must conform to fundamental criteria. Kakari-geiko serves to instill a positive attitude of mind in the execution of attacking techniques, and a setting of the mind so that the "four evils," fear, doubt, surprise, and worry, which retard the free flow of action, are eliminated. The "four evils" must be replaced by a sense of confidence that is generated through the exponent's participation in *jiyu renshu,* or "free practice." Yamaoka Tesshu, the great master of the Itto Shoden Muto Ryu, required all trainees in his charge to exert themselves assiduously in kakari-geiko, using a shinai approximately the length of a real sword. Yamaoka permitted no jiyu renshu for trainees with less than three years experience, fearing that it would "break their form."

There is no secret in modern kendo that is a key to success except hard effort in training. An adherence to the pattern of shugyo has been, without exception, the manner by which all experts have made progress. Kendo training involves mental discipline but is essentially physical. Therefore kendoists are apt to be oriented toward the physical side of discipline. The example of the masterful Yamaoka is a case in point. Yamaoka's body to all appearances was an ordinary one, but it was in fact extremely powerful, as it had been developed by relentless training in *suburi,* a basic exercise in which footwork unifies body movement and striking with a shinai; Yamaoka daily engaged in suburi made with an extremely heavy bokken. He also excelled at *ude-zumo,* or arm wrestling. Yamaoka took pride in his great sense of balance, often inviting astonished guests to try to knock him backward out of his house and into his garden as he stood balanced on the edge of a large window in his room. Friends found him rooted like a tree, and even the strongest of them could not dislodge him.

Yamada Jirokichi, a former headmaster of the Jikishin-kage Ryu, makes some pertinent points concerning physical technique in his *Kendo Ron:*

3. Kendo has a wide scope. . . . Don't rely on small techniques.
4. Reflect on yourself. . . . Don't fear [the opponent's] technique, and in confronting a superior [in technique], do not be beaten [mentally] before you start.
5. It is most important to train oneself in being persistent, and to develop the ability to make instant decisions.
6. Sword and mind must be united; technique alone is not enough, nor is spirit alone sufficient.
7. Sincerity of effort is the key to attainment. When we wish to deliver [blows to the] *men, kote,* or *do* against a stronger opponent, we must not trifle with sincerity but do our best.

> 8. The kendo match is made with the thought of a real sword in hand. Never regard the shinai as being less than a real sword.
> 9. Learning through use of kan [intuition] brings revelation of the truth.
> 10. It is prior to the match that the winner and the loser are decided; the proper mental attitude prior to the match must be studied and mastered.
> 11. Postures must be natural . . . [and] should display a fullness [ki] of personal style. Always pay attention to your style, concentrating on fundamentals of stance, holding the shinai, movement, and balance.

In the *Shuyo Shosei Ron* he writes:

> 3. To get ahead, train hard. Sakakibara [the fourteenth headmaster of the Jikishin-kage Ryu] swung a heavy *shimbo* [staff]; Takahashi Deishu used the *tessei no yari* [iron spear] while balancing on a fence rail.
> 7. He who is careless in little [seemingly unimportant] things is careless in all, and can't accomplish greater things.
> 8. Strength alone is to be despised, for it will fail him who relies upon it alone.
> 12. After achieving technical mastery, persist in hard training.
> 13. The feeling of wanting to quit can be mastered [overcome] by a strong will.
> 18. Exhausting training is the key to attainment.
> 20. Food [nutrition] is important. . . . Seek the right kinds and amounts [of food]; likewise, refrain from alcohol.
> 22. Do not sacrifice your occupation [life's work] for kendo, but absorb your occupation into kendo.
> 23. Hold no prejudice. . . . Never despise or overrate an opponent. Make an intuitive reading of the opponent [his capabilities and limitations].
> 25. Adversity in life is essential to training [shugyo]. Be frugal in habits.

Jirokichi's points are replete with significance for modern kendoists, who would do well to study them and apply them in their daily lives.

That a purely physical kind of kendo has no lasting value unless it is supported by sound theory is a truth that is appreciated by all modern kendo authorities. Classical kenjutsu and kendo embody theory in kata, the formal techniques of swordsmanship, which are exercised in a prearranged manner, and make the use of kata their primary training method. Though kata is not a primary training method in modern kendo, nevertheless it is a vital need for the development of advanced kendoists.

The Japanese police were the first to develop a standard kata for use in modern kendo. With the influx of many skillful swordsmen hired as instructors for policemen, it soon became evident that the many styles of kenjutsu that these swordsmen followed could not be accommodated in a single training program. Therefore, in 1886 a technical commission consisting of the foremost police swordsmen was formed and charged with the task of formulating a standard kata for police use. The commission agreed to accept the following ten techniques:

1. *hasso* of the Jikishin-kage Ryu
2. *henka* of the Kurama Ryu
3. *hachiten-giri* of the Hozan Ryu
4. *maki-otoshi* of the Rishin Ryu
5. *kadan no tsuki* of the Hokushin Itto Ryu
6. *a-un* of the Asayama Ichiden Ryu
7. *ichi-ni no tachi* of the Jigen Ryu
8. *uchi-otoshi* of the Shindo Munen Ryu
9. *hasetsu* of the Yagyu Shinkage Ryu
10. *kurai-zume* of the Kyoshin Meichi Ryu

In 1906 the Butokukai convoked a meeting of its technical commission in order to formulate its own standard kata. High-ranked swordsmen from the Shindo Munen Ryu, Musashi Ryu, Jikishin-kage Ryu, and Kyoshin Meichi Ryu were members. After much study the commission announced the Dai Nippon Teikoku Kendo Kata (Great Japan Imperial Kendo Kata) in 1912. This kata consisted of twelve techniques, nine made with the *odachi* (long sword) and three with the *kodachi* (short sword). This kata, renamed the Nihon Kendo Kata (Japan Kendo Kata), continues in use today as the basis of all modern kendo theory and is supported by the Zen Nihon Kendo Remmei (All-Japan Kendo Federation).

KENDO TODAY Modern kendo is practiced by approximately eight million devotees around the world. It is truly international in scope. The organization of the International Kendo Federation (IKF) in 1971 was the beginning of the spread of kendo's wholesome social values on an organized international basis. Earlier, on the occasion of the World Goodwill Kendo Meet in Tokyo in 1967, Kimura Tokutaro, president of the Zen Nihon Kendo Remmei, announced: "We wish to assemble all the people of the world on the common basis of kendo and compete in friendly rivalry and deepen friendship and thus make a contribution toward world peace and prosperity based upon *budo seishin* [the spirit of budo]." The late Shoriki Matsutaro, tenth-dan judoist of Kodokan judo and president of the Nippon Budokan, amplified Kimura's thoughts: "I am confident that this [meet] will deepen mutual friendship and that many a comradeship beyond boundaries will be established and hence contribute toward international amity and peace in the world."

Kimura, retired president of the International Kendo Federation, regards the propagation of budo seishin through kendo as the primary aim of the organization. He endorses the use of kendo as a sport only to the extent thet sport can be a vehicle for conveying the intrinsic spirit of kendo. Kendo must not be regarded as pure sport, however, for to do so is to dismiss and so show disrespect for tradition, the very foundation of this modern discipline.

CHAPTER SIX

JUDO

> There is no boundary in the way of flexibility,
> and the heart shall see no enemy.
> Mifune Kyuzo

Modern judo is commonly described as a sport, a fighting art, a spiritual discipline, a system of physical education, and a recreational activity. It is to some extent all these things, and more. Exponents fully dedicated to judo consider it to be a way of life. But a full appreciation of the true nature of judo is yet to be attained by the vast majority of its six million exponents. This is because personal interests have narrowed the scope of judo; many of its important aspects have been played down in favor of a few specialized ones.

In order that judo may be seen in its true light, it is necessary to examine the original Kodokan Judo, because this is the link between Japanese feudal-age or classical judo and the sport-contest kind of judo that is so internationally popular today.

Kano Jigoro (1860–1938) was the founder of Kodokan Judo. In the personality of Kano the man, his rational genius as an educator and his personal philosophy as an idealist were of great importance in determining the nature of the original Kodokan Judo. Kano the educator sincerely believed that the prosperity of any nation depends on the fullness of that nation's energy, the latter determined by the excellence of the moral quality of its citizens' minds and the vigor of their bodies. As a boy Kano suffered from bad health. Because of his physical weakness he was often the victim of bullies, who beat him unmercifully. Because he was deeply concerned over the deplorable state of his health, Kano sought to correct it. He embarked on a program of physical exercise, participating in baseball, rowing, gymnastics, and hiking. Two years later Kano noted with great satisfaction that he had improved his health and now possessed a reasonably strong body. Nevertheless, the real turning point in Kano's life came with his decision to study *jujutsu* (the art of flexibility).

Kano enrolled in the Tenjin Shin'yo Ryu in 1877 under the tutelage of Fukuda Hachinosuke, who had been a disciple of Iso Mataemon, the founder of the ryu. The Tenjin Shin'yo Ryu was devoid of any martial aim in the Meiji era, but it still had the reputation of being an effective art of self-defense. Fukuda provided rigorous training for his few disciples, who soon proved to be less devoted to their study than was Kano. At every training session Kano found his interest in jujutsu increasing, although the severity of the physical exercise was taking its toll. The specialty of the Tenjin Shin'yo Ryu was *ate-waza,* or "striking techniques," and *katame-waza,* or "grappling techniques." Kano's tattered and torn *uwagi* (training jacket), preserved today by the Kano family as one of its treasures, gives evidence of the vigor with which he undertook his training. His injuries were many. Outside the dojo, Kano was frequently chided by companions for self-doctoring wounds received in jujutsu training. They complained that "Kano's ointment," a concoction that Kano applied liberally to his bruises and abrasions, smelled so bad that his presence was known to them even before he came into sight.

Fukuda's death brought Kano under the technical guidance of Iso Masatomo, a son of the founder of the Tenjin Shin'yo Ryu. But Iso's death forced Kano to continue his study of classical bujutsu elsewhere. He joined the Kito Ryu in 1881 and enlisted the services of an instructor named Iikubo Tsunetoshi. The Kito Ryu, too, at this time lacked martial fiber. Iikubo's teachings, called *ran* (implying "freedom of action"), were considerably different from the jujutsu of other ryu. Iikubo demanded only moderately vigorous physical training, more attention being given to abstract symbolism in connection with physical technique. Emphasis in the Kito Ryu was laid on *nage-waza,* or "throwing techniques."

The cumulative effect of training in the styles of the Tenjin Shin'yo Ryu and the Kito Ryu not only further improved Kano's physique but gave him an insatiable appetite for yet more knowledge about jujutsu. He made an academic study of other classical bujutsu ryu, especially the methods of unarmed combat prescribed in the martial curricula of the Sekiguchi Ryu and the Seigo Ryu. At this time Japan was influenced by a current of thought that had turned most of its urban citizens against traditional institutions, customs, and beliefs. Kano lamented the fact that classical jujutsu had thus fallen into disuse. With the decline of jujutsu, the prestige of many legitimate experts was also lowered. Many skilled exponents, because of their social and even economic plight caused by the lack of disciples, turned to giving burlesque performances or to issuing challenges to all comers for the amusement of an admission-paying audience. Kano, however, regarded jujutsu as an object of national culture, a cultural asset worthy of the respect of the nation. He therefore resolved to restore jujutsu to its rightful place.

Kano began his self-appointed task by recasting jujutsu in a very special way, one that was both attractive and useful to the members of Meiji society. In 1882, Kano emerged with a synthesized system and established himself, under the humblest of circumstances, at the Eisho-ji, a temple in the Shitaya area of Tokyo. Kano called his new system Kodokan Judo, and began teaching nine disciples in a dojo of only twelve *tatami* (rice-straw mats used for flooring, each approximately three feet by six feet).

Kodokan Judo is a highly eclectic system. Kano liberally borrowed ideas from established classical Japanese sources. In selecting the name Kodokan, for example, Kano was well aware of the existence of a Kodokan at Mito, Ibaragi Prefecture. The Mito Kodokan was founded by daimyo Tokugawa Nariaki in the nineteenth century to further academic learning; there scholars like Aizawa Seishisai and Fujita Toko developed the chauvinistic kind of nationalism that inspired the overthrow of the Tokugawa bakufu and the nationalistic ideology of the leaders of Meiji and later eras. Kano's word "Kodokan" is homophonous with that of the Mito Kodokan, though the first ideogram of the two words differs. However, the general meaning of both Kano's Kodokan and that of Mito indicates a common spirit of cultural endeavor. Kano's Kodokan means: *ko* (lecture, study, practice), *dō* (way or doctrine), and *kan* (hall or place), that is, "a place for studying the way."

The general concept and purpose of classical budo as a spiritual discipline used as a vehicle for attaining self-perfection appealed to Kano. He clearly intended his Kodokan Judo to be the vehicle to *michi o osameru,* or "attain the way." Kano deliberately chose the word "judo" in preference to "jujutsu" to describe his system in order to emphasize the importance of the philosophical aspect inherent in dō as "a way of humanity." But Kano also had more mundane reasons for this choice. He wrote: "Many jujutsu ryu often indulged in such dangerous practices as throwing by rather unfair means, or by wrenching limbs. This led not a few people who had occasion to witness those wild exercises to deprecate jujutsu as being dangerous and harmful to the body. Moreover, there were some ill-disciplined jujutsu ryu, the disciples of which made themselves obnoxious to the public by willfully throwing down innocent people or by seeking quarrels. It thus turned out that the word jujutsu carried with it an unfavorable association in the minds of some in higher classes. Hence my desire was to show that my teaching, in marked contrast to jujutsu teachings [as] interpreted by the men of those classes, was quite free from danger and was not to be used as a means for reckless aggressiveness. . . . [My system] if taught under the name jujutsu might prove unacceptable to persons of the higher classes."

In Kano's words, aside from his obvious disdain for the reputation of Meiji-era jujutsu, we can also feel the degree of his preoccupation with social class-consciousness. The fact that Kano came from an affluent and influential merchant family, together with his high level of education, made him extremely aware of social class differences in terms of class morals. It was this awareness that caused him to teach Kodokan Judo only to people of the highest moral qualities; Kano never intended his system to be taught indiscriminately to any and all people.

Kano's use of the word "judo" presented a problem. Some two centuries earlier, the Jikishin Ryu had become the first ryu known to have used the word "judo," but several other classical ryu soon followed suit. This fact made Kano insist on the use of the prefix "Kodokan" in order that his judo teachings might be distinguished from the judo of the classical styles.

THEORY OF KODOKAN JUDO   Kano accepted the practical aspects of *ju no ri,* or "the principle of *ju* (flexibility)," which had already been developed and was in use by the exponents of many classical bujutsu and budo. There were many interpretations of ju, however, some of which Kano regarded as gross misunderstandings of the working of this principle. These errors, if applied to Kodokan Judo, distort its theory, making it unrealistic and incapable of practical implementation. When the principle of ju is wrongly interpreted, there is an obvious conflict between theory and practice. In many ways these erroneous opinions still influence modern-day judo, and thus the principle of ju is worth further examination.

Classical bujutsu and budo exponents use the expression *Ju yoku go o sei suru* to describe the basis of the spirit and mechanics of their many different component systems. Kano's acceptance of this aphorism as applicable to Kodokan Judo shows him to have been one of its strongest expositors. From his detailed study of jujutsu, Kano found evidence of the fact that there was not a universal acceptance of the principle of ju, although only a minority failed to subscribe to it. He further discovered that among those jujutsu systems in which the principle was accepted, there were many interpretations that were unscientifically based.

"Ju yoku go o sei suru" may be loosely translated as "Softness controls hardness" or "Weakness controls strength"; it implies a certain naturalness of manner and action that is made the *sine qua non* of the execution of all techniques. For Kano, however, the meanings of "ju yoku go o sei suru" stem from Taoist teachings as expressed in the *Lao-tzu* (also known as the *Tao Te Ching*). This is an extremely important point, for it determines the intrinsic meaning of ju as applied to Kodokan Judo. The *Lao-tzu* declares that "reversing is the movement of the Tao," and makes of this phenomenon a law of nature that supports the idea that "the most yielding things in the world master the most unyielding." There is no direct mention of softness or hardness, nor of weakness or strength, which suggests that no precise limits are possible for either yielding or unyielding. Thus, in the multiple situations in which yielding and unyielding operate, the act of yielding can be made with strength, specifically, a flexible kind of strength. That which yields is not necessarily soft or weak in a quantitative sense, though its act of yielding may be so in a relative sense, and it only is temporarily softer and weaker than that which opposes it by being unyielding.

Kano was too much of a realist to be confused by abstract Chinese philosophy. From his study of the Kito Ryu he learned to appreciate the ancient and complex Chinese doctrine of *yin-yang* (*in-yo* in Japanese). The oneness of these two elements comprises the basis of the Kito Ryu theory of mechanics. *Ki,* meaning "to rise," is equated with yang (yo), a positive factor; *to,* meaning "to fall," is equated with yin (in), a negative factor. Yang implies light; yin implies shade. The action and interaction of these mutually participating and sustaining, inseparable aspects of nature regulate the use of strength in the execution of Kito Ryu techniques. Thus, varying interpretations of the expression "Ju yoku go o sei suru" did not disturb Kano's keen mind. He recognized the distinctions being made between softness and hardness, weakness and strength, as being formal distinctions, not absolute ones. Kano was also aware of the failure of some jujutsu ryu to make the necessary practical interpretation, thus being led down the path of solely aesthetic endeavor, resulting in ineffective techniques.

Kano's fervent desire as a youth to attain physical fitness allowed him to recognize and appreciate the merit of physical strength in athletic endeavor. In fact, Kano embodied his respect for physical strength in the element of *rentai-ho* (method of physical training), one of the aspects of his "three-culture principle" (see page 118), which makes Kodokan Judo a system of physical education. It was Kano's idea to argue not against the development and use of physical strength but rather the misuse of that strength. Kano endorsed his disciple Arima Sumitomo's comment: "Instances often occur in which it is found advantageous for one to employ an unusually large amount of strength or to exert strength directly against strength in defeating an enemy.... It follows, therefore, that a strong man can avail himself of judo to a more decided advantage than a less strong man." It was natural that Kano placed great reliance upon the Tenjin Shin'yo Ryu interpretation of ju—the submissive quality of the body that subordinates it to the mind—that makes it a principle of flexibility of mind in meeting and adapting oneself rapidly to sudden emergencies. This concept had already been expressed as *karada o shite seishin ni jujun narashimeru jutsu,* or "the art of making the body obedient to the mind," by Terada Kan'emon, the fifth headmaster of the Kito Ryu and founder of the Jikishin Ryu. Thus, for Kano, the principle of ju was never without practical physical implications; for the body, directed by the flexible mind, is to react with similar mechanical flexibility as it adapts itself to a situation encountered suddenly.

The principle of ju as applied to the mechanical execution of judo techniques was for Kano the basis for the act of combining one's strength with that of the opponent so as to bring about the latter's defeat. Jujutsu systems earlier recognized the same principle in the same way, as can be seen by the expression *Kureba mukae, sareba okuru,* which means "When the opponent comes, welcome him; when he goes, send him on his way." The *go-go ju, ni-hachi ju* (five and five is ten; two and eight is ten) theory of jujutsu evolved from that, and is summarized as follows: "If the enemy pushes with five units of strength, pull with five units of strength; the result is ten units. If the enemy pulls with eight units of strength, push with two units of strength; the result is also ten units."

Kano applied scientific reasoning to such jujutsu expressions and clarified their somewhat cryptic quality by postulating a unit-of-strength theory of his own: "What then does this 'gentleness' or 'giving way' really mean? . . . Let us say that the strength of a man standing in front of me is represented by ten units, whereas my strength, less than his, is represented by seven units. Now, if he pushed me with all his force I would surely be pushed back or thrown down, even if I used all my strength against him. But if instead of opposing him I were to give way to his strength by withdrawing my body just as much as he had pushed, taking care at the same time to keep my balance, then he would naturally lean forward and thus lose his balance. In this new position he may become so weak, not in his actual physical strength, but because of his awkward position, as to have his strength represented for the moment by only three units instead of his normal ten. But meanwhile, I, by keeping my balance, retain my full strength, as originally represented by seven units. Here, then, I am momentarily in a superior position, and I can defeat my opponent by using only half of my strength, that is, half of my seven units, or three and one-half, against his three. This leaves one-half of my strength available for any [other] purpose. If I had greater strength than my opponent I could of course push him back. But even if I wished to, and had the power to do so, it would still be better [more efficient] for me first to give way, because by so doing I should have greatly saved my energy and exhausted my opponent's."

Kano's application of the principle of ju, then, is that of using the body not to collide with forces applied by the opponent but rather through clever maneuvering to combine with them to upset the opponent. Kano, well versed in dynamics, also approved of Arima's statement: "The degree of power is determined by the weight of a given body and the speed of its motion, so that the greatness of weight and the agility of movement are important factors in judo. Viewed in this light judo is not an art to be wondered at; on the contrary, it merely employs strength in the most effective way." The principle of ju for many jujutsu ryu, as well as for Kano, incorporates two aspects, those of yielding and resisting. Kano objected to those who believed that yielding was the only facet of the principle. He notes: "The way of gaining victory over an opponent is not confined to gaining victory only by giving way. . . . Sometimes an opponent takes hold of one's wrist. How can someone possibly release himself without using his strength against this opponent's grip? The same thing can be asked when somebody is seized around his shoulders from behind by an assailant. . . . These are forms of direct attack." In suggesting that Kodokan Judo techniques operate on the basis of both yielding and resisting, Kano also explodes the fiction that Kodokan Judo is purely a defensive system: "If [that] were true it would imply that judo techniques are useless unless the opponent attacks first, and if this were so it [judo] would indeed be a restricted form of combat."

Kodokan Judo, like many jujutsu systems, operates on the basis of kobo-itchi, that is, the aspects of attack and defense are but one and the same thing, priority of aspect being determined in a given situation. Kano demonstrated the aggressive nature and superiority of Kodokan Judo over the Yoshin Ryu jujutsu, based on defense and led by Totsuka Hikosuke. In 1886 under the auspices of the Tokyo police, a tournament was arranged between adherents of the Yoshin Ryu and Kodokan Judo. Fifteen men were selected on either side to demonstrate their respective styles of combat. The Kodokan won a brilliant victory, losing only two matches and drawing one. Saigo Shiro played no small part in this triumph. Using his technique of *yama arashi* (mountain storm), Saigo devastated his opponents with masterly throws. It is not generally known, however, that Saigo's technique was one he had learned earlier from the Daito Ryu style of aiki-jujutsu (discussed in chapter eight).

AIMS OF KODOKAN JUDO   There has always been an assumption by many exponents of Kodokan Judo that the system that they practice is superior to any other in the field of hand-to-hand tactics. Indeed, Kano himself gives evidence of his belief that Kodokan Judo is in all ways superior to anything ever developed in the Japanese martial arts and ways. We see this best in Kano's choice of the formal name Nippon Den Kodokan Judo, an expression that implies "the best budo of Japan." This prestigious and boastful appellation appears on all certificates of dan rank. The validity of its implied meaning, of course, cannot be substantiated, but it is indicative of the confidence and faith that Kano placed in his beloved Kodokan Judo.

Having clearly defined the principle of ju, categorically denying that yielding or giving way is its only mode of operation, Kano states: "If thus the principle of giving way cannot cover all the methods used in contests . . . is there any principle which really covers the whole field? Yes, there is, and that is the principle of maximum efficient use of mind and body." In his academic study of jujutsu, Kano discovered the expression *Shin-shin no chikara o moto no yuko ni shi o suru*. This stresses the importance of the economical use of energy, both mental and physical. Restated by Kano, it is the following: "Whatever be the object, the best way of attaining it shall be the best use of energy directed to that purpose or aim." This statement Kano announced in 1923 as *seiryoku zen'yo,* or the principle of "the best use of energy." This principle is the basis of the Kodokan ideal.

In this principle Kano sees energy as a living force, not simply as physiological vigor. Through judo training one learns how to abide by the principle. But higher values were in Kano's mind as he exhorted all exponents of Kodokan Judo to follow the principle. Training in Kodokan Judo for the purpose of acquiring a physically sound body (rentai-ho), or for the purpose of developing expert contest skill (*shobuho*), is termed *kyogi* judo by Kano, that is, judo in the "narrow sense," because it stresses only technique. Kyogi judo is to be replaced by *kogi* judo, or judo in the "wide sense," in which *shushin-ho,* or mental cultivation in terms of moral standards, leads to the perfection of the self. Thus, physical perfection of the self is not sufficient in itself, for no matter how healthy an exponent becomes through his practice of judo, no matter how skillful he is, "If he does not benefit society," says Kano, "his existence is in vain." Rentai-ho, shobu-ho, and shushin-ho form the three elements of what Kano referred to as his "three-culture principle," a principle that makes Kodokan Judo a form of physical education.

Kano wished judo training to be undertaken not only in the dojo but also outside it and so make of its physical aspects the focus of human endeavor for the progress and development of man. Whereas the exponents of kyogi judo may be technically mature, it is only with their realization of kogi judo that they become socially mature. Kano's outlook here is conditioned by the Confucian precept of "extending one's scope of activities to include other people and activities." In this way it amplifies the avowed purpose of classical budo, which in some ryu is quite vague in terminology except when dealing with the seeking of individual perfection. Kano defines Kodokan Judo, in terms of the principle of seiryoku zen'yo, thus: "Judo is not a method of making the best use of mental and physical energy for purposes of attack and defense alone, rather it is a method by which this principle [seiryoku zen'yo] can be assimilated and applied in all spheres of life." Following this train of thought, Kano evolved his second great principle, which he called *ji-ta kyoei,* or the principle of "mutual prosperity" (mutual assistance, cooperation, and welfare).

The principle of mutual prosperity became the keystone of Kano's hopes for international social harmony. The basic elements of Kano's ji-ta kyoei are found in the tenets of the classical bujutsu and budo ryu. Exemplary among these tenets are the teachings of the Yagyu Shinkage Ryu (Edo line), which features swordsmanship of a kenjutsu type. Kenshi of the Edo Yagyu Shinkage Ryu regard their training in kenjutsu as being kogi kenjutsu, and more commonly refer to it as *seiho* or *heiho.* They seek self-perfection through training according to prescribed sword techniques, but such an endeavor is always only a means to a greater end. In the doctrine of the Edo Yagyu Shinkage Ryu, seiho is the declared aim of the exponent who seeks to perform "good deeds" for Japanese society. Kano's emphasis on doing good for society, however, has a considerably broader sphere of application, that is, the entire international community. Kano expected that exponents of Kodokan Judo everywhere, through their common interest in training and learning, would learn to use the principle of seiryoku zen'yo, and to understand that this is possible only when there is mutual cooperation. This realization, in turn, leads them, in Kano's words, "to a very high state where the differences between oneself and others have been transcended," and they are able to apply the principle to the daily activities of their lives, there to influence others so as to make their lives similarly wholesome and useful to mankind.

TECHNIQUES AND TRAINING METHODS   Any honest and thoroughgoing analysis of Kano's original Kodokan Judo techniques reveals the fact that all of them without exception were in some manner already being used by the older classical bujutsu or budo systems. Thus what was collectively designated by Kano as the Kodokan *go kyo no waza,* or "the five principles of technique," as well as those techniques standardized in the Kodokan katame-waza, the category of grappling techniques, stem from the mechanics and theory of sources with which Kano was familiar. Modern judoists using effective contest throws like *seoinage, haraigoshi,* and *osotogari* to down their opponents, or judoists who gain a contest victory through the immobilization of their opponent with techniques like *kesagatame, jujijime,* and *ude hishigi jujigatame,* owe a real debt to sources older than Kodokan Judo; this is no less true in the practice of *ate-waza,* the assaulting techniques of Kodokan Judo in which the exponent uses various parts of his body as weapons against the anatomical weaknesses of the opponent. Rudimentary forms of Kano's original Kodokan techniques can be seen in the tactics of the Yagyu Shinkage line of "empty-hand" combat (itself derived from the influence of the Kage Ryu and the Tenshin Shoden Katori Shinto Ryu), the Kito Ryu (based on the Teishin Ryu), the Jikishin Ryu (influenced by the Kito Ryu), the Tenjin Shin'yo Ryu (based on the Yoshin Ryu, the Shin no Shinto Ryu, the Fukuno Ryu, the Isogai Ryu, and the Miura Ryu), the Sekiguchi Ryu (greatly influenced by sumo tactics), and those ryu, such as the Seigo Ryu, that deal with *kumi-uchi,* combat by grappling.

As regards Kano's originality in devising new techniques for his Kodokan Judo, he was an adapter rather than an adopter of existing ones. It is in this sense that Kano demonstrated considerable originality of thought. Two criteria conditioned Kano's efforts in the design of Kodokan techniques: (1) to base all techniques on scientific principles, and (2) to remove all crude and dangerous practices from techniques. Both of these important considerations were prompted by the social needs of Meiji society.

Kano's refinement of old techniques along scientific lines was based on the fact that the empty-hand techniques with which he was familiar appeared to him to be unscientific. But on the basis of what is known today of those techniques, the validity of Kano's criticism is suspect; perhaps it would be fairer to criticize the technical ability of the men in Kano's time who used those techniques. Nevertheless, in view of the wide range of opinions with regard to the principle of ju, there were many techniques performed in Kano's time that used this principle in an unacceptable manner, and he did seek to make it possible to use mechanical efficiency in the techniques that he adapted for use in Kodokan Judo.

Kano's concern for the personal safety of those using Kodokan Judo techniques brought about a refinement of techniques that were once battlefield methods or methods of self-defense for use in civil scuffles in which the safety of the loser was unimportant. The resulting refinement of such techniques for use in Kano's judo made of them a kind of sport-play activity. And so Kano established certain rules governing the execution of techniques, and clearly described and defined certain prohibited actions.

Perhaps Kano's biggest contribution to empty-hand techniques was that of requiring opponents to grip each other by the garments when executing them. While this feature can be found in some of the older bujutsu and budo forms, gripping is almost absent in the truly classical arts of combat, the bujutsu, where it would have proved to be not only a dangerous practice but one that would rarely have been possible because combatants usually wore some kind of armor. The act of gripping fulfills both of Kano's aims in his adaptation of older techniques for Kodokan Judo. Not only does gripping lend more efficient leverage against the opponent, but it affords a high margin of safety for the one being thrown; in the latter case the thrower can control the pattern and rate of fall of his opponent, making a safe landing possible instead of leaving his victim to gravity.

In many ways Kano stands as a heretic vis-à-vis the classical bujutsu and budo traditions. For example, in devising Kodokan Judo training methods he defied the classical concept of *yugen* insofar as this term implies "mysterious skills." To some degree this is a direct refutation of yomeigaku philosophy, which formed the very backbone of all classical learning methods. Kano did not agree that it was necessary to acquire technical and spiritual maturity both through experience and through penetration of the hidden depths of the *okuden,* or secret teachings; for if this were admitted, Kano's own study, particularly that made in a purely academic way, would mark him as being deficient in many respects in his knowledge of classical bujutsu. Kano also placed less reliance on kan, or intuition, in learning, replacing it with rational thought and analysis based on a "method of instruction in conformity with modern science."

Kano decried the lack of systematic teaching methods that would make things like learning *ukemi* (taking falls) a less dangerous task. In most jujutsu systems the thrower would hurl down his victim and the latter would have to fall as best he could. Kano had seen with his own eyes the crippling results of this practice. He therefore devised a special manner in which ukemi was to be learned without running undue risk of injury. It is this feature of Kodokan Judo that satisfies one criterion of good physical education, that of safe and systematic teaching methods, and further identifies the orthodox Kodokan manner of teaching. Thus the tendency of some modern judoists to omit systematic ukemi exercises from training is not the "new development" that it is sometimes claimed to be by its advocates; it is rather a reversion to the old, crude, and unsystematic practices of jujutsu.

The central point on which Kodokan Judo rests as a system of physical education is Kano's demand for a state of equilibrium among the elements of his "three-culture principle," those of rentai-ho, shushin-ho, and shobu-ho. In regard to the last, Kano says: "I did not attach exclusive importance to the contest side of training . . . but aimed at a combination of contest exercises and training of mind and body." Skill, for Kano, is an important aspect of training, to be sure, but as a goal of judo training it is inferior to that of skill used as a means to the greater social aims of Kodokan Judo. Kano also clearly announced his dislike for Spartan training methods that rely upon "survival of the fittest." "Correct judo training," says Kano, "must not cause overexertion."

In order for Kodokan Judo to satisfy other criteria of good physical education, Kano insisted that all training must give full regard to the harmonious development of the human body. Such a development is impossible in a contest-oriented kind of training in which the major emphasis is on *ran-dori,* or "free exercise." Kano's own experience with the *ran* system of the Kito Ryu had given him the idea for ran-dori; in the Kito Ryu, trainees were urged to *ran o toru,* "take freedom in action." But Kano saw ran-dori as being incomplete in itself. He concluded: "What is deficient in ran-dori must be supplemented by kata [prearranged form]."

Kata, long the basis of classical bujutsu and budo, was extremely important for Kano, who not only made it the theoretical base for Kodokan Judo but insisted that judo cannot be a good system of physical education without sufficient use of kata in the training schedules of all exponents. Kata confers on judo the means by which it becomes balanced physical education, transforming kyogi judo—ran-dori, or contest-centered judo —into kogi judo, a cultural or educational discipline, which is the essence of Kodokan Judo. Kano's deliberate designation of *nage no kata* and *katame no kata,* the prearranged forms of throwing and grappling, respectively, as *ran-dori no kata,* or prearranged forms of ran-dori, shows his intention that these two kata are to be used as the theoretical basis for ran-dori training.

Kano declared ran-dori, kata, and shiai to be the primary elements of judo training but also made judicious use of lectures and *mondo,* question-and-answer periods, in directing the technical development of his disciples. The value of these latter two training methods in stimulating the intellectual development and moral training of judo exponents is very real. Kano considered that the personal character of all of his disciples was the real test of their value, and always required them to conduct their lives in a dignified manner. By his own outstanding example Kano inspired all who came to the Kodokan.

Kano's ideas on human virtues can be categorized as (1) those developing and influencing others and (2) those affecting one's own life. The former category includes the cultivation of a sense of honor, the avoidance of luxurious habits, a sense of justice, a sense of righteousness, kindness and discernment, an adherence to good etiquette, and honesty; the latter category includes the development of good mental health, control of the passions, achievement of physical fitness, the development of courage, preparedness, mental acuity, persistence and determination, readiness in emergencies, temperance in all things, and esteeming not victory over an opponent but the way in which victory is striven for.

JUDO TODAY   Kano remarked: "Nothing is of greater importance than education; the teaching of one virtuous man can reach many, and that which has been learned by one generation can be passed on to a hundred." Modern-day exponents of judo will do well to reflect on Kano's words in light of the original form and concepts of Kodokan Judo that have been described. Because Kano believed that Kodokan Judo could contribute to the peace of the world and improve the general welfare of mankind, he made very determined attempts to internationalize judo. He traveled abroad eight times to further this goal. While in London in 1933, Kano spoke of his plans for a world judo federation and the dissemination of the teachings of Kodokan Judo throughout the entire world: "The spirit of judo, which has as its ideal world peace, concurs with the international spirit; and in this respect, if an international judo federation comes into existence, it will mean the establishment of a real international organization." In 1952, though he did not live to see it, Kano's dream of an international judo body was realized. That organization, the International Judo Federation, is the senior world body for judo and is composed of national federations from over seventy nations. The aims and purposes of the federation, as stated in article four of its statutes, are as follows:

1. To promote cordial and friendly relations among the members, and to coordinate and supervise Judo activities in all countries of the world.
2. To protect the interests of Judo throughout the world.
3. To organize and conduct World Judo Championships and Judo competitions in the International Olympic Games Program, in conjunction with the Regional Unions.
4. To organize the Judo movement throughout the world on an international basis, and to promote the spread and development of the spirit and techniques of Judo.
5. To establish technical standards.

Prior to the end of World War II, judo in Japan rose to an all-time high of technical perfection. Although exponents looked forward to competition, the real purpose of all training was seishin tanren, or spiritual forging. The prohibition against carrying on martial arts and ways declared by SCAP in 1945 included judo and resulted in its technical stagnation. When judo was finally reinstated in 1947, Kano Risei, adopted son of Kano Jigoro and third president of the Kodokan, made resolute efforts to rebuild the technical integrity of Japan's judo under the aegis of the Kodokan. He organized the Zen Nippon Judo Remmei (All-Japan Judo Federation) in 1949 and assumed leadership over the administrative and technical aspects of judo.

Although aware of the cultural values of Kodokan Judo, Kano Risei's policies nevertheless placed emphasis on judo as a competitive sport. This emphasis began with the organization of the first truly national Japanese judo championships in 1948. Judo in Japan today is primarily a sport, much to the dissatisfaction of many traditionalists who view judo as a Japanese cultural activity. Nevertheless, the way all judo training is conducted today continues to be one in which experts for world and Olympic competitions are formed.

CHAPTER SEVEN

KARATE-DO

> True karate-do is this: that in daily life, one's mind and body be trained and developed in a spirit of humility; and that in critical times, one be devoted utterly to the cause of justice.
>
> Funakoshi Gichin

There are more than seventy different Japanese systems of karate-do; some thirty more systems prefer to designate their teachings karate-jutsu. There is, however, in all of these systems, to varying degrees, the influence of what was originally a plebeian Okinawan form of combat. Distinctive Japanese taste has influenced the original Okinawan teachings to produce a characteristically Japanese kind of karate-do that is primarily devoted to the study and practice of unarmed methods of hand-to-hand sparring and grappling. Japanese karate-do, properly taught, is a balanced system of spiritual discipline, physical education, self-defense, and competitive sport.

Cultural exchanges between Japan and the Ryukyu Islands have existed since prehistoric times. But the fact that these islands had nothing much to offer the outside world until the Chinese developed gunpowder in the ninth century A.D., and later, from the twelfth century onward, required sulphur in large quantities for their war against the Mongols, kept China and Okinawa from entering earlier into large-scale trading or tributary relationships.

In the seventeenth century the Japanese overlords of Okinawa made possible a limited knowledge in Japan of both Chinese and Okinawan combative arts. But it is only in the Meiji era that we have evidence of the Japanese government's interest in Okinawan fighting arts. An alert Japanese army doctor noticed the unusually well-proportioned and strong physiques of certain Okinawan conscripts in Okinawa; subsequent investigation revealed that such physiques were due to the practice of what the Okinawans called *te*, meaning "hand." Te is a category of hand-to-hand combat including both unarmed and armed combat. It developed under the strong influence of Chinese *wu shu* (martial arts), especially those of the *ch'uan-fa*, or "fist way," types brought to Okinawa by Chinese monks, merchants, and traders. Okinawan te developed as a plebeian form of fighting.

The Japanese officials on Okinawa approved the inclusion of te in the physical education curriculum of Okinawan schools in 1902 because it served a military purpose, that of conditioning future conscripts. Te, as adapted for the purpose and general aims of physical education, eventually became known as *karate-jutsu*, the ideograms for which mean "Chinese hand art."

No historical proof has been found to show that Okinawan te or karate-jutsu was systematically taught in Japan before the Taisho era, though it is probable that individuals traveling between the Ryukyu Islands and Japan's southernmost main island, Kyushu, had some knowledge of these arts. The present emperor, while touring Okinawa in 1921 as the crown prince, witnessed a demonstration of karate-jutsu and was so favorably impressed that he included the event in his formal report to the Japanese government. Official Japanese curiosity about Okinawan combative arts led the Ministry of Education to invite an Okinawan expert to Japan. Funakoshi (Tominakoshi) Gichin (1869–1957) of Shuri, an elementary school teacher, was selected to travel to Japan because he was the most literate exponent of the Okinawan art of te; but there were many other native exponents more skillful than he. Funakoshi had appeared at the Butokuden in Kyoto in 1917 in a preliminary effort to familiarize Japanese government officials and the members of the Butokukai with te and karate-jutsu. But it was not until his second visit, in 1922, that he made the first public demonstrations of karate-jutsu in Japan.

To increase his chances of interesting the Japanese public in karate-jutsu, Funakoshi deliberately made his appearances only before intellectuals. He gave impressive demonstrations and lectures on the physical and spiritual merits of karate-jutsu to audiences composed primarily of artists and attorneys; Funakoshi reasoned that professional people who possessed keen minds generally tend to have unfit bodies. He stressed the fact that training in karate-jutsu strengthens even the weakest body, and that a person of small stature like himself could develop and maintain good health through such training. Funakoshi selected volunteers from his audiences to test his resistance to blows and to efforts to force him to lose his balance; no member of any audience succeeded in making Funakoshi wince or tumble. His calm and dignified appearance had a remarkable effect upon all who witnessed his demonstrations, and it was not long before his teachings gathered a considerable number of devotees. Funakoshi also demonstrated and lectured on karate-jutsu at Kano Jigoro's Kodokan and at universities, where his dynamic presentation of his art greatly inspired educators and students alike.

Funakoshi's method of introducing karate-jutsu in Japan brought only a small portion of the Okinawan art before the Japanese public, that portion which Funakoshi deemed to be most appropriate to his purpose and most likely to gain the approval of his intellectual audiences. His popularity as an instructor grew rapidly, and with it the public's curiosity to learn more about this effective method of hand-to-hand combat. By 1924, Keio Gijuku University in Tokyo had adopted karate-jutsu as physical education; Tokyo Imperial, Shoka (Hitotsubashi), Waseda, Gakushuin, Takushoku, Chuo, Meiji, Nihon, and Hosei universities soon followed Keio's example. The great popularity of karate-jutsu among Japanese university students soon gave this art a larger following in Japan than on Okinawa.

Funakoshi remained in Tokyo directing the establishment of a new style of karate-jutsu based on the mechanics of the Shuri te that he had learned from Azato Anko. Mabuni Kenwa, a former fellow student of Funakoshi during the time that both were studying Okinawan te under a teacher named Itosu Yasusune, arrived in Japan to organize the development of his own style of karate-jutsu in 1928. Itosu was an exponent of the Shuri te originated by Matsumura Munehide; the latter was also the teacher of Azato. In spite of these fundamental relationships, Funakoshi's style of karate-jutsu differed vastly from Mabuni's style, especially after Mabuni trained under the guidance of Higaonna Kanryo (1888–1951), a master of Naha te. Thereafter, Funakoshi and Mabuni went their separate ways as instructors of distinctly different styles.

Though Funakoshi favored the Shuri te style, he made a number of modifications to it. His son Yoshitaka acted as Funakoshi's instructor; his teachings were radically new and formed the basis of the original Japanese style of karate-jutsu. Mabuni developed what he first called the Hanko ("Half-heart") style. Later he preferred the name Shito; this name derives from the alternate readings of ideograms found in the names of his former teachers, *shi* for the *ito* of Itosu, and *to* for the *higa* of Higaonna. On Okinawa, in the absence of Funakoshi and Mabuni, Miyagi Gogyun (Chojun), a senior disciple of Higaonna, became a leading master of a style of karate-jutsu that he called Goju; this name derives from the influence of the Chinese ideograms *go,* meaning "hardness," and *ju,* meaning "softness." Miyagi selected this name for his teachings because his Goju techniques are based on maintaining a balance of resistive and flexible actions.

During his stay in Japan, Funakoshi developed a long line of disciples, each of whom has played a very influential role in the development of a modern Japanese kind of karate-do technique expressing the individual styles of these men. Most prominent among Funakoshi's senior disciples in Japan are Takagi Masatomo, Nakayama Masatoshi, Ito Ken'ichi, Otsuka Hidenori, and Konishi Yasuhiro. Moreover, Yamada Tatsuo is of primary importance in the development of the Japanese style of kempo, "fist way." Mabuni's disciples, too, have greatly affected the Japanese development of karate-do, but their teachings remain more under the influence of Okinawan technique than do those of Funakoshi's disciples. Kokuba Kosei is one such outstanding disciple. After study with Mabuni, Kokuba followed Motobu Choki, a Shuri te specialist who learned from Mabuni, Itosu, and Azato; Kokuba also studied for a time with Funakoshi. Both Mabuni's and Miyagi's teachings, as interpreted by Sawayama Masaru, have also influenced the development of Japanese kempo; but it is Miyagi's last Japanese disciple, Yamaguchi Gogen, who must be credited with founding a typically Japanese Goju style of karate-do.

The rapid proliferation of Japanese karate-do cannot, however, be credited to the teachings of any one man or the influence of a single sect. Many skilled exponents have influenced the formation of Japanese karate-do and have shared in promoting its growth. From the traditionalist's point of view, however, Funakoshi must be considered the "father" of Japanese karate-do, insofar as he is responsible for making various important innovations in Okinawan karate-jutsu that have brought this art closer to Japanese taste. In 1933 Funakoshi changed the concept of *kara,* which was originally written with an ideogram meaning "China." By substituting another ideogram, also pronounced "kara," Funakoshi changed the meaning to "void" or "empty." Thus, Funakoshi's new karate-jutsu meant "empty-hand art." Two years later Funakoshi discarded the word "jutsu" in favor of "do." Thus karate-do was born in Japan, and the literal meaning is "empty-hand way." In Okinawa, Funakoshi's changes angered many exponents, who considered them to be gross insults to tradition. But by 1938 almost all Okinawan exponents were accustomed to calling their systems either karate-jutsu or karate-do.

To facilitate the dissemination of his teachings, Funakoshi established a central dojo in Tokyo in 1936 and, after much deliberation, gave it the name Shotokan. The ideograms that are read "Shoto" are Funakoshi's pen name as a calligrapher; *kan* means "hall." Funakoshi never referred to his style of karate-do as the Shotokan Ryu; in fact, he was categorically opposed to the use of the feudal term "ryu" for his newly developing karate-do. Thus the use of the expression "Shotokan Ryu" among modern exponents to bolster claims to authenticity through affiliation with Funakoshi's teachings has no valid basis. Funakoshi's son Yoshitaka, however, organized the Shoto-kai (Shoto Association), and this organization became the basis for the founding of the Nippon Karate Kyokai (Japan Karate Association) in 1957.

The presence of Okinawan masters of karate-jutsu in Japan brought about a reasonably wide dissemination of their original teachings, but it also caused an even wider interpretation of these teachings by masters and disciples. Intense rivalries among masters were generated as each tried to outdo the others in skill; these rivalries were inflamed by loyal disciples who sought to establish the superiority of their master or sect over all others. The scope of techniques, as well as methods of training, were greatly expanded by this professional jealousy and friction.

With Japan's entry into war with China in 1937, and its participation in World War II, karate-jutsu and karate-do were officially recognized as valuable adjuncts in the training of soldiers and sailors. The mass participation of some of Japan's finest young men resulted in a prodigious development of new unarmed karate-like techniques. After Japan's defeat, and during the period when most martial arts and ways were prohibited, karate-like systems continued to flourish; the Allied Powers believed these systems to be little more than methods of physical education in the manner of "Chinese boxing." The technical progress of karate-jutsu and karate-do in the 1950s and 1960s was characterized by the formalization of the techniques, tactics, and training methods of each sect. This in turn made obvious the very great differences among the various sects, and created in many experts the desire to formulate a Japanese national standard for karate-do. Toward this end the participation of great numbers of high school and university students in karate-do competitions brought popular appeal to the sport aspect of karate-do and made it a sport of national importance.

ESSENCE, AIMS, AND TECHNIQUES The very strong influence of Chinese ch'uan-fa on Okinawan te and karate-jutsu is carried over in lesser degree to the Japanese styles of karate-like technique. Te that developed at Shuri was under the direct influence of *wai-chia*, the so-called "external systems" of ch'uan-fa; that at Naha was affected by the *nei-chia*, the "internal systems"; while te at Tomari was a combination of the two forms. Japanese karate-do absorbed many features of the external styles but was relatively uninfluenced by the internal forms.

The concept expressed in the *Lao-tzu* as "The most yielding things in the world master the most unyielding" indicates the most important characteristics of the internal systems. The effect of the "soft" and pliable actions of the internal systems depends on *nei-kung*, or "internal power," which in turn is released through the interaction of the will (*i*), vital energy (ki), and muscular strength. Internal systems make much of *wu-kung*, exercises that gear glands and mind to physical effort. External systems rely on the use of *wai-kung*, or "external power." They are characterized by "hard" and rigorous muscular exertion in which quickness of eye, hand (fist), and foot are all essential. No system of ch'uan-fa, te, karate-jutsu, or karate-do is an absolutely "soft" or "hard" system, but may be categorized as being one or the other depending on the priority given to one or the other aspect in the execution of techniques.

Okinawan combative arts are not intrinsically under the influence of Buddhism because at the time of the founding of these arts Buddhism was not popular in Okinawa. The linking of Okinawan fighting arts and of Japanese karate-jutsu and karate-do to Buddhist religion or philosophy, especially Zen, is a modern innovation and one that is considerably newer than the systems it allegedly spiritually invigorates. In particular, the quasi-Buddhist teachings that are sometimes associated with Japanese karate-do are without foundation in the original form established by Funakoshi. These teachings are largely due to the personal interests of those exponents who seek to satisfy their consciences in justification of hand-to-hand combat, or who otherwise seek to bring esoteric aspects into their art in support of claims to higher ideals than are contained in systems involving purely physical sparring and grappling. The fanciful imaginations of writers who are largely without experience in karate-like disciplines have enhanced the erroneous belief that karate-do and Buddhism are inseparable.

Funakoshi had very specific things in mind when he replaced the original ideogram "kara," meaning "China," with that meaning "empty." The fact that pure Japanese karate-do does not involve the use of weapons other than parts of the body gives literal substance to the translation of "karate" as "empty-hand." But the obvious conflict of that rendering with the fact that Okinawan karate systems always include the use of specific weapons was one reason why Funakoshi's change of ideogram angered the traditionalist exponents in Okinawa. Funakoshi clarified the apparent paradox and gained support from his fellow countrymen. He declared that the use of the ideogram "kara" (empty) was based on the concept of "hollowness," meaning "unselfishness." Thus the "emptiness" suggested by the newly chosen ideogram refers to the state of rendering oneself "empty," or egoless, for the purpose of an unhindered development of spiritual insight. This new meaning for "kara," Funakoshi insisted, gave a philosophical essence to what heretofore had been basically a physical art. But Funakoshi never intended that farfetched philosophical abstractions be made of his concept of kara. He leaves a clear definition in his writings: "As a mirror's polished surface reflects whatever stands before it and a quiet valley carries even small sounds, so must the student of karate-do render his mind empty of selfishness and wickedness in an effort to react appropriately toward anything he might encounter. This is the meaning of kara, or 'empty,' of karate-do." Beyond this expression of the meaning of "kara" there seems little need for the many and varied interpretations given to it by modern karatephiles.

As early as 1926 both Higaonna and Itosu on Okinawa had argued that te should be revised as a shugyo, a system of austere discipline, making of its then essentially combative and physical nature a spiritual one. Both of these great masters insisted that te was not an art to be used for harming human beings but one in which technique combines with spirit to solve daily problems and avoid physical conflicts. Neither Higaonna nor Itosu taught people whose individual characters were known to be bad. But it was the impetus given to karate technique by Funakoshi, who clearly taught it as an exercise for the mind and body to form personal character, that led to the establishment of Japanese karate-do in 1935.

The Okinawan prototypes of Japanese karate-jutsu and karate-do evolved from the efforts of people from the lower social classes whose morals, ethical standards, general interests, and level of education all differed vastly from those of the aristocratic Japanese warriors. This plebeian environment in which karate techniques developed in Okinawa, together with the fact that they also developed in a plebeian environment in twentieth-century Japan, make it obvious that there is no direct connection between Japanese karate-like systems and the classical Japanese martial arts. It is also apparent from detailed studies made of the pre-Edo period bushi's fighting arts that these professional warriors had little interest in the empty-hand aspects of combat because the accepted manner of engaging the foe entailed armed combat; unarmed scuffling was regarded as peasant activity, beneath the dignity of the bushi's social position. Bushi, armed with lethal weapons like the long sword, were capable of rendering all unarmed techniques ineffective.

The great social changes that occurred during the Edo period included the decay of the classical warrior institutions, the appearance of a class of men known as samurai many of whom were not only effete but also only nominally warriors, and the rise of the commoners to a position of social importance. Methods of unarmed combat, though at times useful to the samurai when engaged in civil scuffles, did not constitute their major martial study. But the commoners' interest in empty-hand arts was both natural and widespread. They had long been denied the use of weapons, a fact that makes their preference for unarmed combat understandable. But it is quite apparent from the historical records that many commoners sought to gain social prestige through participation in disciplines in which weapons were used in such martial ryu as they were permitted to join or were able to found for themselves.

In this manner the commoners became familiar at first hand with the spirit and practices of the warriors. They borrowed liberally from the warriors' martial culture the aspects they greatly admired or believed to be essential to their own systems of discipline. In some ways the commoners were original, but by and large they were adapters, not adopters, of warrior systems. They were also guilty of misrepresenting warrior beliefs, customs, ethical standards, and martial practices through exaggeration or lack of understanding. But the commoners' interest in empty-hand disciplines, made with an inquiring attitude of mind, continued through the Meiji and Taisho eras. This set the scene for the rapid acceptance of Okinawan karate-jutsu among the general citizenry of Japan.

Japanese karate-jutsu and karate-do exhibit certain characteristics of the classical warrior spirit and ethos. Funakoshi used the expression *mizu no kokoro,* which means "a mind like water," to emphasize the importance of making the mind calm when facing an emergency or an adversary. This imagery indicates that the calm mind, like still water, accurately reflects all that comes before it. Thus the exponent who gains this mental state will be both psychologically and physically prepared to deal with whatever action an adversary takes. But Funakoshi's use of this expression is not entirely original, for it stems from a plethora of metaphysical concepts involving fudoshin (immovable mind) that were in common use by Japanese swordsmen in the sixteenth and seventeenth centuries. Another favorite expression of Funakoshi is also rooted in the classical warriors' traditions: *tsuki no kokoro,* or "a mind like the moon," which refers to the necessity of maintaining surveillance over one's surroundings at all times. By this symbolism is meant that, like the wide range of illumination produced by the unclouded moon as it sends its light earthward, so the mind must be aware of all conditions surrounding the body. This attitude is expressed in classical martial arts as zanshin, and is also included in the function of *kan-ken futatsu no koto,* perceiving with both the eyes and the intuitive mind.

Nakayama Masatoshi, as a disciple of Funakoshi in 1931, witnessed the master's rigid discipline in connection with tsuki no kokoro. Funakoshi was quick to criticize his disciples for any relaxation in their alertness. In training he would deliver sound kicks and blows to those trainees who failed to maintain a proper bearing. Even outside the dojo he was a taskmaster. "He would quickly tip up a bowl of rice into the face of any disciple who handled it in such a way as to weaken his defense," says Nakayama, and, without injuring the user, would also "show how an adversary could jam improperly handled chopsticks down one's throat even as the user ate with them." Funakoshi never ceased to maintain vigilance. "Even while walking outdoors," recalls Nakayama, "he would never turn a corner close to a wall but make a wide circuit to avoid being surprised."

Funakoshi's concern with the practical aspects of self-defense did not result in an overemphasis on proficiency in physical technique. Important as technique obviously was for Funakoshi, training meant the individual's confrontation with obstacles in order to develop an improved power of persistence in endeavor and the consequent ability to overcome hardship. The performance of karate-do, in this sense, is a vital matter for Funakoshi, and is highly reminiscent of the Taoist religious doctrines in which nature is to be confronted; exercise is the means by which mind and body are improved and the span of life is increased.

When asked about it, Funakoshi invariably characterized karate-do as a system of defense, but always within the concept of kobo-itchi, where *hen-o,* or response to an emergency, includes *sen no sen,* the highest form of attack initiative, as well as *go no sen,* the lowest form, depending on the appropriateness of one or the other in a given situation. What mattered most to Funakoshi was that the trained exponent should refrain from contention, but that if pressed, he should respond naturally, instinctively, and spontaneously to the threat of the attack. But above all, Funakoshi declared karate-do to be a medium for character building and the final goal of training to be the perfection of the self, which is implicit in the classical interpretation of dō. The maxims displayed in the dojo of the Japan Karate Association summarize Funakoshi's highest hopes for karate-do: (1) character, (2) sincerity, (3) effort, (4) etiquette, and (5) self-control.

In gentle contrast to Funakoshi's concept of karate-do, and in marked opposition to many of the karate-like systems that have developed since Funakoshi's death, is the ideology of Konishi Yasuhiro, who founded the Shindo Shizen Ryu in 1934. Konishi trained under both Funakoshi and Motobu Choki. For Konishi, the Taoist philosophy of life is the basis of all training. He explains: "People often use the word 'conquest' in speech. When a mountain climber comes to the summit, he says immediately that he conquered such and such a mountain. And if one endures such hardships as heat or cold well, he says that he mastered the conditions. This is all merely an illusion. What seemed like having conquered is really . . . a state of accommodation without any opposition to nature. It is a state of God and man united in one body. This results in [inner] peace and is a natural state in which [the distinction between] enemy and friend does not exist."

Konishi, also the holder of a kendo *kyoshi* (teaching license), brought various ideas from the realm of swordsmanship into his teachings, which he prefers to call karate-jutsu. In particular, emphasis on zanshin, the ability of an exponent to gain dominance over an opponent through an alert state of mind and the maintenance of proper physical posture, characterizes Konishi's techniques. Thus the spiritual aspect dominates the physical. A decidedly strong bias of antiviolence cloaks Konishi's karate-jutsu in its stringent ethic, a fact that makes clear that jutsu forms are not without higher ideals despite what advocates of dō forms sometimes erroneously believe.

Training in the manner demanded by Konishi is made for the purpose of developing a wholesome human being, one who is both mentally and physically sound. Through dedication to training carried out over a protracted period of time, *shin* (mind), *gi* (technique), and *tai* (body) are united in the proper proportions. When this is accomplished the trainee becomes aware of his moral obligation to be useful to society.

Kata, or prearranged formal exercise, is the basis for discipline in Konishi's karate-jutsu; it is therefore the starting point of all training. Through the sufficient use of kata a trainee gains control over his mind and body and thus comes to understand that karate-jutsu technique is to be applied only for the purpose of controlling undesirable personal traits in oneself and in others. Karate-jutsu must never be used to foster a malicious spirit. But kata alone, notes Konishi, is not sufficient to produce the fullest development of the individual. Accordingly, trainees are required to participate in controlled bouts with fellow trainees; to this end competition becomes one facet of training.

Otsuka Hidenori (b. 1892), who founded the Wado Ryu in 1939, has developed what is perhaps the purest form of Japanese karate-do. The essence of Otsuka's teachings derives from his long experience with classical bujutsu. He began to study the jujutsu of the Shindo Yoshin Ryu when very young—in 1898, at the age of six—and attained the menkyo (license) level of proficiency in 1921 under the tutelage of Nakayama Tatsusaburo Yokiyoshi. Otsuka began his study of karate-jutsu under Funakoshi in 1922. A deep concern for human welfare is evident in Otsuka's teachings. For him, *ten-chi-jin, ri-dō* ("heaven-earth-man, principle-way") is a harmonious union to be respected and sought through adherence to austere discipline (shugyo). A *waka* (a standard verse-form containing thirty-one syllables) describes Otsuka's aspirations for those who engage in any bujutsu or budo:

Bu no michi wa	Have no regard for martial
tada aragoto to	aspects [when training],
na omoi so	but rather adhere to the
Wa no michi kiwame	way of peace [harmony and
Wa o motomu michi	tranquillity].

Karate-do for Otsuka is thus primarily a spiritual discipline. All exponents of the Wado Ryu demonstrate great ability in coping with armed and unarmed attack. This ability stems from the fact that Otsuka has welded the facet of yielding according to the principle of flexibility (ju no ri) to karate-like techniques. This results in many of the harsher resistive elements of sparring technique that characterize most styles of karate-jutsu and karate-do being removed from the Wado style. But the "softness" of Wado Ryu technique is less subtle than that of the internal systems of genuine Chinese ch'uan-fa. The absence of "softness" in technique represents, in Otsuka's opinion, an uneconomical use of the body, for a great expenditure of energy always accompanies the use of "hardness." Otsuka is one of the Japanese pioneers in the development of the relaxed-arm thrust punch coupled to a rapid withdrawal of the punching fist to effect a focusing of energy. As regards the popular practice of hardening certain parts of the body by deforming them in order to reduce their sensitivity to pain, Otsuka totally rejects such inane ideas.

Yamaguchi Gogen has developed his Japanese Goju style of karate-do as *seishin no mono,* that is, "a thing of the spirit." There is in the balance of "hard" (go) and "soft" (ju) actions displayed by Yamaguchi's performance of technique a confirmation of what is suggested by the name Goju, and also what is perhaps the best example of the influence of Chinese nei-kung (internal power) on a Japanese style of karate-do. Exponents of Yamaguchi's Goju karate-do, therefore, are expected to place emphasis on the development of internal power through the use of special exercises. These exercises are performed to bring posture, movement, and breathing into a harmony that teaches the body to act as a whole, unified in concentrated effort. Breathing is vigorous, but is performed slowly and in a rhythm that is precisely timed. Inhalation is made as if "smelling" the air, while exhalation is made forcefully and with the emission of sound that stems from air forced outward by the muscular contraction of the abdomen.

The pursuance of dō, or the way, through the discipline of karate-do is for Yamaguchi a display of patience, fortitude, and perseverance. Karate-do in its broadest sense "is a way of peace," he claims. "Karate-do means not to be beaten, but also not to strike others." Human morals differ among different individuals and peoples, but karate-do, says Yamaguchi, can guide all people to right behavior. The dō is thus a way to live correctly, and he who fails to do so, Yamaguchi believes, is a coward. Training in karate-do, when properly carried out, leads one to the discovery of a nonaggressive way of life.

KARATE-DO TODAY The amazing proliferation of karate-like systems in Japan has led to the involvement of more than two million Japanese exponents in a bipolar sphere of activity. Karate-do is concerned largely with sport, and has the largest following; karate-jutsu is fundamentally devoted to the study of self-defense.

In Okinawa, Itosu is generally credited with being the first to teach karate-jutsu as a sport, allegedly having done so in 1905 for middle school students after the Japanese authorities authorized this art for inclusion in the physical education curriculum. But it is the Japanese who are the pioneers in the use of karate-do as a sport; Okinawan karate-jutsu was in no sense viewed as a sport until it succumbed to Japanese influence. In Japan, Funakoshi's Shotokan initiated *jiyu kumite,* or "free sparring," in 1936, a development that eventually led to the adoption of competitions and championships in 1957. Today, the majority of Japanese engaged in karate-do train for the purpose of becoming skillful in competition; all else is secondary. Nakayama Masatoshi, currently the chief instructor of the Japan Karate Association (JKA), posts a warning about this trend and prefers that karate-do be carried out in the manner intended by its founder, Funakoshi: "This [sport] development is, of course, welcome, but training merely to win a match can lead to the deterioration of this dynamic and powerful art. The need to build true proficiency on a solid foundation, I feel, is more important than ever. I believe that karate-do should be viewed from a broad viewpoint. From the aspect of its development as a modern discipline, and from the aspect of physical education also, the ultimate goal of karate-do should be the attainment of a [wholesomely] developed moral character built through hard and diligent training."

The adapting of karate-like techniques from being suitable only in fighting to fit the requirements of sport as Japanese karate-do began with the teachings of Funakoshi's son. The elder Funakoshi's techniques were oriented toward self-defense. They were characterized by the use of wide stances and depended on actions made at close range. Short, powerful kicking attacks, made at low target areas in order to avoid the possibility of counterattacks, were Funakoshi's favorite opening tactics; these were followed by the clever use of throwing techniques. The younger Funakoshi, though, taught a style based more on upright and fluid postures, it being assumed that the opponent was much farther away. He made abundant use of the tactics of full-leg-extension kicking at high target areas, as seen in today's *mawashi-geri* (round kick), *yoko-kekomi* (side-thrust kick), and *ushiro-geri* (rear kick). Throwing techniques were rarely used. This is the basis of the present-day style of JKA exponents.

Japanese karate-do in general, under the influence of the younger Funakoshi, eventually became only a quasi-combat form because both weapons and throwing techniques were discarded. Furthermore, many of the techniques developed, if used under the conditions of serious combat, are reckless and liable to cause serious injury to the user. Nevertheless, because the execution of techniques in the JKA style requires the exponent to commit his body fully in either attack or defense, this style produces a forceful action with a tremendous appeal to energetic young people. It is a style well suited to competition. Thus the JKA style has affected almost all sects of karate-do, literally forcing them to follow similar patterns of technique if they wish to attract new members and keep pace with the growing popularity of the JKA sport style.

Reaction to the loss of combative integrity in Japanese karate-do was not long in coming. Two present-day experts exemplify the efforts made by numerous others to preserve the essentially combative nature of karate-like techniques, which in the dō form has been greatly weakened.

It may be that history will prove that Korean-born Oyama Masatatsu, a naturalized Japanese, was a courageous, brilliant synthesizer of karate techniques, though at present his popularity with Japanese karate-do officials is not great. Oyama began his study of Japanese karate-do under the influence of Yamaguchi Gogen's Goju teachings. Oyama already had extensive knowledge of Chinese Shaolin and Korean combat arts (*subak, tang-su, kwonpup, tae-kwon, tae-kwonpup,* and *pakchigi*), but his study of Goju karate-do focused his experience and enabled him to devise his own eclectic system. Oyama's teachings, now contained in a style called Kyokushin, are developed essentially with the idea of combat in mind, in a style spiritually toned by Zen concepts. The Kyokushin style is definitely a dō form, constituting as it does for Oyama "a way of courage"; but Oyama is uncompromising in regard to the fact that all karate-like systems were originally combative arts and must remain so if they are to deserve the name "karate." The idea of *hitotsuki hitogeri,* meaning "one punch, one kick," to achieve victory over an opponent pervades Oyama's teachings. Kyokushin karate-do is also wide-ranging and efficient; its training methods are as unique as they are severe. Elements of Korean, Chinese, Japanese, Okinawan, and Siamese (*toi-muay*) fighting arts have been welded by Oyama in a sincere attempt to build an efficient system of self-defense.

Kyokushin karate-do is primarily an empty-hand system, but the study of weapons is not rejected. Even in competition, Oyama is insistent on the maintenance of combative reality. For Oyama a simple touch of hand or foot, no matter how quickly and skillfully it may be made against an opponent, is not a telling blow; nor is a well-executed attack that is purposely stopped short of its target by the focus of one's forces. To decide the winner of a contest in karate-do fashion, Oyama insists, contact must be permitted (as in boxing), and such contact must produce either a knockout or the resignation of a combatant. Of course, Oyama would provide some margin of safety for the contestants; specific rules and the use of protective armor, he believes, fulfill that necessity.

One of the most brilliant exponents of karate-do on the modern Japanese scene is Hayashi Teruo, founder of a style called Kenshin Ryu. Hayashi is a disciple of Kokuba Kosei, Mabuni's apt and vigorous exponent of the Shito Ryu. Hayashi also studied under the supervision of Nagamine Shojin of the Shorin Ryu, and Higa Seko of the Okinawa Goju Ryu. A thorough expert technician of Shito Ryu karate-do in his own right, Hayashi nevertheless decries the lack of combative realism in modern karate-do. The overemphasis on the use of empty-hand techniques is, for Hayashi, a serious mistake that keeps karate-do from being fully a form of combat.

Fascinated by the primitive weapons of Okinawa, Hayashi was led to study with Okinawan te master Nakaima Kenko of the Ryuei Ryu. Under Nakaima's expert guidance Hayashi mastered the use of the *bo* (six-foot hardwood staff), *sai* (double-forked iron truncheon), *nunchaku* (wooden flail), *kama* (sickle), and *tui-fa* (wooden handle). These weapons are characteristic of Okinawan te in its most primitive form, as well as other native combative arts. The term *ko budo,* "ancient martial ways," is a generic term coined in the twentieth century. It may be used to describe collectively all Okinawan combative systems, but it is more accurate to say "Okinawan ko budo," in order to distinguish them from Japanese ko budo (the classical bujutsu and budo), which are entirely different and basically unrelated systems. The use of the term ko budo should not be limited, as it popularly is, to the describing of the ancient weapons systems of Okinawa.

Hayashi's intensive study of primitive Okinawan weapons has had a profound effect on karate-do. Ironically, Hayashi has been responsible for a renewal of interest on Okinawa itself in what was a dying art just a few years ago. This in turn reestablishes the fact that weapons are an essential part of Okinawan karate systems. In Japan, Hayashi's efforts to popularize the use of Okinawan weapons in karate-do have caused various sects that were once devoted entirely to the study of empty-hand techniques to begin a study of such weapons. One innovation in the study of weapons that Hayashi has made is proving to be popular: the conducting of *kumite,* or sparring, with weapons. This new feature of Japanese karate-do will help to bring a feeling of true fighting into what has been primarily a sport.

With the existence of the many styles and sects of karate-do it is to be expected that severe rivalry among them would mar the Japanese scene. There is no widespread agreement over how karate-do is to be taught or propagated, or what technical characteristics are truly representative of Japanese style. But some attempts to bring order into the confusion that now prevails have resulted in the rise of a central organization that is stronger and more influential than all the others that have been formed in the past. In the founding of the Federation of All-Japan Karate-do Organizations (FAJKO) in 1964 lie the hopes of many of Japan's foremost exponents of karate-do for the formulation of a truly national standard through which Japanese karate-do may be propagated.

The federation, however, is not yet truly a national organization, for the majority of karate bodies have no affiliation with it; but such affiliates as it does have are the most influential groups in Japan. The FAJKO is headed by three local federations and six sects. The local federations are the All-Japan Self-Defense Force Karate-do Federation, the All-Japan Collegiate Karate-do Federation, and the All-Japan Workers Karate-do Federation. The sects include the Japan Karate Association, Goju-kai, Wado-kai, Rembu-kai, Rengo-kai, and Shito-kai.

FAJKO's function is to set standards of technique, advise on methods of teaching, and decide the qualifications necessary for instructors; it is also concerned with the ethical standards of its individual members. In order that the Japanese style of karate-do may be properly propagated throughout the world, the FAJKO contemplates strengthening its ties with the international community. As I write there are vast problems, both administrative and technical, that hamper this quest, and Japan's role in international karate-do is yet to be fully determined.

A spokesman for the FAJKO, Eriguchi Eiichi, summarizes the Japanese version of the purposes of modern karate-do: "The ultimate goal of karate-do in the true sense of the word is to build a peaceful world . . . a world free from discord and conflicts. It does not merely mean acquiring technical skill to conquer the opponent in a hand-to-hand fight. It means more than winning matches. . . . Karate-do begins with courtesy and ends with courtesy. If superior to their teachers in skill, the disciples should never forget to respect their teachers. The fists are meant not for killing, but for protecting life."

CHAPTER EIGHT

AIKI-DO

> As winds in empty air
> diffused strength lose,
> Unless thick old-grown
> woods of their strength oppose.
> 　　　　　　Lucian

Aiki-do is not a system of hand-to-hand combat that has been handed down as such from antiquity. The word "aiki-do" is a generic term coined in the twentieth century. It is representative of a group of modern disciplines that have broad aims, such as spiritual discipline, religious cultism, physical education, self-defense, recreational activity, and sport. More than thirty different sects of aiki-do exist today. These are all, in spite of claims that there are spiritual and technical differences among them, related endeavors, for they represent the interpretations and partial transformations made by various individuals of what were originally the teachings of one man.

It is most unrealistic to take the position that there is only one aiki-do, and that the other systems that also use this name are false forms; to do so is to deny the existence of the natural process of evolution followed by any classical or modern discipline; to deny, in fact, the very process through which aiki-do itself was created. In view of this evolutionary process, it is also important to distinguish between the present forms of aiki-do and the earlier prototypes. It is necessary, therefore, to disregard the traditional, unproven claims of aiki-do's connections with the remote past, and to realize that its earliest historical prototype was developed in the Edo period.

Takeda Takumi no Kami Soemon (1758–1853), a scholar, taught theology and Neo-Confucian (Chu Hsi) doctrine to the daimyo of the Aizu han (present-day Fukushima Prefecture); these teachings were known as *aiki-in-yo-ho,* or "the doctrine of harmony of spirit based on yin-yang." The Aizu han was a stronghold of the Chu Hsi doctrine because Hoshina (Matsudaira) Masayuki (1611–72), a grandson of Tokugawa Ieyasu, the first Tokugawa shogun, was a staunch advocate of this bakufu-approved school of Neo-Confucianism when daimyo of the Aizu han. The Aizu warriors were thus all educated in the Chu Hsi ethic. Their interpretation of bushido was a strict code embodying Chu Hsi concepts.

The fighting men of Aizu were formidable in combat, and greatly respected for their outstanding martial ardor. These warriors engaged in martial arts stemming from various ryu. Goto Tamauemon Tadayoshi (1644–1736) founded the Daido Ryu, the martial curriculum of which included *tojutsu* (kenjutsu), *kyuba* (mounted bow-and-arrow combat), *sojutsu* (spear art), and *kajutsu* (the art of gunnery and explosives). In 1671 Goto entered the Aizu han, and his teachings became compulsory subjects in the education of all warriors. The skillful swordsmen of Aizu also studied iai-jutsu (quick-draw swordsmanship) of the Mizuno Shinto Ryu, founded by Kobayashi Koemon Toshinari (died between 1703 and 1736). A secondary system of jujutsu-like combat was also included in the teachings of the Mizuno Shinto Ryu.

The general erosion of martial virtues among the majority of the samurai of the Edo period was somewhat less noticeable among the Aizu warriors, who continued to maintain a reasonably high level of readiness for combat with classical weapons. All of their secondary systems of hand-to-hand combat were subsumed under the generic term *oshikiuchi*. This system was based on the dualisms of the Neo-Confucian philosophy as taught in the aiki-in-yo-ho doctrine. Only samurai with high social and financial status were permitted to study oshikiuchi. Leadership for the propagation of oshikiuchi eventually devolved on Saigo Tanomo Chikamasa (Hoshina Chikamasa; 1829–1905), who became a minister of the Aizu han and the head of Shirakawa Castle.

The dissolution of the han in 1871 and the prohibition against wearing swords in 1876 resulted in a loss of popularity for classical swordsmanship. But the often tumultuous social conditions of the early Meiji era made the study of empty-hand self-defense arts both popular and necessary. Saigo Tanomo Chikamasa was at this time a Shinto priest at the Nikko Toshogu shrine, and it was there that he met Takeda Sokaku Minamoto Masayoshi (1858–1943), a highly skilled swordsman.

Sokaku originally studied the Ono-ha Itto Ryu heiho (kenjutsu) in 1870, under the guidance of Shibuya Toma, a former physician of the Aizu han. He also gained experience in the swordsmanship of the Kyoshin Meichi Ryu against Momono-i Shunzo in 1874. But it was not until Sokaku joined the Jikishin-kage Ryu in 1875 and trained under Sakakibara Kenkichi that his skill with the sword became polished and earned for him the nickname of Aizu no Kotengu, "the little *tengu* [a mythological goblinlike being credited with great powers] of Aizu." Sokaku was at the Toshogu shrine on business in connection with the death of his elder brother, who had been studying there. Saigo Tanomo Chikamasa was so favorably impressed with Sokaku that he hired him to be his personal bodyguard; but the aging Saigo's motives for employing Sokaku may have included his hope that Sokaku would study oshikiuchi. Be that as it may, this turn of events enabled Sokaku to devote his entire energy to the study of martial arts.

He attained licences of proficiency in the okuden, or secret teachings, of both the heiho of the Ono-ha Itto Ryu and the sojutsu of the Hozoin Ryu in 1877. While touring Japan and testing his ability against numerous swordsmen from other ryu, Sokaku's fame as a strong swordsman grew.

Sokaku's fighting mettle was seriously tested when he was twenty-three years of age. Barely five feet in height, Sokaku must have presented a strange sight as he trudged along the Tokyo streets with his training gear slung from his valuable sheathed Bizen sword, which he carried over one shoulder. The general decline of interest in swordsmanship and the marked tendency of the average Meiji-era Japanese citizen to worship things from the West prompted several young construction workers to call out to Sokaku as he passed by: "Hey, isn't swordsmanship a bit old-fashioned these days?" Sokaku's curt reply, "Keep your mouth shut," angered the workers, who immediately attacked the tiny Sokaku. When one of the workers seized Sokaku by the lapels of his kimono, Sokaku instinctively reacted by dumping to the ground the training gear that he was carrying, and used the sheathed sword to push his adversary backward. In the ensuing struggle the sword came free of its scabbard and severely cut the worker across his chest. The other workers retreated at the sight of blood, but their fear was quickly overcome by rage. Their calls for help quickly brought other construction workers to their side. More than twenty men, armed with daggers, sword canes, and tools, set upon Sokaku. Sokaku had no choice but to use his sword to defend his life. He cut down all those who came into range. A crew boss, upon seeing Sokaku's great skill with the sword, ordered more reinforcements, and it was not long before almost three hundred workers encircled the desperate Sokaku.

His retreat cut off, Sokaku found himself in the middle of an unruly mob. They hurled stones, tiles, hatchets, and whatever other tools they could find. Sokaku remained calm, dodging and running from side to side until he became exhausted and stumbled to the ground. The workers set upon him at once. One of them hacked at Sokaku's fallen body with a *tobi-guchi,* a sharp-beaked, long-handled fire-fighting tool. Sokaku faced certain death. At this instant mounted policemen rode in on the bloody scene and saved Sokaku's life. After the workers were dispersed, the police found twelve slain and many more wounded; Sokaku lay unconscious, soaked in blood but still clutching his precious sword. Subsequent court action resulted in Sokaku's acquittal of all charges brought against him by the workers. Saigo Tanomo Chikamasa advised Sokaku: "The way of life has changed from what it once was in the Edo period. The age of the sword is over. That altercation occurred because you were armed. Put down your sword and learn jujutsu." It was to be a long time before Sokaku would heed that advice.

In 1877 Saigo Tanomo Chikamasa sponsored Shida Shiro (b. 1868) and took him to Aizu to teach him oshikiuchi. After three years of arduous training, Shida moved to Tokyo to further his education. While studying at the Seijo Gakko, a training school for army personnel, Shida enrolled in the Inoue Dojo of the Tenjin Shin'yo Ryu in 1881. Two years later he caught the eye of Kano Jigoro, who was also a disciple of the Tenjin Shin'yo Ryu. Kano was at this time struggling to build a reputation for his Kodokan

Judo. Shida's skill in hand-to-hand encounters convinced Kano that it would be a good idea to offer Shida an assistant instructorship at the Kodokan; and Shida accepted. Upon marrying Saigo Tanomo Chikamasa's daughter in 1884, Shida became an adopted son of the Saigo family and therewith changed his name to Saigo Shiro. Saigo was an inspirational force in the early days of the Kodokan. He has been immortalized in novels and films as Sugata Sanshiro. In 1886, when the Kodokan stood defiantly against the challenges cast at it by jujutsu ryu seeking to destroy it and the upstart Kano along with it, Saigo Shiro demonstrated his great skill. Using the technique of yama arashi (mountain storm), which is based on the principles and techniques of oshikiuchi, Saigo decisively defeated all comers and was instrumental in making both Kano and his Kodokan Judo famous.

Kano appointed Saigo Shiro to be director of the Kodokan while he was in Europe in 1888. This responsibility brought with it an increase in Saigo's remorse over conflicting loyalties. He owed much both to his original sponsor and teacher, Saigo Tanomo Chikamasa, and to Kano, who had placed such great trust in him. To resolve his problem, Saigo Shiro left Tokyo for Nagasaki in 1891 and set about making his own life in a way that would be unfettered by debts of loyalty to either Saigo or Kano. He abandoned the study of both oshikiuchi and judo. By 1899 he had become the vice-president of the Hinoda Newspaper Company in Kyushu, and for the next twenty years, until his death, he devoted himself entirely to the study of *kyujutsu* (the art of the bow), finally attaining the rank of *hanshi* (master teacher).

Saigo Shiro's precipitous departure made the elder Saigo look for another worthy disciple whom he could entrust with the complete teachings of oshikiuchi. While serving as a priest at the Reizan Shrine, the elder Saigo selected Sokaku for this honor and began teaching him the once exclusive art of the Aizu warriors in 1898. Sokaku's zest for martial learning, coupled with his skill in classical swordsmanship, led him to rapid mastery of oshikiuchi. In the same year in which he began his study under Saigo, Sokaku was authorized to instruct people selected from the former samurai class in Aizu. Shortly before the elder Saigo died, he encouraged Sokaku to spread the spirit and techniques of oshikiuchi on a wider basis. In compliance with his master's wish, Sokaku gradually modified the original oshikiuchi teachings. In response to an official request he traveled to Hokkaido in 1908 to instruct police units in hand-to-hand combat.

Sokaku regarded oshikiuchi in its modified form as jujutsu. To lend prestige to his teachings he appended the name Daito Ryu (not to be confused with the Daido Ryu of the Aizu han) to them. Daito Ryu jujutsu, under Sokaku's leadership, remained a conservative but effective system of self-defense. One of Sokaku's most promising disciples was Ueshiba Morihei (1883–1969).

Ueshiba was the eldest son of a Wakayama Prefecture farmer. The young Ueshiba traveled to Tokyo to enroll in the Tenjin Shin'yo Ryu under Tozawa Tokusaburo in 1898. It is said that Ueshiba's interest in other classical bujutsu led him to study Yagyu Shinkage Ryu jujutsu under Nakae Masakatsu in 1902. During the Russo-Japanese War Ueshiba served as a conscript soldier in the Imperial Army. This afforded him the opportunity to travel and come into contact with various arts of combat and self-defense. Throughout his army service Ueshiba continued his practice of jujutsu, and was eventually awarded the menkyo-kaiden, the highest licence of proficiency, by the Tenjin Shin'yo Ryu in 1908. After his release from the army, Ueshiba traveled to Hokkaido with the intention of engaging in agriculture, and it was there that he enrolled himself in the Daito Ryu to learn jujutsu under Sokaku in 1915.

Ueshiba was a diligent disciple, earning the menkyo, or teaching license, for mastery of thirty-six techniques in 1917. He also continued his study of the Yagyu Shinkage Ryu, allegedly earning the menkyo for his mastery of the jujutsu-like portion of its teachings in 1922; in the same year he was authorized by Sokaku to become an instructor of Daito Ryu methods, then taught as aiki-jujutsu.

But the enterprising Ueshiba was dissatisfied with the classical bujutsu that he had studied. He sought to focus on higher ideals (dō) rather than on the practical aspects of hand-to-hand combat (jutsu). Yet his early form of aiki-jujutsu emphasized practical measures of self-defense. In a special demonstration of his skill made before Admiral Yamamoto Gombei at the latter's residence in 1925, Ueshiba favorably impressed his elite audience. Ueshiba opened a dojo in the Shinjuku area of Tokyo in 1932 and dedicated himself to the task of widening the basis of aiki-jujutsu. He sought through participation in training to establish a direct contact with nature, improve himself, and thereby better society. His influence upon his disciples was a strong one, and his teachings became popular with a wide segment of Japanese society. Ueshiba studied academically the Shinkage Ryu (not to be confused with the Yagyu Shinkage Ryu) jujutsu, as well. In 1938 Ueshiba emerged with his own distinct kind of aiki-jujutsu, which was designed to be suitable for use in the social circumstances of his times. He called it aiki-do.

Thereafter, a split occurred in the main line of the Daito Ryu aiki-jujutsu. Sokaku's line, the traditional or conservative sect, fell behind Ueshiba's newly risen progressive sect in terms of popularity. Each of these sects functioned differently, and because Ueshiba's aiki-do differs greatly from the aiki-jujutsu of Sokaku's traditional sect in purpose, technique, and training methods, Ueshiba is the actual originator of aiki-do.

ESSENCE, AIMS, AND TECHNIQUES   All systems of aiki-like techniques are traditionally classified in terms of their mechanics as a subset of jujutsu, because in fundamentals they are based on ju no ri, or the principle of flexibility. But in view of the different ideals that underlie the teachings of aiki-do, it is more accurate to give these many systems a classification of their own; for this reason aiki-do appears in this book in the section devoted to dō forms.

The rationalism of Neo-Confucian doctrine is fundamental to all aiki-do teachings. This fact exemplifies the effect of a Chu Hsi education on Aizu warriors and the influence of the aiki-in-yo-ho doctrine on their martial disciplines. The Aizu art of oshikiuchi, and consequently of Sokaku's aiki-jujutsu, are both steeped in the dualisms of the Chu Hsi doctrine. The concept of ki, which is the essence of all aiki-do, is not without an antecedent in the Chu Hsi dualisms, where it is described as "material force" in connection with its complement, ri, or "principle." Ki is also explained by the Neo-Confucian Kaibara Ekken, who qualified the dualisms of Chu Hsi and viewed ki as a monism. The doctrine of *aiki-ho* is found in the teachings of the Yagyu Shinkage Ryu, wherein the concept of aiki is made analagous to the action of a willow branch as it flings off snow that has accumulated on its surface. And in the practical application of aiki technique, ki is stressed in the teachings of the Tenjin Shin'yo Ryu, which were studied by Saigo Shiro and may have influenced the Meiji-era development of oshikiuchi.

The words ki, aiki, and ki-ai have been treated as technical terms within the classical bujutsu ryu. They are no more than matters to be attended to in rigorous training. Though recognized as important matters, ki, aiki, and ki-ai received no special emphasis or treatment by fighting men, nor were they considered secret teachings. These terms may be found in the *makimono* (hand scrolls) of many classical martial ryu in connection with okuden, but it is the nature of the techniques comprising the okuden, not the terms ki, aiki, or ki-ai, that made such teachings secret.

During the Meiji era, scholars and writers with imaginative minds and greatly inflated ideas about ki, aiki, and ki-ai recorded their opinions. The oldest book to discuss aiki is *Budo Hiketsu—Aiki no Jutsu* (The Secret of Budo—The Art of Aiki), published in 1899, which states: "The most profound and mysterious art in the world is the art of aiki. This is the secret principle of all the martial arts in Japan. One who masters it can be an unparalleled martial genius."

Other books gave equally inflated descriptions of the terms ki, aiki, and ki-ai, but in the *Jujutsu Kyoju-sho Ryu no Maki* (Textbook of Jujutsu, Volume on Ryu), published in 1913, there appeared what is perhaps the best definition of aiki: "Aiki is an impassive state of mind without a blind side, slackness, evil intention, or fear. There is no difference between aiki and ki-ai; however, if compared, when expressed dynamically aiki is called ki-ai, and when expressed statically, it is aiki."

Thereafter the term aiki became well known to the public and enjoyed widespread popularity among exponents of various ryu who attached it to the disciplines they practiced. Even karate-jutsu, newly introduced into Japan from Okinawa, came under the influence of aiki. In the *Sokuseki Katsuyo Karate Goshin-jutsu* (Instant Application of Karate, the Art of Self-defense), published in 1917, we find: "The secret principle of aiki is to defeat the opponent without a fight by getting the better of his ki." Another book, the *Goshin-jutsu Ogi* (The Secret Principles of the Art of Self-defense), published the same year, echoes the teachings of the Yagyu Shinkage Ryu: "Aiki-ho is the technique used to stop the enemy's attack by gaining the initiative over him."

The records of the Tachikawa Library, Tokyo, show that in the middle of the Taisho era, or around 1920, books concerned with such subjects as aiki-jujutsu and *ki-ai-jutsu* (the art of ki-ai) were immensely popular with the public. The book *Ninjutsu Kaisetsu-sho* (A Commentary on Ninjutsu), published in 1921, was one such popular book; in it are discussions of both aiki and ki-ai. Sokaku viewed ki, aiki, and ki-ai with a conservative outlook. He was primarily interested in their practical application. His personal definition of the essence of aiki is recorded in succinct form: "The secret of aiki is to overpower the opponent mentally at a glance and to win without fighting."

Ki is a concept that is both natural and simple. Those who would make of it something mysterious and akin to magical power do a great disservice to what is essentially a common thing. All human beings possess ki. It is only that one must learn to release and utilize ki, wherein lies the difficulty of expressing its nature and functions. Aiki-do has for its purpose the training of the individual so as to enable him to release and consciously control the use of ki; in this purpose aiki-do is no different from any of the systems of classical bujutsu and budo.

But ki has many and varied meanings. It has been translated as "vitality," "breath," "spirit," "aura," and "nervous energy." Its function in the human body has been described as "electricity that flows back and forth along the wires of our nerves" and as "the psychophysiological power associated with blood, breath, and mind, the biophysical energy generated by respiratory rhythm." All that really matters to the exponent of aiki-do is that ki exists as a force that is both summonable and controllable, and that gaining control over ki is identified with spiritual progress. On a more mundane level, ki is related to the coordination of mind and body, and it enables one to react appropriately in an emergency.

Ueshiba Morihei is, to date, the greatest expositor of ki in modern Japanese disciplines. Though all exponents of aiki-do recognize the workings of ki, none of them places stronger emphasis upon it than Ueshiba. Ueshiba follows Kaibara's monistic interpretation of ki, which describes it as a "creative life-force." To that definition Ueshiba has added moralistic philosophy based on the Mo-ist doctrine of "all-embracing love." Ueshiba sought religious sanction for his teachings, and chose the Mo-ist standard of that which is "beneficial to country and people" when designing his aiki-do. Man and nature, according to both Ueshiba and Kaibara, are "allied and inseparable." An understanding of nature, therefore, is indispensable for the understanding of man. Man comes to understand nature, believes Ueshiba, by devoting himself assiduously to disciplined, righteous living, for which the practice of aiki-do is the *sine qua non*.

Another Mo-ist concept, that of *jen,* or *jin* in Japanese, underscores a major aim of Ueshiba's aiki-do. Jin may be defined as "benevolence" or "human-heartedness" and is the supreme Confucian virtue through which man and nature are interrelated. To make this clear, Ueshiba sees benevolence as transcending humanity, and the personal effort in being benevolent thus becomes "love for all things." In this thought Ueshiba echoes Kaibara, who writes: "All men in the world are children born of heaven and earth, and heaven and earth are the great parents of us all.... Man's duty is ... to serve nature.... Benevolence means having a sense of sympathy within, and bringing blessings to man and things." Ueshiba borrows still more from the Mo-ist doctrine of "all-embracing love" by making jin equivalent to "cosmic love," which is identified with the creativity of nature.

Ueshiba's ideal man follows Kaibara's thought, which states that man "should be humble and not arrogant toward others, control his desires and not be indulgent of his passions, cherish a profound love for all mankind born of nature's great love, and not abuse or mistreat them. . . . All . . . are objects of nature's love. . . . To cherish them and keep them is therefore the way to serve nature in accordance with the great heart of nature."

The physical techniques of Ueshiba's aiki-do reflect and encompass his religious philosophy. He regards the basic dynamics of the universe as supreme examples of *ai*, or harmony and affinity (cosmic love). Inasmuch as all matter in the universe follows circular, not linear, lines of movement, Ueshiba designed all his aiki-do techniques on circular movement. Aiki-do is mind and body unified harmoniously in a system of mechanics that is based on force applied along lines of continuity: a concept of natural rhythm, a free flow of personal expression that offers no conflict with nature. Just as personal expression is infinitely varied, techniques of aiki-do are theoretically infinite in number.

There is no conflict between the practical use of Ueshiba's aiki-do and his philosophy of love for human beings when it is understood that Ueshiba intended aiki-do to remove all thoughts of aggression from people's minds. All techniques are applied without any thought of defeating or injuring an aggressor. Ueshiba rejects the concept of kobo-itchi that underlies all classical bujutsu; this concept asserts that, in combat, attack and defense are one and the same thing, and which of the two receives priority depends entirely on the situation. Ueshiba substitutes instead the concept of absolute *go no sen*, a defensive initiative. Through application of this concept Ueshiba's aiki-do becomes purely defensive in nature, a response to aggressive actions, and this fact makes it theoretically impossible for two exponents who abide by this concept to attack each other.

Ueshiba's aiki-do is not a system of conflict with an aggressor, but rather the means by which a state of *ai*, or harmony, is established between the adept of aiki-do and his antagonist. Only after an aggressor has launched his attack does the defender become physically active. He does so first by avoiding the attack, then blending with it so as to use the attacker's own force to overcome him. An assailant is literally led to his own destruction. Leading is accomplished by use of ki, which is "extended" by the exponent of aiki-do and joined harmoniously to the ki of the attacker. A great sensitivity to the attacker's state of mind and his direction of movement must be developed, for until the exponent can "read" the attacker's mind and recognize the direction in which he is applying his forces, the exponent cannot harmonize (ai) with him and lead the attacker to realize the folly of his actions. If an attacker is injured in assault against an expert exponent of aiki-do, the attacker has literally injured himself.

In sharp contrast to Ueshiba's spiritually oriented aiki-do is Sokaku's traditional aiki-jujutsu, the primary purpose of which is to provide a method of hand-to-hand combat. Sokaku's aiki-jujutsu is based on a technical essence that enables the exponent to apply severe measures against an assailant. Ample use is made of *atemi*, or blows directed against anatomical weaknesses; and atemi always precede the seizure and subduing of an assailant. Physical strength, economically used (ju no ri) in conjunction with technique, is desirable and greatly respected by all exponents of aiki-jujutsu. The classical

27. An early photograph of Funakoshi Gichin *(seated, second from left)*. Also shown are his son Yoshitaka *(seated, second from right)* and Nakayama Masatoshi *(seated, far right)*. (Photo courtesy of Nakayama Masatoshi)

28. Funakoshi Gichin (left) in action as an old man. The speed of his punch is indicated by the blurring of his right arm in the photograph. (Photo courtesy of Nakayama Masatoshi)

29. Otsuka Hidenori, founder of the Wado Ryu style of karate-do, shown at the age of seventy-four in 1966, at the time of his decoration by the emperor for his distinguished service to karate-do. (Photo courtesy of Otsuka Hidenori)

30. This rare photograph shows Funakoshi Yoshitaka as a young man training at the makiwara (straw-wrapped pole). (Photo courtesy of Nakayama Masatoshi)

31, 32, 33. Otsuka Hidenori (right), shown at the age of eighty-two, evades a punch and counterpunches to his opponent' chest. Note Otsuka's "soft," seemingly effortless deflection of the punch, characteristic of Wado Ryu karate-do. (Phot courtesy of Otsuka Hidenori)

149

34, 35. Nakayama Masatoshi (right), chief instructor of the Japan Karate Association, uses a forearm block followed by an elbow strike against his opponent. This is an extremely difficult combination calling for split-second timing. (Photo courtesy of Nakayama Masatoshi)

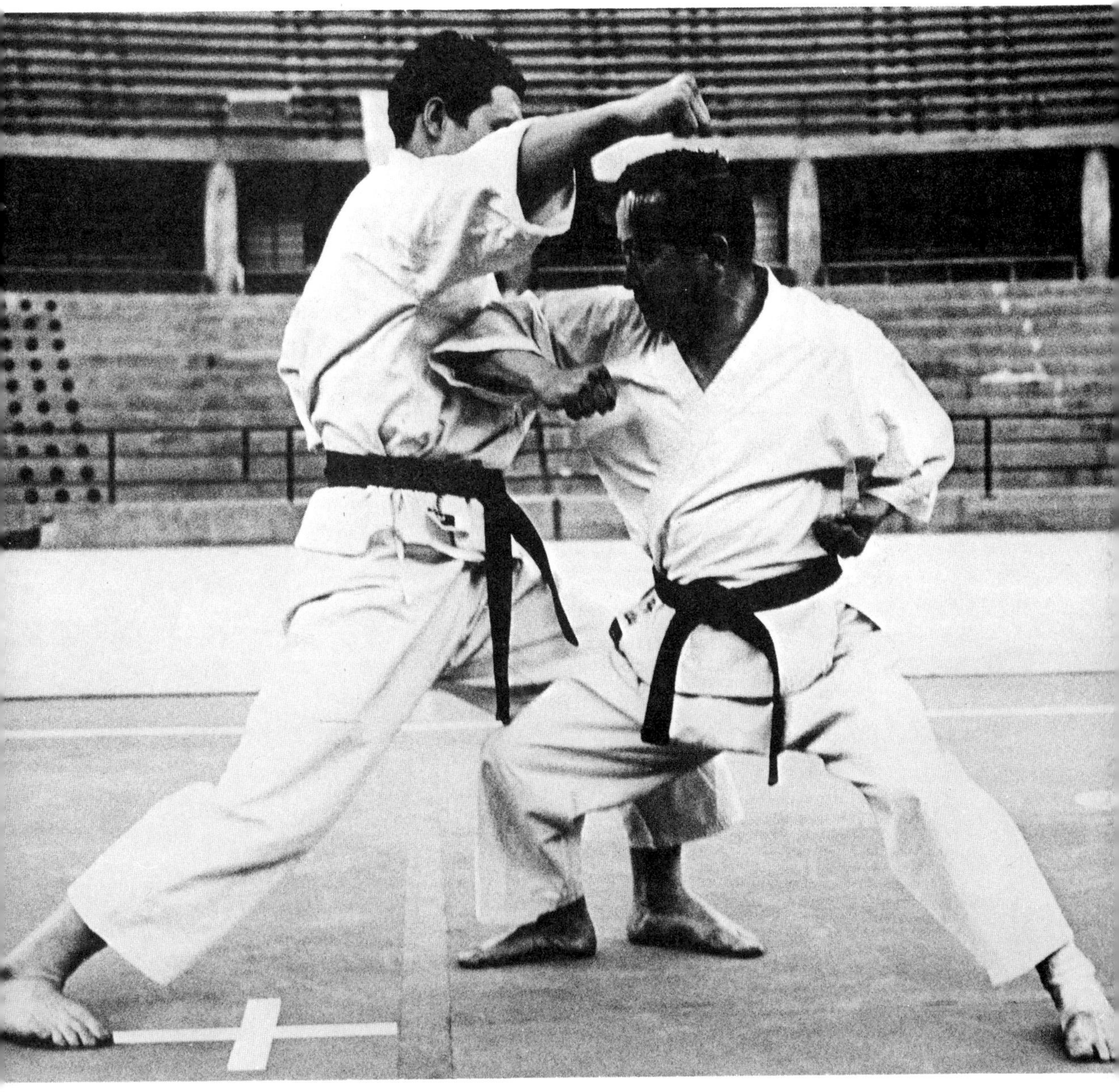

36. Hayashi Teruo (right), founder of the Kenshin Ryu of karate-do and a master of the use of Okinawan weapons, here uses the tui-fa (tonfa) against an opponent armed with a live sword.

37. Yamaguchi Gogen, popularly known as "the Cat," at the time of his decoration by the emperor for his distinguished service to karate-do. (Photo courtesy of Yamaguchi Gogen)

38. Takeda Sokaku, first disseminator of Daito Ryu aiki-jujutsu *teachings*.

39. Ueshiba Morihei, *founder of modern* aiki-do.

40. Ueshiba Kishomaru, son of Morihei and present head of the Aikido Hombu Dojo, Tokyo.

41. *Ueshiba Kishomaru throws his opponent from a seated position.*

42, 43. *Tomiki Kenji (in shirtsleeves), founder of the Tomiki style of* aiki-do, *begins (left) and executes a* shiho-nage *throw. Tomiki believes that all aiki-do techniques must be applicable when the exponent is wearing ordinary clothing.*

44. Shioda Gozo, founder of the Yoshin style of aiki-do, deflects an attack and strikes his assailant before throwing him.

45. *Two exponents of Nippon Shorinji Kempo, the Japanese version of Chinese* shaolin, *spar in the grounds of a Shinto shrine.*

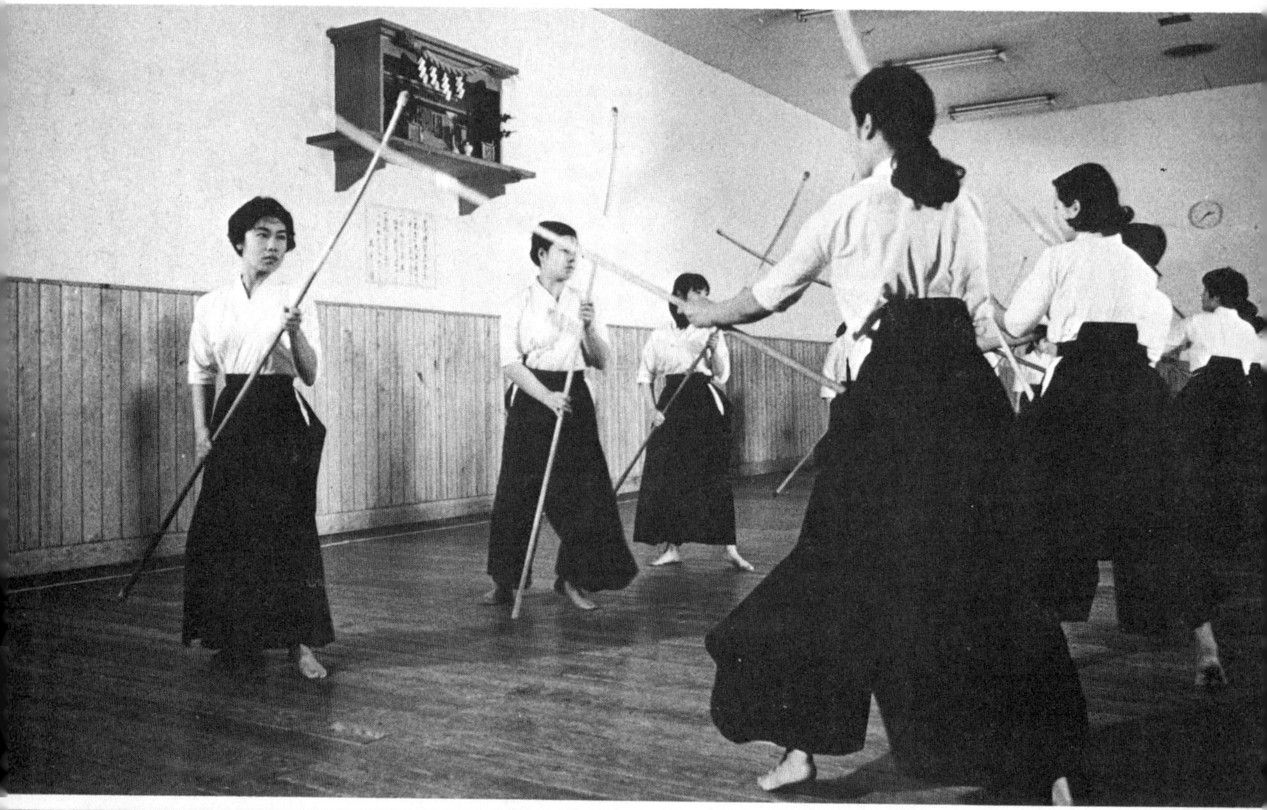

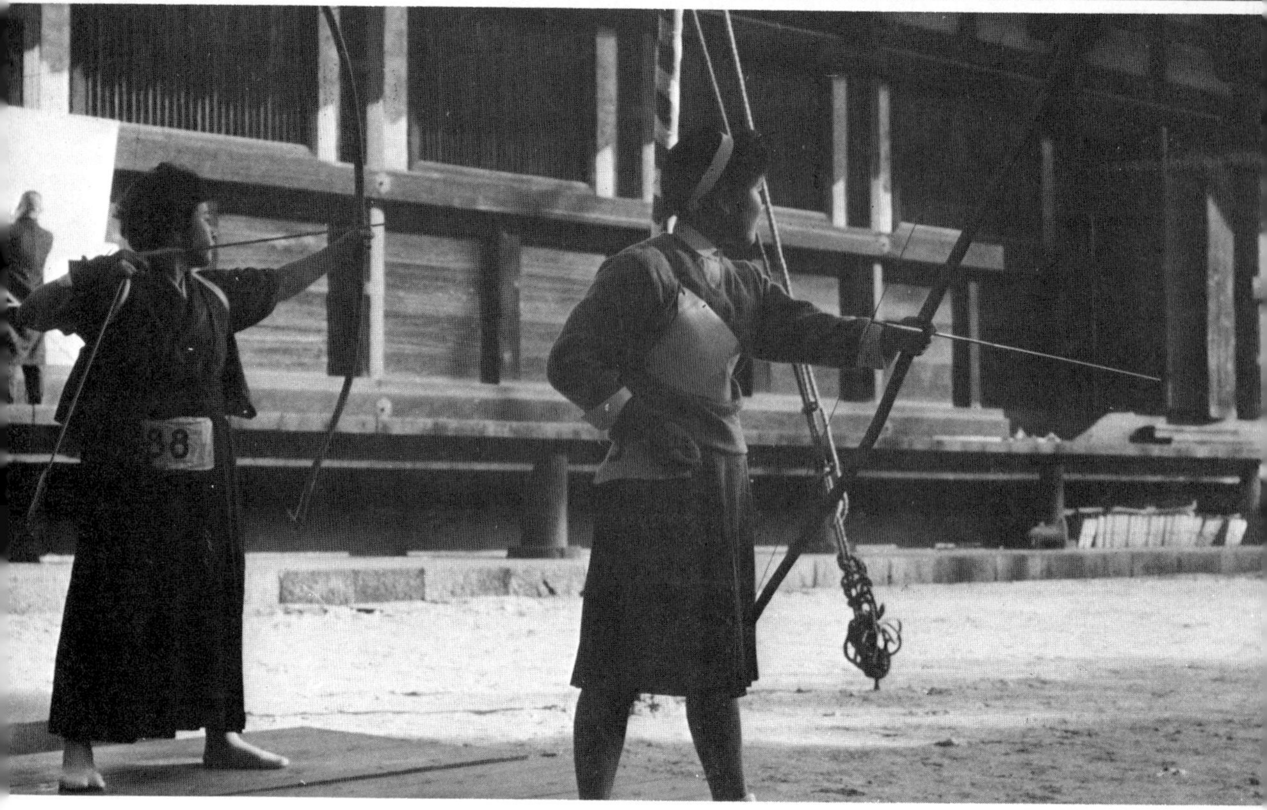
38

46, 47 (above). Left: Women engage in naginata-do *training at the Bukodan, Tokyo. There is a small Shinto shrine on one wall. Right: Two women contend in a* naginata-do *competition. Note the shin guards worn over the* hakama *(divided skirt) as required in modern* naginata-do.

48. This kyudo *tournament at Sanjusangendo, Kyoto, pits a classical exponent against a modern advocate. (Photo courtesy of Asahi Shimbun)*

49. *Two competitors in the 1973 National Bayonet Championship at the Budokan, Tokyo, score simultaneously, the man at left with* nodo, *a thrust to the throat, and his opponent with* shita-do, *a thrust to the lower torso. (Photo courtesy of Zen Nihon Juken-do Remmei)*

50. *The competitor at right scores with* do, *a thrust to the torso, at the 1973 National Bayonet Championship at the Budokan, Tokyo. (Photo courtesy of Zen Nihon Juken-do Remmei)*

method of instruction—master to disciple on a personal basis—characterizes the teaching method of the traditional sect. This conservative method of teaching guarantees a high degree of technical excellence in disciples that is unobtainable when disciples are taught by the mass-class method; at the same time, of course, it greatly limits the number of disciples.

In view of the nature of Sokaku's aiki-jujutsu, Ueshiba's aiki-do is a highly weakened form of hand-to-hand combat. Aiki-do is essentially noncombative in nature because it does not function according to the concept of kobo-itchi; further, the omission of atemi from its techniques removes aiki-do from the category of practical hand-to-hand combat styles. Taught through group-instruction methods, aiki-do has for its purpose the development of a healthy mind and body together with a wholesome spirit. All exponents of aiki-do aim to live in harmony with themselves and with those around them. Thus, when the idea of combat is dismissed from mind, Ueshiba's aiki-do is an outstanding system of discipline for the pursuance of those spiritual and sociological aims it has made its own. Sokaku himself viewed aiki-do somewhat more mundanely than Ueshiba: "Aiki-do is to adjust your movement to that of the opponent, and to defeat him by making use of his power imposed through the smooth circle movement. It is much like an elegant dance of the old days."

AIKI-DO TODAY The teachings of the Daito Ryu aiki-jujutsu continue today, but because aiki-jujutsu is taught under the general rubric of *aiki-budo,* the foregoing summary of its nature appears in this section rather than in the one that is devoted to bujutsu; this also facilitates a comparison between Sokaku's aiki-jujutsu and Ueshiba's aiki-do.

Takeda Tokimune is the current headmaster of the Daito Ryu. The leading proponents of this traditional sect are Horikawa Kotaro, Sagawa Yukiyoshi, Hisa Takuma, Matsuda Hosaku, and Yamamoto Tomekichi. Matsuda has further trained two other leading experts in aiki-jujutsu, Okuyama Yoshiji (Yoshiharu) and Oba Sachiyuki; the former is the founder of the Hakko Ryu jujutsu, a modern bujutsu. Okuyama, in turn, includes in his long line of disciples Nakano Michiomi, who, as So Doshin, is the founder of the Nippon Shorinji Kempo system.

Ueshiba's teachings, being considerably more progressive in nature than those of any instructor of the traditional aiki-jujutsu sect, have resulted in a considerable number of expert stylists of aiki-do, among whom the most senior are his son Kishomaru, Tohei Koichi, Murashige Yuso, Shioda Gozo, Mochizuki Minoru, Tomiki Kenji, Hirai Minoru, and Inoue Yoichiro.

Kishomaru, a mild-mannered man, succeeded the elder Ueshiba on the latter's death in 1969. Aiki-do for Kishomaru is not a jutsu form concerned with combative effect but follows the classical concept of dō. There is no carnival hocus-pocus in Kishomaru's interpretation of ki, or in his performance of aiki-do in general; in fact, he deplores the actions of those who sometimes use this approach to popularize aiki-do. "Aiki is a natural flow," says Kishomaru, "in which human beings unite through adjusting to the circle [cycle of nature]. This exercise leads to self-protection and self-perfection." Not all of the elder Ueshiba's disciples follow precisely his kind of aiki-do, and many have established their own distinctive styles in which the emphasis on ki is greatly reduced. The foremost innovators of Ueshiba's aiki-do are Shioda, Tomiki, Hirai, and Inoue. Shioda's Yoshin aiki-do is oriented towards combat and closely approximates the traditional sect of aiki-jutsu in regard to technique, though its spiritual purpose is attuned to that of Ueshiba's. Tomiki style aiki-do is a system of physical education that contains practical elements of self-defense and is practiced competitively. Hirai's Korindo aiki-do is concerned with self-defense. The Inoue system is called Shinwa *taido,* a blend of self-defense and sport.

Other less senior disciples of Ueshiba, too, have developed their own patterns of aiki-do. Otsuki Yutaka has founded the Otsuki Ryu aiki-do, and Hoshi Tetsuomi is the founder of a system that he calls *kobu-jutsu;* both of these systems are primarily concerned with self-defense. Tanaka Setaro is the founder of the Shin Riaku heiho, also a system of self-defense. Disciples of Tanaka are currently at work designing still other systems of hand-to-hand combat based on aiki-do. The so-called Shindo Iten Ryu is still being formalized, while the Yae Ryu of Fukui Harunosuke is steadily gaining followers. Ueshiba's last disciple through direct teaching, Noguchi Senryuken, is the founder of the Shindo Rokugo Ryu, a form of aiki-do that deals primarily with self-defense.

CHAPTER NINE

NIPPON SHORINJI KEMPO

> Nor do not saw the air too much with your hand, but use all gently.
>
> Shakespeare

Nippon Shorinji Kempo is, in the words of So Doshin, a prominent developer of this art in Japan, "kempo reexamined and systematized from a new angle . . . amplified by the addition of a religious philosophy." The expression "Shorinji Kempo" is the Japanese pronunciation of the ideograms that in Chinese are read "Shaolin-ssu ch'uan-fa." A translation of these Chinese ideograms into English reveals that they refer to "the fist way of the Shaolin temple," that is, to but a part of the total teachings of the Shaolin martial-art tradition of China.

Because So Doshin's Shorinji Kempo is today given wide currency as being the transplantation of the Chinese Shaolin tradition onto Japanese soil, it is necessary to examine it by comparing it with the ancestral Chinese form.

So Doshin is the name adopted by Nakano Michiomi (b. 1911), the founder and religious leader of the most widely known sect of Shorinji Kempo in Japan. Nakano was born in Okayama Prefecture, the eldest son of a customs officer. On the death of his father, young Nakano was sent to live in Manchuria with his grandfather, who was an ultranationalist employee of the South Manchurian Railway Company. This was at a time when the militarists of Japan were organizing their policies for territorial expansion on the Asian continent. Both Nakano's father and grandfather were friends of Toyama Mitsuru, the founder of the ultranationalistic Black Dragon Society, and were involved in the operations of the society. On the death of his grandfather, the young

Nakano was recalled to Japan, where he came under the direct guidance of Toyama and other zealous members of the Black Dragon Society.

After undergoing training as a member of the society, Nakano was sent back to Manchuria in 1928 to conduct intelligence operations there. To disguise his mission, Nakano is said to have become the disciple of a Taoist priest, the latter himself an agent of secret Chinese societies and involved in religious and political activism. Nakano supposedly gained his first knowledge of Chinese ch'uan-fa from this Taoist priest, who, Nakano believes, was connected with a northern branch of the Shaolin teachings. Nakano began "to practice it [ch'uan-fa] eagerly."

Nakano states that his first training in ch'uan-fa was of a kind supported by the White Lotus Society. This secret society stemmed from a sect of T'ien-t'ai (Tendai in Japanese) Buddhism that is said to have been organized in 1133; indirectly, its genealogy goes back to the fourth century. The White Lotus Society emphasized repentance, suppression of desires, vegetarianism, and abstinence from alcohol; it further forbade the taking of human life. Its appeal to the members of rural Chinese communities was tremendous. Among the features of the White Lotus Society was the compulsory training of its memners in *wu shu* (bujutsu in Japanese); both armed and unarmed methods of combat were contained in the curriculum of the White Lotus Society. The members of this society were especially skilled in the use of the *chiang,* or straight-bladed spear. To justify the growing militant spirit of its members, the White Lotus Society rationalized it by declaring that this spirit was necessary to resist the invading Jurched barbarians in support of the Sung dynasty (960–1279); similarly, the society rebelled against the Mongols of the Yuan dynasty (1270–1368) in support of the Ming, and also against the Manchus during the time of the Ch'ing dynasty (1644–1911).

The White Lotus Society operated through various branches, such as the Red Scarf Society, the Eight Trigrams Society, the Yellow Society, the so-called Shantung "boxers," and the Society of the White Robe. Yet another prominent branch was that of the Tsai-li (Principle-Abiding) Society, which was steeped in Buddhist doctrines and Taoist practices, and imbued with Confucian ethics. Another important branch of the White Lotus Society was the I-kuan Tao (Way of Pervading Unity), which was active during World War II at the time that Nakano was conducting his operations for the Black Dragon Society. The I-kuan Tao members were militant "boxers" who believed that the Tao, as the One, is the root of all things and beings, and is the principle that penetrates and pervades all existence. According to I-kuan Tao philosophy, the universe evolves from *li,* or principle, which is both infinite and prior to *ch'i,* or material force; the universe operates in accord with yin-yang, the negative and positive aspects of the cosmos. The I-kuan Tao was especially active in the Japanese sectors of north China and Manchuria during Nakano's stay in those areas.

Nakano's original experience with ch'uan-fa was perhaps gained largely through his association with *pai* (traditional sects of Chinese wu shu) dominated by White Lotus Society members. Nakano states that the training which he received appeared to him to be of a rather disorganized nature. Inasmuch as Chinese wu shu is well organized and systematically taught to disciples who are considered to be of the "inner group," that is, closest to the master, Nakano's statement is virtually an admission that he did not penetrate deeply into ch'uan-fa study. But in his role as an agent for the Black Dragon Society Nakano claims to have traveled widely throughout north China. This no doubt gave him many opportunities to come into contact with a great variety of ch'uan-fa experts and to acquire considerable experience in various martial skills. In Peking, Nakano allegedly came into contact with one Wen Lao-shi, "the twentieth master of the north Shaolin Giwamonken" (Japanese pronunciation) style of ch'uan-fa, and became his pupil. Chinese records assert that Wen Tai-tsung was the undisputed master of the northern Shaolin style called I-ho-ch'uan, or "Righteous and Harmonious Fists." Wen had studied at Sung Shan, the highest of five mountain peaks in Honan. His followers comprised the main body of the "boxers" who set off the Boxer Rebellion (1898–1901).

While Nakano's claim to be a disciple of Wen is plausible given the hectic conditions of those times, history refutes his claim that in 1936 he was honored by the aged Wen and named the twenty-first leader of the Shaolin tradition, and that therefore he is "the only true successor to the Shorinji [Shaolin-ssu] tradition." This false claim greatly detracts from Nakano's integrity, for no Chinese historian or wu shu authority has ever heard of him in this role. So it must be assumed that Nakano's claim is but a fabrication made to enhance his personal prestige and the position of his Shorinji system in Japan. For Nakano to suggest that he, a foreigner, could succeed to a position of leadership over a Chinese martial arts tradition is deliberately to ignore Chinese tradition and to insult the intelligence of those whom he would have believe his claim.

There has never been any legitimate sect of Chinese Shaolin in Japan. Nevertheless, Shaolin ch'uan-fa ("kempo" in Japanese) has always fascinated the Japanese people, and the word "kempo" has been loosely used by the Japanese since ancient times to describe any and all forms of unarmed sparring tactics that have, or claim to have, a Chinese influence on their techniques, no matter how slight this may be. As a result of their attraction to Chinese sparring methods, the Japanese have developed a diversified kempo movement in their own country, all styles and sects of which are patterned after Japanese, not Chinese, standards of taste. So far as actual Chinese influence on Japanese kempo is concerned, a Japanese version of Shaolin tactics was already well established at the time that Nakano alleges to have studied ch'uan-fa in China. The oldest sect of Japanese Shorinji Kempo is that founded by Takemori Taizen, whose dojo in Toyama Prefecture began operation in 1930; the current headmaster is Takura Teramasa.

When Russia captured Manchuria in 1945, Nakano managed to escape with the aid of various secret societies. He was repatriated the following year. The Japanese domestic scene under Allied occupation made a lasting impression on Nakano. He resolutely set about to provide a means for the restoration of national morality and pride in the Japanese people. He began by entering the Hakko Ryu, founded in 1938 by Okuyama Yoshiji (Yoshiharu). Okuyama, a disciple of Matsuda Hosaku of the Daito Ryu, taught Nakano jujutsu based on the teachings of the Takeda style of aiki-jujutsu. Nakano gained considerable skill in this modern form of jujutsu, but soon left the Hakko Ryu and set out on his own. As So Doshin (Doshin being the Chinese-style reading of Michiomi, his personal name), Nakano combined his knowledge of jujutsu with the many kinds of ch'uan-fa he may have studied in China and Manchuria. After completely revising, expanding, and systematizing his knowledge of these arts, Nakano emerged in 1947 with his new system, called Nippon Den Sei To Shorinji Kempo.

THEORY OF SHORINJI KEMPO The philosophy of Kongo Zen lies at the spiritual root of So's Shorinji Kempo. *Kongo* refers to a diamond, *Zen* to the meditative discipline and doctrine of Chinese Ch'an (Zen) Buddhism. Kongo Zen, says So Doshin, is a "new philosophy that turns inward as well as radiates outward, that combines gentleness with hardiness and compassion with strength." In it will be found the influence of T'ien-t'ai, or Lotus, Buddhism (so called because of the sect's emphasis on the Lotus Sutra), shown by insistence on a strongly philosophical content, the identification of the relative with the absolute, and the emphasis on concentration and insight as the means for perceiving ultimate truth.

Kongo Zen focuses attention on man, who is but an expression of, and participant in, "the infinite circle of reality." As such, "man is endowed with a share of its vast potentiality." Ultimate reality is not what man makes of it but rather what it intrinsically is. Kongo Zen considers reality something that is beyond man's knowledge; therefore it is incapable of being reduced to human categories of thought or being, as is always the case with any kind of man-made image.

Kongo Zen is also a godless philosophy. It recognizes no supreme power over man. "The only power man can turn to for guidance in life is knowledge, knowledge of the world and mankind as they really are." The individual must seek to express his potential in terms of wisdom, strength, courage, and love in order that his life may be lived to best advantage. Wisdom is equated with humility and respect for knowledge, a state of self-awareness in which understanding is guided by morality; strength is having a vigorous body; courage is initiative, self-confidence, invincible spirit; and love is a reverence for life and humanity, as well as the unselfishness and integrity of a stable personality.

The principle of yin-yang appears in the theory of So's Shorinji Kempo, where it takes on a monistic aspect as the interaction of heaven and earth—of the positive, "male" principle of reason and strength together with the negative, "female" principle of compassion and love. In connection with yin-yang, Kongo-zen maintains that truth is found only in "the middle path of harmony," where matter and mind are inseparably united. In the study of Shorinji Kempo, each exponent must reevaluate his former way of life and then strive for a harmonious balance between physical and mental needs. This cultivation of the self does not require that the individual forfeit his self-identity but rather that he develop his unique identity, at the same time appreciating the fact that all human beings must be interdependent if they wish to better their lives. Thus Kongo Zen prescribes a "functional togetherness."

Kongo Zen asserts that morals and ethical values must be grounded in the true nature of things, not in man-made laws. The true state of reality lies in the middle path, and this is the only valid criterion for directing man's life. This middle path is both the means and the end in human life.

Because Kongo Zen denies Confucian dualism, it rejects giving any value to the states of life and death, and with that the concern for seishi o choetsu, or transcending thoughts of life and death, which is the keystone of classical bujutsu and budo forms. In Kongo Zen, human life is viewed as something that passes through numerous states. Man is but an embodiment of a continuity of changes that occur from moment to moment and are never repeated. Thus the exponent of So's Shorinji Kempo learns to regard life in terms of the middle path and makes of it a life of "becoming" rather than one of "is" and "was." Each moment of life is its own lifetime, different from all other moments. But because all changes or stages of life are interrelated and connected, the preciousness of each single moment is paramount. Each individual must make an earnest endeavor to make every moment of his life worthwhile.

AIMS OF SHORINJI KEMPO   The founder's own words best summarize the purpose and aims of his Shorinji Kempo: "Shorinji Kempo offers a new hope for true peace, progress, and prosperity, and for the fulfillment and happiness of every individual on earth." Disciples are therefore enjoined to engross themselves in activistic discipline and through the process of self-activity to strive humbly for unbiased knowledge in order that they may come closer to the ultimate truth.

In view of its broad and lofty purpose, So's Shorinji Kempo is a way of life and a system of discipline that is dedicated to an attempt to encourage people to cultivate themselves so that they can live in harmony with one another. Each disciple of So's Shorinji Kempo learns to regard his way of life as a relentless journey made over the middle path, the only possible way to traverse a good life. Because the spiritual aspect of Shorinji Kempo frees man from the anxiety of concern over an absolute God who judges him, punishes him, rewards him, and in general dictates to him what is right and wrong, man learns not to trust in providence but to sort things out for himself. Man is his own master. He is responsible for all that is good or evil in society. In order that good may triumph over evil, however, man must draw from his inner resources to discover a morality that is rooted in the true nature of things, and then actively strive to create a meaningful life that is a "heaven on earth" where people can live in harmony and happiness.

So's brand of Shorinji Kempo aims to alleviate personal suffering throughout the world. It proposes to accomplish this not through the Buddhist practice of self-abnegation, not through a reordering or remaking of nature in conformity with man's wishes, as is the Taoist religious doctrine and also the Christian practice, nor through a combination of these two practices. Shorinji Kempo sees the need both to better the external social world and to gratify the physical needs of man as he cultivates his internal mental and moral self. Three factors are believed essential to this end: (1) unity of *ken,* or body in action, and *zen,* the composed mind; (2) unity of strength and love, which ensures that strength is fitted to right reason; and (3) living half for oneself and half for others. In regard to the first factor, training that is undertaken for the sake of either the body or the mind alone is incapable of producing a mature and cultivated person. With the second factor, right and justice that are enforced by strength are opposed to passive submission to force. And as for the third factor, with its emphasis on the interdependence of all individuals, each person must seek to curb his ego, gain freedom of self through his experience in discipline, and through that course of discipline reach the final goal of thinking of others while at the same time promoting his own affairs. The Confucian concept of extending one's scope of activities to include others is quite evident here.

Because of its stated purpose and aims, So's Shorinji Kempo is clearly a budo form, a martial way, not a bujutsu, or martial art. Although So Doshin occasionally loosely uses the expression "martial art" when identifying his Shorinji Kempo system, his stress on its passive qualities identifies his system as that of a martial way. He insists emphatically that Shorinji Kempo is not designed to incite violence or to inflict injury on others. He views Shorinji Kempo not as a tool of attack, nor as a method by which to win competitions; and he declares that it is not a method of becoming physically rugged, a cultivation of brute strength or strange powers for the purpose of achieving self-satisfaction through the display of skill for the entertainment of onlookers. Shorinji Kempo, says So, is dedicated to the creation of "human beings with social consciousness equipped with the power to eliminate evil elements in society and to terminate and prevent conflicts."

TECHNIQUES AND TRAINING METHODS   So Doshin's attempt to link his system of Shorinji Kempo with the traditional Shaolin art of China results in a distortion of historical truth. This, in turn, has a bearing on the nature of Shorinji Kempo techniques.

So Doshin sees Bodhidharma (c. 470–c. 534), the famous Indian monk who is traditionally regarded as having introduced Ch'an teachings to China, as the first to introduce Shaolin to Chinese monks. This is the traditional legend, to be sure, but it is only a legend, and one that no self-respecting scholar today will support. It has been proved by researchers that the only form of physical exercise that can possibly be attributed to Bodhidharma is found in a book that is attributed to him, the *I-chin Ching* (The Doctrine of Relaxing Tension). Another work, mentioned in the preface to the *I-chin Ching*, the *Hsi-sui Ching* (The Doctrine of Cleansing the Marrow), expounded by Hui-k'o, successor to Bodhidharma, is not extant. The *I-chin Ching* describes exercises which, because no foot movement is involved, cannot be technically classified as ch'uan-fa; the main concern of these exercises is regulation of breathing.

There are other glaring mistakes in So's presentation of Shorinji Kempo as linked to Chinese Shaolin. For instance, the Ch'ing dynasty did not ban ch'uan-fa, as So states, nor has it entirely disappeared in China today under Communist rule. Neither is So Doshin correct when he states that ch'uan-fa was taught only to Buddhists; anyone might learn it, and its spread even to illiterate commoners of the agricultural and merchant classes of China was the main reason it became a powerful social force.

So Doshin's statement that his system of Shorinji Kempo does not countenance the use of weapons also goes against Chinese traditions. The use of weapons is an integral part of all Chinese wu shu, Shaolin included. The very religious society of which So Doshin was allegedly a member while in China required its members to become skillful with weapons, especially the spear. That So Doshin is not so skilled is a most unusual fact, especially for one who claims to be the true successor to Chinese Shaolin tradition. It is interesting, however, to note that in So's earliest efforts to promulgate Shorinji Kempo, the use of the *nyoi* (a special kind of short stick) and the *shakujo* (priest's staff) was taught.

Six hundred and ten techniques make up the repertoire of Shorinji Kempo as taught by So. On the whole, they bear little resemblance to Chinese Shaolin. For example, the footwork taught is utterly wrong. In every leading style of Chinese Shaolin the heel, not the ball of the foot, is put down first when advancing. The seizing techniques of So's Shorinji Kempo lead to exaggerated and inefficient throwing methods in comparison to the more functional but less spectacular Chinese Shaolin methods, or even to the Japanese judo nage-waza. Though experts in Shorinji Kempo decry the use of high-kicking methods, most responses to attack that involve kicking tactics are aimed at high target areas. Shorinji Kempo kicks, as taught by So, resemble those made in the general style of kicking that prevails throughout Japanese karate-do circles, and certainly are not those of Chinese Shaolin. The so-called *gassho-gamae*, the basic Shorinji Kempo salutation stance, performed before and after each practice, has no basis in Chinese Shaolin tradition, that is to say, no pai uses it exactly as So requires it to be performed; in So's method the hands are positioned too high, tending to mask the eyes and view of the defender, thus leading to weaknesses in his defense.

Gojutai no waza, the technique of togetherness, or "hardness and softness," is the basis of the Shorinji Kempo techniques taught by So. The fact that ju, or "softness," is not really an absolute condition in combat makes it necessary for the go, or "hard," techniques of blocking, thrusting, and kicking to be used. There is considerable overlap in the use of "softness" and "hardness" when receiving attacks and making counterattacks.

Goho, the "hard" or positive system of training, depends on the exponent's mastery of stances. Stances are considered the foundation of all techniques and are the initial step in all training. Stances are more than just physical postures; they are an expression of mind and spirit. Correct stance is related to the proper distance between the defender and assailant; the eyes are to be held in the *happomoku* position, that is, not focused on any single point. Blocking techniques are the most basic ones in the Shorinji Kempo style of defense. They precede any other counteraction. The defender may apply the force of a block either at right angles to or circularly against his opponent's attack; or he may blend with that attack without disturbing its direction. Thrusts, or striking actions, are delivered with the hands and arms moving in an upward direction; the arm is relaxed until the moment of thrust, and on impact with the target the shoulder comes into line with the striking point on the arm or hand being used.

Thrusts are directed only against the assailant's anatomical weak points, but this is not an absolute rule in Chinese Shaolin. In So's Shorinji Kempo techniques, preference is given to short thrusting actions, a feature that contrasts with the northern Shaolin preference for long thrusting actions. Kicks made in So's Shorinji Kempo style have little regard for the protection of the user's groin, which in Chinese Shaolin tactics is always covered with a hand or arm while kicking is being performed. Northern Chinese Shaolin styles, under the influence of *lohan* (scholar-priest) stances, postures, and tactics, are particularly uncompromising on the defense of the groin region while making a kicking action.

Juho, the "soft" or passive system of training in So's Shorinji Kempo, is based on the need to neutralize an assailant who seizes the defender by his garments or body. These tactics lock and stabilize the aggressor's body so that he is unable to gain an advantage. This method depends first on yielding to the attacker's force, then using subtle leverage against him, and is evidence of the influence of aiki-jujutsu (jujutsu) on So's system. Once an assailant has been neutralized, techniques of avoidance may be used. These are based on leverage designed to break the assailant's grasp; the assailant may also be struck before or after avoidance tactics have come into play. The basic avoidance techniques are supplemented by twisting (joint-locking) and throwing techniques. The latter category of techniques differs from the nage-waza of judo in that hip action is not a prerequisite; nor is grasping of the attacker's garments required.

So Doshin's Shorinji Kempo system of defense depends not on great physical strength but on the application of scientific knowledge. An important phase of advanced study is *keimyaku-iho* (blood vessel and nerve therapy). This study teaches that 708 "holes" called *keiraku-hiko,* or "secret nerve-connection holes," exist on the human body, but only 142 major "holes" are exploited. Only the most trusted disciples of the Shorinji Kempo system are selected for this secret phase of study. The method of teaching is oral transmission, so as to avoid compromise. The use of the "holes" permits the defender to render his assailant paralyzed or unconscious.

All training in So's Shorinji Kempo is conducted by licensed and recognized instructors, who actively participate in training with their students. The intuitive yomeigaku method is characteristic of most teaching. Disciples learn to *manabu,* that is, to learn by copying the instructor's actions, a process that when carried out efficiently ensures that correct form and principle will be achieved. Thereafter, the experienced trainee takes his training a step beyond rote learning and gives originality to his movements by combining separate techniques into a working style that expresses his character. All learning depends on accumulated experience, great effort, discipline, patience, endurance, and an unbending will to succeed.

Training in So's Shorinji Kempo centers on the *embu,* or partner-practice, method. In this form of practice exponents are paired off, one taking the role of a defender, the other of an attacker; then roles are exchanged. This method of instruction develops each trainee's reactions to encounters, encouraging him to concern himself with realistic actions. There is no thought of "winner" or "loser" in such training, but rather the thought that the partners train together in mutual harmony and progress. This embu method instils a sense of harmonious cooperation between trainees, who through their actions learn the reality of interdependence. This is the method of dynamic encounter to teach dynamic harmony.

The embu method is carried out in *giwaken,* or prearranged forms. This corresponds to the Chinese *tao-chien* and the Japanese *kata,* in which performers know beforehand what actions each is to make and what the final results are to be. But the traditional Chinese Shaolin training does not insist on partner-practice, as does So's Shorinji Kempo; in fact it requires *lien tao-chien,* solo training, until the level of the performer's skill is high enough to merit pitting it against a training partner in the role either of an attacker or of a defender.

Hardening or toughening methods are used by all Chinese Shaolin exponents so as to make various parts of their body resistant to pain and injury. The absence of this kind of training in So's Shorinji Kempo system is justified on the basis that its teachings stress the use of techniques applied only against the assailant's anatomical weak points; here the use of force does not require more than ordinary strength and toughness. Chinese Shaolin systems require all exponents to use hardening methods because in hand-to-hand encounters there is no guarantee that one can avoid being struck anywhere on the body. Such Shaolin systems also require all exponents to use medicines after every training session; medicines applied externally to ease crippling effects of contact shock, as well as internal medicines in the form of herbal teas to assist repair of body tissues damaged in training, are indispensable.

Zazen, the practice of meditation of T'ien-t'ai Buddhism, Ch'an, Japanese Zen, and Taoism, is used by the exponents of So's Shorinji Kempo to complement their physical training. The static conditions under which meditation is undertaken balances the dynamic actions of kempo and are believed to cultivate the rhythm of breathing necessary to revitalize the body in connection with the restoration of normal circulation of the blood and the calming of the mind.

Another practice, called *seiho,* is used to preserve the soundness of bones and nerves and promote good blood circulation. It consists of techniques applied to vital points on the body after strenuous training; this practice induces muscles to relax and relieves the tension of the body caused by muscular exertion.

SHORINJI KEMPO TODAY So Doshin's Shorinji Kempo is but one of at least twelve systems in Japan that claim to have ancestral roots in Chinese Shaolin. Of the almost half a million exponents who are dedicated to the study of kempo in Japan, So's system boasts the support of over three hundred thousand devotees.

In spite of his ludicrous claims that he teaches a traditional form of Shaolin, So Doshin's system is an important one. It should, however, be seen for what it is, a Japanese version of Chinese Shaolin and the foundation of a new social philosophy. A decision rendered by Japanese courts in 1972 against So's use of the name "Shorinji Kempo" was brought about by Chinese pressure groups that disproved So's claim to Chinese affiliations. As a result, So now calls his system "Nippon Shorinji Kempo," which means "Japanese Shaolin Fist-way." Its spiritual and ethical values are admirable, socially acceptable in their present form not only to the Japanese but to people of other countries as well. Nippon Shorinji Kempo, if kept free from the egocentric practices of sport, can continue to be a useful and powerful influence on modern society. It is hoped that, in the words of its founder, Nippon Shorinji Kempo will be "a catalyst" for transforming the world into a unified and peaceful international community.

CHAPTER TEN

OTHER MODERN BUDO

Practice is the best of all instructors.
Publilius Syrus

KYUDO   Skillful bowmen have since ancient times been held in high esteem in Japan, and *kyujutsu,* or the art of the bow, was one of the most important subjects in the martial curriculum of classical warriors. The ability to deliver an arrow accurately in any direction from either a mounted or a dismounted position was diligently cultivated by the classical bushi. Before the Edo period the bow was a major weapon of war. The introduction of firearms in 1542, however, changed this. By the early Edo period, kyujutsu was regarded primarily as a spiritual discipline.

Morikawa Kozan (seventeenth century) of the Yamato Ryu, a martial tradition known for the merits of its kyujutsu and jujutsu, made a systematic study of kyujutsu and reformed the orthodox teachings of his ryu. He made the study of the bow and arrow a spiritual discipline, and is traditionally credited with being the first to use the word *kyudo* (literally, "way of the bow") in 1664 to describe the nature of this discipline.

Morikawa required the exponents of his style of bowmanship to make a systematic study of all its aspects. He divided his curriculum into six parts: (1) *kyu-ri* (logic of the bow), (2) *kyu-rei* (etiquette of the bow), (3) *kyu-ho* (technique of using the bow), (4) *kyu-ko* (making and repairing the bow), (5) *kyu-ki* (mechanical analysis of the bow), and (6) *shi-mei* (the four virtues that deal with the development of mind and spirit). Part five was the central study. Lectures, demonstrations, and actual practice accompanied the study of each part of the curriculum. Shooting instruction (part three) was based on a thorough mastery of fundamentals, which was accomplished through the method of repetitive practice. Morikawa thus linked the orthodox yomeigaku psychological or experiential learning methods, in which intuitive perception (kan) dominates, with the logical method of learning, in which rational analysis prevails. Morikawa's idea of converting kyujutsu to kyudo was not universally popular with warriors, and the criticisms made against it were many. The majority of ryu that featured the use of the bow continued to refer to their systems as kyujutsu.

A majority of Edo-period bowmen adhered to the orthodox values of kyujutsu and made *tekichu shugi,* or striking the target, the main part of their study; their interest was confined to the practical limits in which the bow could be used as a weapon. But other ryu began to give more attention to rei-ho, or etiquette, in the training of samurai; and some few ryu declared the development of *seishin* (spirit, mind, soul) to be the object of all training, as inspired by Morikawa. As the Edo period advanced the bow became obsolete as a weapon of war, and many ryu consequently declared a spiritual objective for their kyujutsu. By the middle of the nineteenth century there was a tendency among the common citizens who had been attracted to the art of bowmanship to enjoy it mainly as a sport or game.

There was no general agreement about the technical aspects of bow and arrow techniques among expert bowmen during the Meiji or Taisho era. This lack of harmony made it impossible for a national standard for kyudo to be formulated, although this had long been the aspiration of many bowmen. It was left to the Butokukai to attempt to bring order into the general state of confusion that prevailed among bowmen. A technical committee was established in 1933 for the purpose of creating a national *kei,* or form, for kyudo. The aspect of *sharei,* or etiquette of shooting, proved to be no great problem, but that of *shaho,* the actual method of shooting, was a vexing one. In particular, *uchi-okoshi,* the act of raising and drawing the bow, caused long and heated debate. When agreement was not forthcoming, the chairman of the technical committee overruled the other members and declared that a compromise form comprising elements of several major styles should be adopted. The Butokukai published the kyudo *yosoku,* or principles, in its *Dai Nippon Kyudo Kyohan* (Great Japan Kyudo Manual) in 1934, but revision of the technical contents of the manual necessitated its republication under the title *Dai Nippon Kyudo Kihan* (Great Japan Kyudo Standards). This further indicates that the lack of agreement that still existed among experts was a wide one that could not easily be eliminated.

The principles of kyudo as expounded by the Butokukai committee underwent patient testing. Kyudo was made a compulsory subject of education in all middle and high schools throughout Japan in 1936. The government approved of kyudo as a means by which to prepare Japanese youth for war; training in kyudo was conducted in schools for purposes of *yoshin rentan,* that is, the cultivation of the mind and the fostering of courage. This widespread use of kyudo, however, revealed serious technical weaknesses and led to many new debates concerning changes to be made. In 1937 the Butokukai declared its form of kyudo the standard one for examinations for obtaining ranks and teaching licenses. Though there were few bowmen who did not criticize the Butokukai standard, they complied with its provisions for the purposes of gaining rank and authority to teach kyudo.

The technical debate continues today. Bowmen of the famed Ogasawara Ryu and the Takeda Ryu prefer to use the orthodox label "kyujutsu" for their art. But the form of kyudo established and enforced by the Zen Nihon Kyudo Remmei (All-Japan Kyudo Federation), founded in 1948, is the national standard in Japan. Under the aegis of this federation, kyudo is more than a system of self-discipline concerned with the development of physical and spiritual benefits. The modern form of kyudo is characterized by a blend of spiritual and sport values, and it is this kind of kyudo that now reaches more than four million enthusiastic Japanese citizens in training programs conducted in schools, industry, and private organizations throughout the country. Though the emphasis on sport in modern kyudo is popular with the young exponents, both male and female, when they attain technical maturity most of them prefer to conduct their training along lines closer to those of classical kyudo, making it the means through which to develop mastery (unity) of mind, body, and bow. Modern kyudo experts believe that the elements involved in shooting the bow, from *kai*, or "meeting," to *hanare*, or "leaving," influence the development of a state of mind in which the bowman learns to accept that which comes along in life with undisturbed calm and composure. It is the attainment of this final goal to which they dedicate themselves in their training.

NAGINATA-DO   Prior to the Edo period the *naginata*, a heavy, long-handled, short-bladed halberd, was mainly a man's weapon for use on the battlefield. In the peaceful Edo period, however, the naginata became obsolete as a weapon of war and was assigned to the women of warrior families for the defense of their residences. Late in that same period a mock weapon resembling the naginata became important in the physical education of women. Chiba Shusaku, founder of the Hokushin Itto Ryu, did much to promote the use of the mock naginata in competitive matches against shinai-bearing kendoists. Throughout the Meiji, Taisho, and early Showa eras the naginata was used in *naginata-jutsu* for women's physical education; during times of national emergency naginata-jutsu was a compulsory subject in the curricula of all schools from primary through high schools. As such, naginata-jutsu, though also exercised as a spiritual discipline, was not entirely shorn of combat value. Yet the lightness of the mock weapon directly affects the manner in which it is used, and thus modern techniques are considerably different from what they were when the classical warriors used this devastating weapon.

Among the almost five hundred different ryu that concerned themselves with naginata-jutsu there were many technical differences. These differences made the formation of a truly national standard of naginata techniques most difficult. The Tenshin Shoden Katori Shinto Ryu, Japan's oldest historically proven martial tradition, the Buko Ryu, and the Ryugo Ryu all used the naginata in jutsu form to develop courage in their exponents and the ability to win in combat. But other ryu were more inspired by the classical concept of the dō. The Hoshin Ryu taught the use of the naginata as the means for attaining *zenchi zen no kami*—for making its exponents "perfect gods," or possessors of "absolute intelligence." The Gassan Ryu and Tendo Ryu saw training with the naginata in a different light; for them it was a means for instilling the spirit of a "universal heaven," or "infinite wisdom," in members. The Seni Ryu, Jikishin-kage Ryu, Seikan Ryu, and Sanwa Ryu used the naginata to develop "an alert and active mind," while the Anazawa Ryu, Masaki Ryu, and Toda Ryu employed naginata training as a means of preserving family name, honor, and the perpetuation of specific sociopolitical loyalties and rivalries.

It was not until 1953, with the creation of the Zen Nihon Naginata-do Remmei (All-Japan Naginata-do Federation), and its approval by the Ministry of Education, that a national standard of naginata technique was made possible. Today the express purpose of all naginata training conducted under the auspices of that federation is fourfold: (1) spiritual discipline, (2) physical education, (3) sport contest, and (4) athletic endeavor.

A combination of technical elements gleaned from the various ryu with modifications of classical naginata techniques produced the national standard that is the modern discipline of naginata-do. Five basic kamae are essential: *chudan* (middle level), *jodan* (upper level), *gedan* (lower level), *hasso* (upright side-body), and *waki* (horizontal side-body). Techniques include striking, slashing, thrusting, blocking, parrying, and screening actions. These techniques are expressed in their pure form through kata, or prearranged exercise, or in shiai, mock combat. Exponents wear protective armor that is similar to that worn by kendoists, with the addition of the *sune-ate,* or shin protectors. In shiai, an exponent armed with the mock naginata engages a similarly armed opponent or one who is armed with the shinai. One attempts to score by making what would be lethal attacks if made with a real naginata; designated target areas are the head, throat, shoulder, solar plexus, trunk, and shin. Rigorous training provides mental discipline and exhilarating exercise for almost two million exponents of naginata-do, a modern discipline the majority of whose exponents is female.

JUKEN-DO   Though the use of the bayonet by the Japanese fighting man is at least as old as the beginning of the Edo period, the systematic use of that weapon in pure Japanese style, known as *juken-jutsu* (bayonet art), was developed during the Meiji era. The bayonet served the Japanese soldier well during the Sino-Japanese War, the Boxer Rebellion, the Russo-Japanese War, World War I, the Siberian Expedition, the fighting in China (1937–41), and World War II. The necessity for effective use of the bayonet on the battlefield led to the development of a standard method of bayonet fighting, which was taught in the Toyama Gakko, a special military training school in Tokyo. The prohibition against martial disciplines imposed by SCAP in 1945 included juken-jutsu.

The fact that the bayonet, like older weapons, such as the sword, bow and arrow, and naginata, could be used as a means for attaining spiritual discipline as well as for the promotion of physical fitness and for sport competition, prompted the revival of interest in the bayonet among military and ex-military personnel. *Juken-do,* or "the way of the bayonet," is the name of the modern discipline that resulted, and with the founding of the Zen Nihon Juken-do Remmei (All-Japan Juken-do Federation) under the presidency of General Imamura Hitoshi in 1956, this modern discipline received official recognition. Its current president, Hatta Ichiro, is a well-known budo and sports figure in Japan. Hatta directs the activities of some 280,000 advocates of juken-do.

Kiso, or fundamentals, of juken-do technique revolve about the *shitotsu,* or straight-thrust tactic. The success of the shitotsu depends entirely upon the exponent's mastery of *jujitsu-shita kisei,* or the "full-minded posture," the equivalent of keeping one's body filled with ki (material force) so that the body is alive and alert in any emergency. Through adequate training the exponent of juken-do learns to unify his mind and technique with his posture, resulting in an effective fighting ability. To measure his skill in combat the exponent engages a training partner in mock combat (shiai). Each combatant is garbed in especially durable protective gear made strong enough to withstand the forcible shock of the thrust made with the *mokuju,* or wooden rifle and simulated bayonet. Rules make all training for matches a well-regulated affair. The object is to register a lethal attack against one's opponent. Three target areas are designated for this purpose: the heart, lower left side, and throat. Kata, or prearranged exercises, may also be practiced.

Juken-do has aims other than the development of a fighting skill. The rigorous discipline provided by training is said to lead to the development of a polite, humble individual. Juken-do training, because of the directness of its technique, which requires a high degree of accuracy in judgment of ma-ai (combative engagement distance), is also said to develop a careful attitude in all exponents, and further, to grant them the ability to make unswerving decisions when acting in times of emergency.

Members of the Japanese Self-Defense Force comprise the majority of the country's juken-do exponents. But there is a substantial interest among ordinary citizens in this spirited art, which has resulted in the establishment of various private, civilian organizations for the furtherance of this modern discipline.

EPILOGUE

THE FUTURE OF MODERN BUDO

Its most foresighted visionaries could not have imagined the effect dō would have on people of the twentieth century around the world. And there is every probability that they would be horrified to see what is taking place today in the name of that austere Oriental philosophy.

The growing aversion of conservative exponents of classical disciplines to the blatant progressivism being shown by exponents of the modern cognate disciplines is very real. This aversion signifies resistance to unwanted change. The reaction of the conservatives is to hide their disciplines from society by choice, not to let them decay through neglect as is commonly charged by the progressives. Giving old ideas new currency is an accepted and reasonable thing to do; it justifies the notion of progress. At any period of history, however, it is always relatively easy to be progressive, just as it often requires considerable reflection and strong determination to stand on the side of conservatism. Because conservatives must continuously swim against the current of general fashion and belief, they have developed a durable spirit that is reflected in their adherence to classical disciplines.

The conservative exponents of classical disciplines declare that the idea of creating modern disciplines from old traditions is a process that must be regulated with great care. While criticizing those who follow the tendency of the modern age to try to find the easy way in life, the conservatives also recognize the fact that it is hard to step out ahead of one's age and at the same time maintain a firm grasp on universal truth. Stepping out ahead is not the same thing as the actions of those proponents of things modern who, though they may act in good faith when they create new modern disciplines, usually end up making arbitrary compromises that have little genuine value and rarely respect tradition. In these cases tradition is used to enhance personal prestige or to give inflated and imaginary value to the systems created. If such people really entered into the spirit of tradition or stepped out ahead of their age, it should be expected of them that they assume a firm stance and not shrink when faced by vilification and opposition; instead they act in such a way that they can change and modify their ideas according to the way the wind is blowing at the moment. The conservatives believe that it is far better to renounce tradition and start to create a new one, putting it to good use in new undertakings. But it is more usual for the developers of new modern disciplines to ride the current of the times because they lack both technical insight and spiritual depth.

In the many new systems of discipline being created today there appears to be little of lasting value. Through a dismissal of classical concepts, in which lie metaphysical truths, and the focusing of attention purely on physical effort, the universal principle of ri, or reason, gives way to *ji,* the particular event. Ji has become all-important in the modern cognate disciplines. The concept of dō also suffers distortion in these disciplines. It becomes a way to see the world subjectively, not a doctrine that teaches the negation of either the self or the individual so that he may become one with the universe, which is the doctrine's essence. The consuming interest of the exponents of modern disciplines in things subjective implies the selfish desire for the things themselves. This in turn leads to feelings of envy and jealousy among exponents, which, if not kept in check through a system of moral training and strict ethical practices, leads invariably to appalling results. Thus in the world of modern budo, where emphasis on subjectivity reigns supreme, there are frequent examples of overattention to superficial matters and neglect of the intrinsic values of dō, on which these new forms are allegedly based. Egocentrism is rampant in exponents of modern budo. All exponents, at some time or another, become embroiled in heated rivalries animated by ambitious leaders vying for dominance of organizations that have been created to further the progress of the various systems. In extreme cases violence has erupted, and in all cases there is an unashamed shattering of the ideal of the spirit of universal brotherhood that supposedly is the higher aim of all modern budo forms.

Examples of the failure of the exponents of modern budo systems to achieve spiritual maturity abound. The dō, originally intended in the classical concept as a "way" to be traveled which, though beset with countless difficulties, is wide and manageable for him who will but persist with training made in the manner prescribed. Modern dō, however, has a much narrower meaning. It has become a lane or a path whose boundaries are dictated by selfish interests and narrow personal tastes. Taste is, or should be, something living and primary, that is, something which is both natural and fundamental to life and which furthermore exemplifies good judgment in selecting and harmonizing things for that life. But the sense of taste demonstrated by most exponents of the modern disciplines has been made artificial by making of it something with which to excite and titillate the ego. Taste is no longer something vital. Its *esse* has been virtually obliterated. And as a result, dō has been recast in the image of those who have insufficient inner force and virtuous integrity to follow a more rugged but spiritually rewarding course of endeavor.

Certain arbitrary rules and shallow theories posited by the exponents of modern disciplines preside over the demise of the classical concept of dō. This orthodox concept assumes the inseparability of moral theory and ethical practice. But the tendency of exponents of modern disciplines is to dismiss that vital relationship in favor of making the modern disciplines into a flamboyant means of amusement for participants and spectators alike. Dō forms so misused become mere entertainment through the elimination of spiritual values. Thus, what was originally spiritual essence expressed in physical exercise and having an objective character, and which can thus be considered something cultural, has been cast aside, and something purely physical, subjective, cheap, and monotonous in nature, and certainly not of a cultural nature, has been allowed to replace it.

Yet another aspect of the modern disciplines is appalling. Because the classical concept of dō has been ignored in favor of a modern interpretation that is more in line with the tastes of men of lesser moral values, the modern disciplines have become quite particularistic in nature, and their exponents completely self-centered through their interest in insignificant acts of a purely utilitarian kind. Such a way of thinking if pushed to its extreme, as was the case with the militarists in the Taisho and early Showa eras of Japan, may be the prelude to social upheaval. The concept of dō, so perverted, can lead to opportunism; this can lead to ethnocentrism or ultranationalism. The worst feature of the modern budo is that many of them put their primary emphasis on the sport aspect. The attitude of considering the dō as sports makes it impossible for the individual exponent to acquire a sufficiently objective, intuitive grasp of dō. The impulsively subjective, rational approach that characterizes sport training dominates the behavior of the individual to such a degree that far from producing the lofty aim of the modern cognate forms—peace and amity among nations—it results more and more in unfriendly feelings and nationalistic disharmony.

Modern disciplines suffer from an inroad of Western ideas. The demand of the Westerner for haste, a quality of dubious value, together with constant criticism of a Japanese standard of taste with which he has little familiarity, if any, have told upon the personalities of some of the Japanese who create modern disciplines. Okakura Kakuzo expresses this deplorable state of affairs well: "The weak-spirited among us follow the trend of world opinion and desert the ranks of conservative upholders of tradition." Westerners' participation in modern budo also has another effect. For the Westerner it is the size of membership and commercial solvency of an organization, and the degree of individual technical skill, that indicate success and progress. What is not realized is that quantity does not constitute greatness, and enjoyment of participation does not always result in refinement. The individuals who make up the great modern roster of exponents of modern budo are, in fact, the slaves of a purely mechanical monster that ruthlessly dominates them. In their self-made traps they are completely unable to reap spiritual benefit.

The exponent of today's modern budo gropes about in a maze of classical traditions that he does not understand, and thus, the cleverest of his kind declare that the classical disciplines must be freed from feudal Japanese superstitions and raised to great heights of rational efficiency so as to yield wealth, prestige, and practical use. Some foreigners proudly declare that they aim to "Americanize," or otherwise nationalize, Japanese budo in terms more suited to their country's way of life. Most foreigners have selfish aims that they disguise by mouthing lofty phrases that are nothing but lip service. The Western trainee also expects to reach a high degree of technical skill and leadership without first having shown his personal soundness through his cultivation of ideals. He trains with varying degrees of sincerity, albeit rigorously. But he does not really know through experience the hardship that is a companion to frugal living and so necessary in the lives of exponents of the classical disciplines. He is quite unable to relinquish the comfortable, easy ways of doing his (for example) "American" style of budo. His dojo is the very personification of his egocentric and flamboyant aims. It is always filled with display; in it will be found finery, murals, the excessive use of pictures, nonutilitarian objects, and decorations, all of which operate as distractions and guarantee the exponents training there every opportunity to miss the intrinsic purpose of training.

The modern disciplines thrive on the restlessness of the people of the modern world as they move from place to place and back again. Modern Japanese budo has been transplanted in the West, where, in regard to the object of training, the distinction between means and ends is rarely recognized, let alone appreciated. The West stands for material progress. Progress toward what? When technical efficiency is satisfied by training in modern disciplines, what then? When the drive for fraternity has culminated in universal love and cooperation among men, what purpose is modern budo to serve? If such is the aim of self-centered exponents of modern budo, where do we actually find the advance so boasted of? It may be that the modern disciplines are yet too young for any criticism to be final, but the words of Okakura are once more appropriate: "The machinery of competition imposes the monotony of fashion instead of the variety of life. The cheap is worshipped in place of the beautiful, while the rush and struggle of modern existence give no opportunity for the leisure required for the crystallization of ideals."

INDEX

NOTE: Page numbers in italics indicate illustrations.

Abe Ryu, 77
Admonition to the Armed Forces (1878), 33
ai (harmony, affinity), 144
aiki, 142, 143, 161
aiki-budo, 161
aiki-do, 49, 137–41; essence, aims, and techniques of, 141–44, 161; present status of, 161–62
aiki-ho, 142
aiki-in-yo-ho doctrine, 137, 138, 141
aiki-jujutsu, 75, 118, 141, 142, 144, 161, 170
Aizawa Seishisai (1827–63), 20, 32, 98, 114
Aizu warriors, 138, 141
All-Japan Collegiate Karate-do Federation, 136
All-Japan Self-Defense Force Karate-do Federation, 135
All-Japan Workers Karate-do Federation, 136
Anazawa Ryu, 176
Araki Ryu, 26
Arima Sumitomo, 116, 117
armed forces, 32, 41, 42, 47; see also Imperial Army
armor, 106–7
Army War College, 43
Asahi Heigo (d. 1921), 40
Asari Matashichiro, 108
atemi (blows), 144
ate-waza (striking techniques), 113
Azato Anko, 126

bajutsu (horsemanship), 45
batto-jutsu (sword-drawing art), 65–68, *82*, *83*
Batto-tai (Sword Unit), 100
Black Dragon Society (Kokuryukai), 40, 42, 48, 163, 164, 165
Black Ocean Society, *see* Gen'yosha
Bodhidharma (c. 470–c. 534), 168
bokken (wooden sword), 23, 80
Book of Rites (Chu Hsi), 61
Boxer Rebellion (1900–1901), 34, 165
Buddhism, 29, 63; *see also* T'ien-t'ai Buddhism
budo (martial ways), 51, 55–58, 59–63, 181; see also *ko budo*, *shin budo*
Budo Hiketsu—Aiki no Jutsu (The Secret of Budo—The Art of Aiki), 142

budo seishin (the spirit of *budo*), 111
bujutsu (martial arts), 55–59
buke (martial family), 78
Buko Ryu, 175
bushi (classical warrior), 21, 30–31, 57, 78, 129; *see also* samurai
bushido (way of the warrior), 30–32, 33, 34, 35, 45
Butokuden (Martial Virtues Hall), 35, 49, *81*, 100, 125
Butokukai, *see* Dai Nippon Butokukai

Cherry Blossom Society, *see* Sakurakai
chiang (straight-bladed Chinese spear), 164
Chiba Eijiro (1832–62), 99
Chiba Sanshu, 75, *88*
Chiba Shusaku (1794–1855), 98, 99, 175
chiburi (removing blood from sword), 67–68, *84*
cho-ichi-ryu (superswordsman), 98
ch'uan-fa (fist way), 125, 128, 132, 164, 165, 166, 168
Chu Hsi (1130–1200), 18, 61; doctrine of, 62, 108, 137–38, 141–42
classical warrior, *see bushi*
commoners, 129–30
Confucianism, 18, 19, 20, 29, 61, 62, 63, 168
conscription, 32–33

Daido Ryu, 138
Dai Nippon Butokukai (Great Japan Martial Virtues Association), 35, 47, 48, 49, 100, 111, 125, 174
Dai Nippon Kyudo Kihan (Great Japan Kyudo Standards), 174
Dai Nippon Kyudo Kyohan (Great Japan Kyudo Manual), 174
Dai Nippon Teikoku Kendo Kata (Great Japan Imperial Kendo Kata), 111
daisho (combination of long and short sword), 25, 26, 28, 67
Daito Ryu, 140, 141, 161, 165
dan-kyu (graded rank) system, 62
do (activity), 62
do (torso protector for *kendo*), 97
dō (way), 45, 60, 61, 63, 104, 105, 114, 131, 132, 133, 134, 141, 175, 178, 179–80
dojo (training hall), 106

dojo arashi (*dojo* storming), 99

Edo Yagyu Shinkage Ryu, 119
Egawa Torazaemon, 24, 98
eiji happo (eight laws of the ideogram "eternal"), 66
Eisho-ji, 114
embu (partner-practice method), 170–71
embujo (place of exhibitions or athletic performances), 59
Emmei Ryu, 102
empty-hand techniques, 120
Eriguchi Eiichi, 136

Federation of All-Japan Karate-do Organizations, 136
fudai (hereditary vassals), 19
fudo no seishin (spirit of the immovable mind), 108
fudoshin (immovable mind), 102, 130
Fujita Toko (1806–55), 20, 25, 98, 114,
fukoku-kyohei (prosperous nation, strong armed forces), 18, 27, 34
Fukuda Hachinosuke, 113
Fukui Harunosuke, 162
Fukuno Ryu, 120
Funakoshi Gichin (1869–1957), 125–26, 127, 128–29, 130–31, 133, *145*, *146*
Funakoshi Yoshitaka, 126, 127, *145*, *147*

Gassan Ryu, 176
gassho-gamae (salutation stance), 169
gekken (severe sword), 100, 101, 103
Gembukan *dojo*, 98
Gen'yosha (Black Ocean Society), 39
gi (moral obligations), 104
gochu (district youth organizations in Satsuma), 24–25
Goju-kai, 136
Goju karate-do, 126, 132–33, 134
go kyo no waza (five principles of technique), 119
go no sen (defensive initiative), 144
Gorin no Sho (Book of Five Circles; Miyamoto Musashi), 51
goshin-jutsu (self-defense methods of *jujutsu* and *judo*), 70
Goshin-jutsu Ogi (The Secret Principles of the Art of Self-defense), 142
Goto Shojiro (1838–97), 22, 23, 32
Goto Tamauemon Tadayoshi (1644–1736), 138
grading system, see *dan-kyu*
grappling systems, 60
Griffis, William Elliot, 21
gunto soho (method of using army sword), 65

Hagakure (Hidden Behind Leaves), 31, 34
Hakko Ryu, 161, 165

han (feudal domains), dissolution of, 26
Hanko (Half-heart) style, 126
han-mi (half-frontal position of *kenjutsu*), 106
happo-giri (eight cutting techniques), 66, 67
Hasegawa Nyozekan (b. 1875), 50
Hashimoto Kingoro, 46
Hayashi Teruo, 135, *152*
heiho (swordsmanship), 101, 119, 162; see also *seiho*
heijo-shin (normal state of mind), 71
Higaonna Kanryo (1888–1951), 126, 129
Higa Seko, 135
Hikida Bungoro (c. 1537–c. 1606), 80
Hikida Ryu (Hikida-kage Ryu), 80
hiki-tate (a restraining method), 70, 71
Hirai Minoru, 161, 162
Hirata Atsutane (1776–1843), 19, 63
Hisa Takuma, 161
hojo-jutsu (art of tying), 74–75, *87*
Hokushin Itto Ryu, 24, 32, 35, 98, 105, 111, 175
hontai (main body, morality), 51–52
Horiguchi Tsuneo, 70
Horikawa Kotaro, 161
Hoshina (Matsudaira) Masayuki (1611–72), 138
Hoshin Ryu, 175
Hoshi Tetsuomi, 162
Hozan Ryu, 111
Hozoin Ryu, 139

iai-do (sword-drawing way), 67–68, 70, *84*, *85*
iai-jutsu (sword-drawing art), 100, 138; see also *batto-jutsu*
Ichiden Ryu, 111
I-chin Ching (Doctrine of Relaxing Tension), 168
idori (a restraining method), 70
I-ho-ch'uan (Righteous and Harmonious Fists) style, 165
Iikubo Tsunetoshi, 113
Ikaku Ryu, 72, 73
I-kuan Tao (Way of Pervading Unity) Society, 164
Imamura Hitoshi, 177
Imperial Army, 43; see also armed forces, Self-Defense Force
Imperial Precepts to Soldiers and Sailors (1882), 33–34, 42, 105
Imperial Rescript on Education (1890), 30, 105
inchi-nawa (tying from the rear), 74
Inoue Dojo, 139
Inoue Yoichiro, 161, 162
International Judo Federation, 122–23
International Kendo Federation, 111
Isogai Hajime, 35
Isogai Ryu, 120
Iso Masatomo, 113
Iso Mataemon, 113

isshin itto (one mind, one sword), 103
Itagaki Taisuke (1837–1919), 22, 23, 32
Itatsu Ryu, 74
Ito Hirobumi (1841–1909), 29, 31
Ito Ittosai (1560–1653), 101, 103, 106
Ito Ken'ichi, 126
Itosu Yasusune, 126, 129, 133
Itto Ryu, 101, 103, 107, 108
Itto Shoden Muto Ryu, 101, 109
Iwakura Tomomi, 102
iwao no mi (rock body) concept, 102

Japanese Expansion on the Asiatic Continent (Yoshi S. Kuno), 21
Japan Karate Association (Nippon Karate Kyokai), 127, 133, 134, 136
Jigen Ryu, 24, 25, 79, 100, 111
Jikishin-kage Ryu, 80, 97, 98, 99, 100, 102, 103, 109, 110, 111, 138, 176
Jikishin Ryu, 116, 120
Jinno Shotoki (The Records of the Legitimate Succession of the Divine Sovereigns; Kitabatake Chikafusa), 61
ji-ta kyoei (mutual prosperity) principle, 119
jiyu kumite (free sparring), 133
jiyu renshu (free practice), 109
JKA, *see* Japan Karate Association
jo (medium-length hardwood stick), 68, 69
jojutsu (fighting-stick art), 70, 72; *see also keijo-jutsu*
ju (flexibility), *see ju no ri*
judo: in Meiji era, 30, 35; in Taisho era, 41; in Showa era, 47, 48, 49, 51, 70; present status of, 93, 96, 122–23; *see also* Kodokan Judo
ju-go awase (combining softness with hardness), 106
jujutsu (art of flexibility), 70, 113, 115, 173
Jujutsu Kyoju-sho Ryu no Maki (Textbook of Jujutsu, Volume on Ryu), 142
juken-do (bayonet way), 160, 176–77
juken-jutsu (bayonet art), 46, 176
ju no ri (principle of flexibility), 115, 116–17, 118, 120, 132, 141, 144
jutte (single-tined iron truncheon), 73
jutte-jutsu (single-tined iron-truncheon art), 72
ju yoku go o sei suru (softness controls hardness), 115, 116

Kage Ryu, 120
kaho (practice method using prearranged forms), 59, 60, 79, 80; *see also kata*
Kaibara Ekken (1630–1714), 33, 108, 142, 143
kajutsu (art of gunnery and explosives), 138
kakari-geiko (attack training), 109
kamae (combative engagement postures), 66, 71
Kamiizumi Ise no Kami (1508–78), 80, 103

Kaminoda Tsunemori, 73, *86, 87*
kan (intuition), 59, 60, 110, 121
Kano Jigoro (1860–1938), *92, 93, 94,* 112–23, 139–40
Kano Risei, 123
karate-do, 48, 49, 51, 124, 126–28; essense, aims, and techniques of, 128–33; present status of, 133–36
karate-jutsu, 124, 125–26, 127, 128, 129, 130, 131–32, 133, 142
Kashima Shinto Ryu, 26
kata (prearranged forms), 59, 62; in *kendo*, 110–11; in *judo*, 121–22; in *karate-jutsu*, 132; in *naginata-do*, 176; in *juken-do*, 177; *see also kaho*
katame-waza (grappling techniques), 113, 119
katana (sword), 80; *see also batto-jutsu, iai-do, iai-jutsu, kenjutsu*
keibo (short wooden club), 71, 72–73, *86*
keibo soho (police-club method), 72–73, 74, *86*
Keichu (1640–1701), 19
keijo-jutsu (police-stick art), 68–69, 74, *86*
kempo (fist way), 126, 165; *see also ch'uan-fa*, Shorinji Kempo
kendo, 62, 77–80, *90, 91,* 97–101; in Meiji era, 30, 35; in Taisho era, 41; in Showa era, 47, 48, 49, 51, 70; essence and aims of, 101–6; techniques and training methods of, 106–11; present status of, 111
Kendo Ron (Treatise on Kendo; Yamada Jirokichi), 103–4, 109–10
Kendo Shugyo no Shiori (Kendo Training; Makino Toru), 105
kengi (sword technique), 78
kengo (strong skillful swordsman), 78
kenjutsu (sword art), 24, 70, 78–80, 97–100, 105, 106–7, 119
ken no michi (way of the sword), 104
kenshi (expert swordsman), 65
Kenshin Ryu, 135
Ketsumeidan (League of Blood), 44
ki (vital force), 62, 108, 110, 142, 143, 144, 161
ki-ai, 108, 142
ki-ai-jutsu (art of ki-ai), 142
kiba-sen (mounted combat), 78
Kido Koin (1833–77), 22, 23–24, 25, 26, 30, 32, 98
kiheitai (mixed-rifle units), 27
Kimura Tokutaro, 111
kiritsuke (cutting action), 67
Kita Ikki (1884–1937), 40, 44
Kito Ryu, 113, 115–16, 120, 121
Kobayashi Koemon Toshinari, 138
kobo-itchi (unity of offense and defense), 71, 75, 78, 117, 131, 144
ko budo (ancient martial ways), 135; *see also budo*
kobu-jutsu, 162
Kobusho (a government training school), 98, 100
kodachi (short sword), 111

186 · INDEX

kodawari (undesirable mental fixations), 51
Kodokan Judo, *96*, 112, 114–15, 139–40; theory of, 115–18; aims of, 118–19; techniques and training methods of, 119–22; see also *judo*
kogaku (school of ancient or classical learning), 18–19
kogi judo, 118, 119, 122
koiguchi (mouth of scabbard), 68
Kokon Chomonshu (1254), 30
kokoro (mind, spirit, mentality), 66
Kokuba Kosei, 126, 135
kokugaku (school of historical or national learning), 19
Kokuhonsha (National Foundation Society), 41
Kokuryukai, *see* Black Dragon Society
Kokusuikai (National Purity Society), 41
kokutai (national polity), 20, 36–37, 41, 44, 45
Kokutai no Hongi (Fundamentals of Our National Polity), 44–45
Kongo Zen, 166–67
Konishi Yasuhiro, 126, 131–32
Korindo *aiki-do*, 162
Kotani Sumiyuki, 50
kote (protective gloves for *kendo*), 97
kote-uchi, 73
Kumazawa Banzan (1619–91), 19
kumi-tachi, see *kenjutsu*
kumi-uchi (combat by grappling), 120
Kurama Ryu, 111
Kurando Marume, 80
Kuroda Ichitaro, 73
kyogi judo, *96*, 118, 119, 122
Kyokushin *karate-do*, 134–35
Kyoshin Meichi Ryu, 98, 100, 111, 138
kyuba (mounted bow-and-arrow combat), 138
kyudo (way of the bow), *159*, 173–75
kyujutsu (art of the bow), 173, 174, 175
kyusho (anatomical weaknesses), 69, 72

Lao-tzu, 115, 128
League of Blood, *see* Ketsumeidan
LeMay, Curtis B., 49

ma-ai (combative engagement distance), 67, 71, 72, 177
Mabuni Kenwa, 126, 135
Makino Toru, 105–6
manabu (to learn by copying), 170
Manchurian Incident (1931), 42–43
Masaki Ryu, 176
Masamune swordsmith family (c. 1250–c. 1600), 102
Matsuda Hosaku, 161, 165
Matsumura Munehide, 126

Matsuzaki Ryu, 100
Meiji educational system, 30
meijin (master), 61–62
men (protective mask for *kendo*), 99
men-tare (flaps of *kendo* mask), 99
michi (way), see *dō*
Mikado Empire (William Elliot Griffis), 21
Minobe Tatsukichi (1873–1948), 37, 43
Mito Kodokan, 114
Mito scholars, 20
Mitsuhashi Kan'ichiro, 100
Miura Ryu, 120
Miyagi Gogyun (Chojun), 126
Miyamoto Musashi (1584?–1645), 51, 102
Mizuno Shinto Ryu, 138
Mochizuki Minoru, 161
Mo-ist doctrine, 143
mokuju (wooden rifle), 177
Momono-i Shunzo (1826–86), 98, 99, 138
monjin (disciple), 60
Mori Arinori (1847–89), 30
Morikawa Kozan, 173–74
Motobu Choki, 126, 131
Motoori Norinaga (1730–1801), 19, 63
mu-dansha (having no graded rank), 62
mukei (having no form), 62
muken (no contact between *shinai*), 62
mune-ate (torso protector for *kendo*), 97
Murashige Yuso, 161
Musashi Ryu, 111
mutekatsu, 101
muto (no-sword), 101
Muto Ryu, 102
Mutsu Munemitsu (1844–97), 32

Nagamine Shojin, 135
Nagaoka Shuichi, 70
nage-waza (throwing techniques), 70, 113
naginata-do (halberd way), *158*, *159*, 175–76
naginata-jutsu (halberd art), 30, 175
Naha *te*, 126, 128
Naito Takaharu, 24, 35
Nakae Masakatsu, 140
Nakae Toju (1608–48), 19
Nakaima Kenko, 135
Nakamura Taisaburo (b. 1911) and Nakamura Ryu, 65–68, *82*, *83*
Nakanishi Chuta (fl. 1751), 97
Nakanishi-ha Itto Ryu, 97, 104, 108, 109
Nakano Michiomi (b. 1911), 161, 163–66; *see also* So Doshin
Nakayama Masatoshi, 126, 130, 133, *145*, *150*, *151*
Nakayama Tatsusaburo Yokiyoshi, 132

National Foundation Society, *see* Kokuhonsha
National Police Reserve, 49
National Purity Society, *see* Kokusuikai
National Safety Corps, 49
Natsume Soseki (1867–1916), 38
nei-chia (internal systems), 128
Neigishi Shingoro, 100
nei-kung (internal power), 128, 133
Neo-Confucianism, 18, 137–38, 141–42
Nihon Kaizo Hoan Taiko (Outline Plan for the Reorganization of Japan; Kita Ikki), 40
Nihon Kendo Kata (Japan Kendo Kata), 111
Nihon no Shinro (Japan's New Role; Oyama Ikuo), 48
Ninjutsu Kaisetsu-sho (Commentary on Ninjutsu), 142
Nippon Budokan (Japan Martial Ways Hall), 51, *81*, 111
Nippon Den Kodokan Judo, 118
Nippon Den Sei To Shorinji Kempo, 160
Nippon Karate Kyokai, *see* Japan Karate Association
Nippon Kendo, *see* kendo
Nippon Shorinji Kempo, *157*, 161, 163, 171–72; *see also* Shorinji Kempo
Nishida Kitaro (1870–1945), 38
Nitobe Inazo (1862–1933), 35
Noguchi Senryuken, 162
noto (returning sword to scabbard), 67–68, *84, 85*
nukazu ni sumu (settling issues without drawing the sword), 102
nukitsuke (drawing sword from scabbard), 67

Oba Sachiyuki, 161
odachi (long sword), 23, 78, 111
Ogasawara Ryu, 175
Ogyu Sorai (1666–1727), 18–19, 63
Oishi Shinkage Ryu, 98
Oishi Susumu (1798–1865), 98–99
Okakura Kakuzo (1862–1913), 44, 180, 181
Okawa Shumei, 46
Okinawa Goju Ryu, 135
Okinawan *ko budo*, 135
Okinawan *te*, 125, 126, 128, 135
Okinawan weapons, 135
Okubo Toshimichi (1830–78), 22, 23–25, 102
okuden (secret teachings), 121, 139, 142
Okuma Shigenobu (1830–1922), 22, 23–24, 27, 31, 38
Okumura Sakonda, 100
Okuyama Yoshiji, 161, 165
Omori Ryu, 65
Ono-ha Itto Ryu, 97, 98, 100, 108, 138, 139
oshikiuchi system, 138, 139, 140, 141
Otani Shimosa no Kami Seiichiro (1789–1844), 98, 99

Otsuka Hidenori (b. 1892), 70, 126, 132, *146, 148, 149*
Otsuki Yutaka, 162
Oyama Ikuo (1880–1956), 48
Oyama Masatatsu, 134–35
Oyomei school, *see yomeigaku*

pai (traditional sects of *wu shu*), 164, 169
police force, 49, 68, 100; kendo for, 110–11
prearranged forms, *see kata*

ran (freedom of action), 113
ran-dori (free exercise), 121, 122
ranking system, *see dan-kyu*
"rape of Nanking," 46
Rembu-kai, 136
Rempeikan *dojo*, 98
Rengo-kai, 136
rentai-ho (physical-training method), 116, 118, 121
rigi ittai (theory and technique are one), 108–9
Rishin Ryu, 111
Russo-Japanese War (1904–5), 35
ryu (martial tradition), 57, 78, 80, 127
Ryuei Ryu, 135
Ryugo Ryu, 175

Saburi Ryu, 23
Sagawa Yukiyoshi, 161
Sahashi Shigeru, 51
Saigo Shiro, 140, 142; *see also* Shida Shiro
Saigo Takamori (1827–77), 22, 23–24, 25, 27, 28, 29, 102
Saigo Tanomo Chikamasa (1829–1905), 138, 139
Saigyo (1118–90), 31
Saimura Goro, 70
Saito Yakuro (1799–1872), 24, 98
Sakakibara Kenkichi (1829–94), 99, 100, 110, 138
Sakamoto Ryoma (1835–67), 32, 98
Sakurakai (Cherry Blossom Society), 44
samurai, 21–25, 26–30, 33, 129; *see also bushi*
Sanwa Ryu, 176
Sasamori Junzo, 108
satori (enlightenment), 51, 102
Satsuma Rebellion (1877), 24, 25, 29, 100
Sawayama Masaru, 126
SCAP, *see* Supreme Commander for the Allied Powers
sei (passivity), 62
seichushi (spirited and loyal samurai), 23
Seigo Ryu, 113, 120
seiho, 119; *see also heiho*
seiho therapy, 171
seijo (handcuffing), 71

188 · INDEX

Seikan Ryu, 176
seiryoku zen'yo (best use of energy) principle, 118, 119
seishin (spiritual energy), 57, 174
seishin tanren (spiritual forging), 24, 66, 102
seishi o choetsu (transcending thoughts of life and death), 58, 60, 105, 106, 167
seitei-gata (standard form of sword-drawing technique), 67
seiza (formal seated posture), 66, 67
Sekiguchi Ryu, 26, 113, 120
Self-Defense Force, 49, 75, 177
sen (initiative in combat), 71
Seni Ryu, 176
senjo (battlefield), 59
sensei (instructor), 60
shakujo (priest's staff), 169
Shaolin-ssu ch'uan-fa, 163, 164, 165, 168, 169, 170, 171; see also Shorinji Kempo
shiai (contest), 60, 80, 97, 122, 176, 177
shiaijo (place of sport contests), 59
Shibae Umpachiro, 100
Shibuya Toma, 138
Shida Shiro (1868–19??), 118, 139–40; see also Saigo Shiro
Shidehara Kijuro (1872–1951), 41
Shigakukan *dojo*, 98
shihan (master-teacher), 60
Shimazu Tadayoshi, 26–27
shimbo (staff), 110
Shimizu Takaji, 68–69, 70, 72, 73, 74, 82, 94
shinai (mock sword), 68, 80, 100, 106, 107, 109, 110
shinai-geiko (training with *shinai*), 80, 97, 98, 100
shinai-shiai (*shinai* contest), 80, 98
shin budo (new martial ways), 57; see also *budo*
Shindo Iten Ryu, 162
Shindo Munen Ryu, 24, 100, 111
Shindo Muso Ryu, 69, 70, 72
Shindo Rokugo Ryu, 162
Shindo Shizen Ryu, 131
Shindo Yoshin Ryu, 132
Shingai Tadatsu, 100
shingi ittai (mind and technique are one), 103
Shingo Izu no Kami, 80
Shinkage Ryu, 79, 80, 98, 100, 103, 107, 141
shinken shobu (combat to the death), 58, 60, 79, 80, 107; see also *shobu*
shin-ki-ryoku doctrine, 108
Shin no Budo (The True Budo; Sahashi Shigeru), 51
Shin no Shinto Ryu, 120
Shin Riaku *heiho*, 162
Shinron (New Proposals; Aizawa Seishisai), 20
shin-shin shugyo (mind-and-body training), 105
Shinto, 29–30
Shinwa *taido*, 162

Shioda Gozo, *156*, 161, 162
Shito-kai, 136
Shito Ryu, 135
Shito style, 126
shobu (fight, match), 59, 60; see also *shinken shobu*
shobu-ho (expert contest skill), 118, 121
Shoriki Matsutaro, 111
Shorinji Kempo, 163, 165; theory of, 166–67; aims of, 167–68; techniques and training methods of, 168–71; present status of, 171–72
Shorin Ryu, 135
Shoto-kai (Shoto Association), 127
Shotokan *dojo*, 127
Shotokan Ryu, 127
Showa era, government of, 43; soldiers during, 44
shugyo (austere training), 102, 103, 109, 110, 119, 129, 132
Shuri *te*, 126, 128
shushin-ho (mental cultivation in terms of moral standards), 118, 121
Shuyo Shosei Ron (Treatise on Mental Training and Life; Yamada Jirokichi), 103, 104, 110
Siberian Expedition (1918–19), 39
Sino-Japanese War (1894–95), 34
So Doshin, 163, 166, 168, 169; see also Nakano Michiomi
sojutsu (spear art), 23, 138
soken (searching methods), 71
Sokuseki Katsuyo Karate Goshin-jutsu (Instant Application of Karate, the Art of Self-defense), 142
sonno-joi (revere the emperor, expel the barbarians), 20
soshi (brave stalwarts), 39–40
sparring, 60, 133; with weapons in *karate-do*, 135
Strategic Air Command (SAC), 49
suburi, 109
suki o mitsukeru (finding weaknesses in opponent's defenses), 79
sumo (type of grappling), 30
sunao (plain and straight), 51
Sun-tzu (Art of War; Sun Tzu), 108
Supreme Commander for the Allied Powers (SCAP), 49, 70, 123, 176
sword drawing, see *iai-do, iai-jutsu, batto-jutsu*
swordsmanship, 61, 101, 119

tachi (sword), 80
tachi-iai (sword-drawing from standing posture), 65
tai (essence), 62
taiho-jutsu, 48, 70–72, 74, 86
Taiho-jutsu Kihon Kozo (Fundamentals of Taiho-jutsu), 70
Taisha Ryu, 80
Taisho era, government in, 36–37, 38; literature in, 37–38

Takagi Masatomo, 126
Takahashi Deishu, 102, 110
Takano Kosei, 104-5, 108-9
Takao Tesso, 100
Takasugi Shusaku, 98
Takayama Ken'ichi, 68, 73
Takeda Ryu, 175
Takeda Sokaku Minamoto Masayoshi (1858-1943), 98, 100, 138-39, 140, 141, 142-43, 144, *153*, 161
Takeda Takumi no Kami Soemon (1758-1853), 137
Takeda Tokimune, 161
Takeichi Hampeita, 98
Takemori Taizen, 165
Takuan (1573-1646), 63, 102
Takura Teramasa, 165
tameshi-giri (test cutting), 65, 67, *82*, *83*
Tamiya Ryu, 100
Tanaka Giichi (1863-1929), 39
Tanaka Setaro, 162
tanren, 51
Taoist concepts, 61, 63
Tao Te Ching, see *Lao-tzu*
taryu-jiai (contest between swordsmen of different *ryu*), 80
te, 125, 128, 129
Teishin Ryu, 120
tekichu shugi (striking the target), 174
Tendo Ryu, 176
Tenjin Shin'yo Ryu, 113, 116, 120, 139, 140, 141, 142
tenno shugi (divine rulership of emperor), 40
Tenshin Shoden Katori Shinto Ryu, 26, 107, 120, 175
Terada Kan'emon, 116
tessei no yari (iron spear), 110
Tetchu Ryu, 100
T'ien-t'ai Buddhism, 164, 166
tobi-dashi jutte, see *tokushu keibo soho*
Toda Ryu, 176
Togo Bizen no Kami (1563-1643), 79
Togun Ryu, 100
Tohei Koichi, 161
toho-sen (combat on foot), 78
Tojo Hideki (1885-1948), 44
tojutsu (swordsmanship; same as *kenjutsu*), 138
Tokino Seikishiro, 100
tokubetsu keibitai (special police unit), 68
Tokugawa Keiki, 102
tokushu keibo soho (handling the special police club), 73-74, *87*
Tomiki Kenji, *154*, *155*, 161, 162
torite (art of seizing and restraining), 74
toshu kakuto, 75-76, *88*
tote-nawa (frontal tying), 74
Totsuka Hirosuke, 117
Toyama Gakko, 65, 176

Toyama Mitsuru (1855-1944), 39, 163, 164
Toyama Ryu, 65
tozama (outside) daimyo, 19
Tozawa Tokusaburo, 140
Tsai-li (Principle Abiding) Society, 164
tsuka (hilt), 107
Tsukahara Bokuden (1490-1571), 101, 108
tsuki (thrust), 23, 108

Ueda Umanosuke, 100
Ueshiba Kishomaru, *154*, *155*, 161
Ueshiba Morihei (1883-1969), 140-41, 143-44, *153*, 161
Uesugi Shinkichi, 37, 43
Ugaki Kazushige, 41
ukemi (taking falls), 121
Ushinawareta Nihon (The Lost Japan; Hasegawa Nyozekan), 50

wa (harmony), 45
Wado-kai, 136
Wado Ryu, 70, 132
wai-chia (external systems), 128
wai-kung (external power), 128
Wang Yang-ming (Oyomei), 19
Watanabe Noboru, 100
Wen Lao-shi, 165
Wen Tai-tsung, 165
Western World and Japan, The (George Sansom), 23
White Lotus Society, 164
World War I, Japan in, 38-39
World War II, Japan in, 47-48
wu-kung (special exercises), 128
wu shu (martial arts), 125, 164-65, 169

Yae Ryu, 162
Yagyu Jubei (c. 1607-50), 79
Yagyu Munenori (1571-1646), 79
Yagyu Shinkage Ryu, 111, 120, 141, 142
Yagyu Tajima no Kami (1527-1606), 80, 101
yama arashi (mountain storm) technique, 118, 140
Yamada Heizaemon (d. 1578), 80, 97
Yamada Jirokichi (1863-1931), *89*, 103-4, 109-10
Yamada Tatsuo, 126
Yamaga Soko (1622-85), 18-19, 24, 31, 34
Yamagata Aritomo (1838-1922), 22, 23, 27-28, 32, 33, 34, 35, 38, 39, 42
Yamaguchi Gogen, 126, 132-33, 134, *152*
Yamamoto Tomekichi, 161
Yamamuro Sobun (1880-1950), 41
Yamaoka Tesshu (1837-88), *89*, 101-2, 103, 104, 109
Yamato-gokoro (spirit of Japan), 63
Yamato Ryu, 173
yari (spear), 23

yin-yang, 115–16, 164, 166
yo (function), 62
yomeigaku (school of intuition or mind), 19, 25, 51, 59, 102, 108, 121, 170, 174
Yoshida Shoin (1830–59), 24, 27, 29
Yoshin *aiki-do,* 162
Yoshino Sakuzo (1878–1933), 38
Yoshin Ryu, 117, 120
yu-dansha (one having graded rank), 62
yukei (having form), 62
yuken (*shinai* contacting *shinai*), 62

zanshin (continued domination), 68, 130, 131
zan-totsu ("close and strike" tactics), 78

zazen meditation, 171
Zen, 62, 108
Zen Nihon Iai-do Remmei (All-Japan Iai-do Federation), 67
Zen Nihon Juken-do Remmei (All-Japan Juken-do Federation), 177
Zen Nihon Kendo Remmei (All-Japan Kendo Federation), 67, 101, 111
Zen Nihon Kyudo Remmei (All-Japan Kyudo Federation), 175
Zen Nihon Naginata-do Remmei (All-Japan Naginata-do Federation), 176
Zen Nippon Judo Remmei (All-Japan Judo Federation), 123

The "weathermark" identifies this book as a production of Weatherhill, Inc., publishers of fine books on Asia and the Pacific. Book design and typography by Ronald V. Bell. Cover design by D. S. Noble. Printing and binding by Quebecor Printing, Book Press. The text is set in Bembo, with Optima for display.